ORNAMENTAL AESTHETICS

ORNAMENTAL AESTHETICS

The Poetry of Attending in Thoreau, Dickinson, and Whitman

Theo Davis

Oxford University Press is a department of the University of Oxford. It furthers
the University's objective of excellence in research, scholarship, and education
by publishing worldwide. Oxford is a registered trade mark of Oxford University
Press in the UK and certain other countries.

Published in the United States of America by Oxford University Press
198 Madison Avenue, New York, NY 10016, United States of America.

© Oxford University Press 2016

First issued as an Oxford University Press paperback, 2020

All rights reserved. No part of this publication may be reproduced, stored in
a retrieval system, or transmitted, in any form or by any means, without the
prior permission in writing of Oxford University Press, or as expressly permitted
by law, by license, or under terms agreed with the appropriate reproduction
rights organization. Inquiries concerning reproduction outside the scope of the
above should be sent to the Rights Department, Oxford University Press, at the
address above.

You must not circulate this work in any other form
and you must impose this same condition on any acquirer.

Library of Congress Cataloging-in-Publication Data
Names: Davis, Theo, author.
Title: Ornamental aesthetics : the poetry of attending in Thoreau, Dickinson,
and Whitman / Theo Davis.
Description: New York : Oxford University Press, 2016.
Includes bibliographical references.
Identifiers: LCCN 2015040573 ISBN 978-0-19-046751-7 (cloth)
ISBN 978-0-19-008098-3 (paper) | ISBN 978-0-19-046752-4 (updf)
Subjects: LCSH: American literature—19th century—History and criticism.
Aesthetics in literature. Phenomenology and literature. Thoreau, Henry
David, 1817–1862—Aesthetics. Dickinson, Emily, 1830–1886—Aesthetics.
Whitman, Walt, 1819–1892—Aesthetics. Aesthetics, American—
Poetics and nineteenth-century American literature.
Classification: LCC PS217.A35 D38 2016 DDC 820.9/357—dc23 LC record available at
http://lccn.loc.gov/2015040573

For Eric

CONTENTS

Acknowledgmentsix

Introduction: To Ornament1
1. Beautiful Thoreau: An Ornament to Nature37
2. Dickinson's Ornamental Form90
3. Whitman and the Distinction of Ornament141

Notes195
Bibliography231
Index243

ACKNOWLEDGMENTS

Portions of this project were presented at SUNY Buffalo, Case Western Reserve University, the Mahindra Center for the Humanities at Harvard University, and at Northeastern University; the audiences at those talks all provided stimulating and useful questions. An early version of the work on Thoreau appeared in *ELH*. Time to write was provided by both Williams College and Northeastern University; a year at the Oakley Center for the Humanities at Williams came with the use of a memorably luxurious office. Kerry Larson read the entire manuscript, and his response helped me find the final shape of the argument. Branka Arsić and an anonymous reader at Oxford University Press also read the whole book and provided me with invaluable feedback. David Weimer was an indispensable resource in preparing the manuscript for publication. My thinking about Dickinson began at a seminar Sharon Cameron taught at the National Humanities Center; as the pages that follow testify to the respect I have for her work, I add here a note of personal appreciation. I am grateful as well to Elizabeth Maddock Dillon, Ingrid Diran, Jason Gladstone, Anna Henchman, Carla Kaplan, John Limon, Ruth Mack, Gage McWeeny, Patrick Mullen, Davide Panagia, Kashia Pieprzak, John Plotz, Chris Pye, Joe Rezek, Eliza Richards, Anita Sokolsky, Karen Swann, and Steve Tifft for the many exchanges—some directly about ornament, some not—that constitute an intellectual world in which a book can be imagined. It is a pleasure to dedicate the book to my father, Eric Davis.

ORNAMENTAL AESTHETICS

Introduction

To Ornament

ORNAMENT'S APPEARANCE

Perhaps Walt Whitman said it best: "Most works are most beautiful without ornament."[1] Or Henry David Thoreau, who did not wish "to ornament a line" of poetry, and avowed in *Walden* that he would rather "sit on a pumpkin" than "a velvet cushion."[2] Emily Dickinson, according to Susan Howe, "swe[pt] away the pernicious idea of poetry as embroidery for women."[3] All three writers have been read as dissenters from nineteenth-century American culture's gem-encrusted poesy and parlors heavy with curtains and curio shelves: they wiped the slate clean, abandoning the artifice and clutter of ornament. Nevertheless, their impatience with ornamentation belies a complex investment in the aesthetic interest of ornamental objects, the form of ornamental poetics, and a mode of aesthetic attending to the world which each conceived of as a form of ornamentation. While most scholarship today identifies ornamentation with either material culture or the material form of language, I argue that Thoreau, Dickinson, and Whitman's ornamental aesthetics belongs to a formally and philosophically distinct tradition of ornamentation in which it is a means of marking out persons, objects, and the world—or reality itself—for attention and praise. At issue in their modes of ornamental attending are questions about how persons and language relate to the world which have been inaccessible to literary scholarship shaped around the philosophy and literature of representation.

References to ornamentation abound in all three writers' work. For example, Thoreau sees "a very pretty little chandelier of a flower fit to adorn the forest floor," and notes how "[a] new carpet of pine leaves is forming in the woods. The forest is laying down her carpet for the winter."[4] In one poem, Dickinson writes, "The Trees like Tassels – hit – and swung"; in another, she imagines the natural world covered in carpet and upholsterers' fabric:

> Of Brussels – it was not –
> Of Kidderminster? Nay –
> The Winds did buy it of the Woods –
> They – sold it unto me –
> . . . .
> The Wind – unrolled it fast –
> And spread it on the Ground –
> Upholsterer of the Pines – is He –
> Upholsterer – of the Pond –[5]

In *Democratic Vistas*, Whitman calls American poems "genuine gold" and "gems," and likens America to a cosmos of "definitely-form'd worlds . . . hung up there, chandeliers of the universe, beholding and mutually lit by each other's lights."[6] Such thematic references to ornamental objects in architecture, interior decoration, and dress indicate these authors' curiosity about ornamentation. But to observe a thematic reference to a carpet, gem, or chandelier is only to open the question: Why did these authors make such comparisons?

A famous sentence from Emerson's essay "The Poet" reads, "For it is not meters, but a meter-making argument, that makes a poem,— a thought so passionate and alive, that, like the spirit of a plant or an animal, it has an architecture of its own, and adorns nature with a new thing."[7] While this sentence is frequently quoted for its rejection of English prosody, it has been less remarked that here Emerson deems the "adorn[ment]" of "nature" to be indispensable to poetics. This sense of poetry as an ornament to the world is central to Thoreau, Dickinson, and Whitman's work, and hence to their commitment to understanding the category of ornament as well. For each writer, ornamental references are touchpoints for the development of a literary practice that is at its heart a reconceiving of what poetry is and how it is in the world. (I mean this, incidentally, about Thoreau's *prose*—he considered himself a poet, and part of my argument is that his prose writing is a form of poetic ornamentation.) Such poetry is thought of as an ornament to the world, and as a part of the world that is also placed upon it.

Furthermore, the investigations of ornamental objects and ornamental poetics in Thoreau, Dickinson, and Whitman feed into a comprehensive sense of ornamentation as an aesthetics in the sense of a range of ways to attend, relate, and respond to the world. (When Emerson thinks of ornament as a kind of "thought," he also moves in this direction, insofar as he thinks of ornamentation as a way that knowing relates to the world.) Reflections on, and experimentations with, how poetry might ornament the world are ways of considering how the authors' human existence—as observers, embodied beings, and searching minds—might bear a laudatory and attentive relation to the world. Thus, Thoreau's curiosity about how a flower can "adorn the forest floor" is linked to his wish to find a way to walk in and appreciate nature so as to grace it. For Dickinson, ornamentation structures her exploration of the transient nature of all phenomena, leading to an at times painfully vibrant sense of the mutually fluctuating contact of mind and object. In Whitman, the glorifying dazzle of ornamentation informs his grandly democratic praise, as poem and poet become "kosmoses," or ornaments to the world ("P," 721). By the world, here, I intend both the sense of what appears to us in our sensory experience, and also the underlying sense of Being, an ontological condition that makes the existence of any particular moment or encountered thing possible. The relationship between these two senses of the world is central to the ornamental aesthetics elaborated in this body of writing.

Ornamental aesthetics turns on two primary types of gesture: paying attention to and placing upon. These two forms fan out into activities and movements of body, mind, and image, which include going toward, moving along with, pressing down upon, attaching to, and being buoyantly raised up by. They all concern the relationship of a kind of attention to an act of physical placement. Attention is a mental act, such as the turning of the mind onto an object; ornamentation then ties attention

INTRODUCTION

with a physical act, such as the placement of a flower on a mantelpiece. The physical placing of an ornamental object upon something—a blue ribbon on a lapel, a gold crown on a head, a flower upon a hillside—serves to encourage or to draw mental attention. But the placement, or application, of ornamentation is itself intentional: one poses a jewel, banner, or bird in order to draw other minds to it. So a redounding between the placing of objects and the intentional drawing of attention to and through them is the heart of ornamentation. It cannot be fully identified with either the object (the ribbon, the banner, the jewel in itself) or the intention of the consciousness that places it. In the writings I consider in this project, the relationship of attention to objects often becomes more complex than the initial formulation I have just outlined: a mental noticing, or placing of the attention, may be followed out or figured as a physical motion toward and placement upon some element or object. But together, noticing and moving toward contact are performed through or figured as ornaments being placed upon things to call them out for a laudatory form of attention. This attention is, in turn, taken as the heart of poetic practice in each author's work.

This is the case both in the representations of non-linguistic ornamentation in the discussions that follow, and in the way that Thoreau, Dickinson, and Whitman consider the relationship of their own minds to the world as ornamentation. Whatever the medium, and whether it is a represented or enacted practice, ornamentation will be seen to turn not on objects themselves, nor even on language itself, but on how objects can be used or positioned, and how they engage and affect a writer, reader, or viewer. The relationship of attention to objects is the heart of ornamentation. Therefore, the qualities of placing and going-in-relation that each author identifies with ornamentation are also a means to explore the mind's placement in relation to other objects. It is central that ornamentation entails relations between persons and objects, and even focuses on the form of that relation: How is attention or praise bestowed on nature? How does a poet approach what interests him? How does an image draw a reader or writer to dwell with it?[8] My central contention is that Thoreau, Dickinson, and Whitman are engaged with a tradition of ornamentation as a practice of relational notice. Such relational notice is involved with a way of understanding the relationship of mind to world that diverges from the representational model through which a subject knows a world of objects other to himself.[9]

Martin Heidegger argued that in modern (since Plato) Western culture, knowing is framed as a form of representation: the way a subject grasps a perceived object and replicates it as an image or representation.[10] For Heidegger, representational knowing is a relationship to an object that is posited as other to the subject. Representational knowing, or knowing through concepts and images, is premised on the primary alienation of the subject from the world that he would know. The world is never present to the subject, and he can only know it through the proxies of images and ideas. Such knowing rests on the correspondence between a statement and an externally existing reality, and on the capacity of the subject to dictate conditions. Considering how Romans instituted the latter understanding of truth as the right—*veritas*—Heidegger writes:

> *Ver* is now the maintaining-oneself, the being-above; *ver* becomes the opposite of falling. *Verum* is the remaining constant, the upright, that which is directed to what is superior because it is directing from above. *Verum* is *rectum* (*regere*, "the regime"), the right, *iustum*. . . . Under the influence of the imperial, *verum* becomes forthwith "being-above," directive for what is right; *veritas* is then *rectitudo*, "correctness," we would say.[11]

This imperial right is related to the correspondence theory of truth, for "both have the character of an assimilation of assertions and thinking to the state of affairs present at hand and firmly established."[12] The correspondence theory of truth (the view that truth lies in the adequation between a subject's statement and an external reality) depends upon two assumptions: that the world is a given reality, and that the subject exists apart from that world.[13] As a consequence of the primary separation of subject from the world, knowing is framed as the subject's work of contacting a real that is always beyond him. He may dominate it by rules of the right, or draw it within the ambit of his mind by means of representation, but he remains essentially alien to it. Knowledge as either right or correspondence is, for Heidegger, compromised by an inherent reliance on "assimilation."[14] I would emphasize that the effort to know by this means demands alienation and contraction from the human being; it is painful to adopt this stance toward the world and oneself, even before considering if or how one's knowing might constrict or dominate its objects.

Heidegger elaborates an alternative understanding of truth through the reading of archaic Greek philosophy. In his reading of the poetic-philosophical fragments of Parmenides, he observes that truth is said to appear in the figure of a goddess, Ἀλήθεια. He objects that while modern readers have agreed to treat this goddess's appearance as a mere "embellishment"[15] to the real account of truth in Parmenides, it is actually the essential mode in which truth resides. To Heidegger it is vital that truth appears through a form, rather than simply being there to be counted, registered, or judged. In this passage, his phenomenology lies in the belief that the truth's appearance in phenomenal form is not a trivial "embellishment," for truth does not exist outside of or prior to its appearance. Phenomenal appearance, which Western metaphysics saw as a trifling, temporary material cover or image of reality, is for Heidegger necessary to the basic laying-forth way that truth is.

Heidegger more than once implies that he is opposed to a Western metaphysical view in which phenomena are forms of ornamentation in the sense of trivial material trappings that cover or obscure truth. To him, phenomenal reality is not ornamentation but essential to truth. And yet, this view is close to a defense of ornamentation, in which "embellishment," like appearance, is central to truth rather than incidental to it. I will throughout this book argue that there is a submerged connection between ornamentation and the bearing of appearance upon truth in Heidegger. The entire manner of thinking in Heidegger emphasizes qualities coincident with ornamentation, including approaching, weighing-on, relationality, transitivity (one ornaments something), being-in-place (ornament goes somewhere), and shedding light (as refracted by gold or gems). And the key phenomenological sense that the contingent, changing, and immersed qualities of experience are in a primary relationship to a deeper truth is, I argue, a way of thinking about the relationship of experience to truth that is more truly ornamental than representational. The immediately experienced world is not quite a symbol of Being—instead, it moves in a privileged relation to it.

For example, Heidegger maintains that ἀλήθεια needs an element of sheltering, which takes on qualities of ornamentation. There is, he writes,

> a kind of concealment that does not at all put aside and destroy the concealed but instead shelters and saves the concealed for what it is. . . . Perhaps there are modes of concealment that not only preserve and put away and so in a certain sense still withdraw, but that rather, in a unique way, impart and bestow what is essential. The essential type of bestowal and bequest is in each case a concealment, and indeed not only of the bestower but of what is bestowed, insofar as the bestowed does not simply surrender its treasures but only lets this come into unconcealment; namely that in it a richness is lodged which will be attained to the degree it is protected against abuse.[16]

Just notice how the concealment that is a necessary shelter has ornamental qualities of "bestowal and bequest," of "treasures," even of "richness." Despite his own moves to declaim against ornament when it means transient, nonessential phenomena, Heidegger's sense of the appearance of ἀλήθεια in phenomenal form is subtly inflected by aspects of ornamentation.

In Plato's metaphor of the cave, writes Kaja Silverman, "Western philosophy began with the turn away from the world of the senses to a suprasensual domain."[17] This was a turn away from the sensory world and to one of "[t]rue vision," reached "when all representational mediation has been removed; only when we are face to face with the self-present, the self-same, that which forever Is."[18] In Silverman's account, metaphysics begins in the premise that in the daily life of appearance and sensation, truth can only be accessed through the imperfect translation of "representational mediation."[19] She emphasizes that in Western philosophy, at its root human experience is an image of truth—not just something temporal and changing and thus untrue, but a shadow-play through which truth might be grasped. Then, with reference to Heidegger, Silverman suggests that phenomenology offers a more accurate view that truth lives *in* appearance, and that a turn away from the world's appearing can only be a turn away from truth.[20] Thus her work would clearly return us to the "world of the senses" and the primacy of representation, understood as the housing of thought in material form.

On one level it is true that phenomenology redeems the sensory and temporal world by making immediate experience the site of reality and truth. As George Steiner writes, "in *Being and Time* '*Dasein*' is 'to be there' (*da-sein*), and 'there' is the world: the concrete, literal, actual, daily world. To be human is to be immersed, implanted, rooted in the earth."[21] In this sense, we can expect that Heidegger's ontology locates truth in materiality and in immediate human feeling and perception. His claims in *Being and Time* that in Descartes "the idea of substantiality . . . not only remains unclarified in the meaning of its Being, but gets passed off as something incapable of clarification," and that Descartes is "unable . . . to let what shows itself in sensation present itself in its own kind of Being," encourage us to think of him as a philosopher finding truth in material substance and sensation.[22]

But stopping with a sense of Heidegger as *simply* committed to "this radical immanence, this embeddedness," as Steiner puts it, would be a misunderstanding, for central as questions of bodily and sensory life are to his work, Heidegger is concerned with their Being.[23] That Being cannot be separated from things' appearance in our conscious, moment-to-moment experience, but it is crucially different from it. Phenomenology returns philosophy to lived experience, that is, even as it continues to dislocate us from it. Heidegger is not quite interested in the truth *in* a moment of feeling or engaging an environment, but in what condition of Being underlies and is the primordial truth of such a moment. For Being does not lie on the face of experience: "[T]hat which remains *hidden* in an egregious sense, or which relapses and gets *covered up* again, or which shows itself only '*in disguise*,' is not just this entity or that, but rather the *Being* of entities."[24] To reach the Being at the heart of experience requires a mode of relating to things that turns away from the very immediacy that we might expect phenomenology to restore. "The peculiarity of what is proximally ready-to-hand is that, in its readiness-to-hand, it must, as it were, withdraw [zurückzuziehen] in order to be ready-to-hand quite authentically."[25] Heidegger locates the essential Being of material, sensory, and psychologically engaged experience through a displacement from the straightforward acceptance of the simple presence of mind to object. This is why phenomenology is at heart an interpretation—it doesn't seek the obvious, staring truth of experience but the underlying conditions of its possibility. These are everywhere assumed and internalized, but not yet brought up into awareness and understanding. In Heidegger's words, "The idea of grasping and explicating phenomena in a way which is 'original' and 'intuitive' ['originären' und 'intuitiven'] is directly opposed to the naïvité of a haphazard, 'immediate,' and unreflective 'beholding.'"[26]

While Heidegger himself encourages us to think of phenomenology as a form of interpretation, it is important not to take this too literally. As Silverman explained, phenomenology departs from philosophical views that treat the experienced world as just a representation of the truth—in other words, Heidegger is no Emanuel Swedenborg. He is interested in "dwelling autonomously alongside entities within-the-world," which is distinguished from finding out what entities refer to or what meaning they carry. If Heidegger defines "*interpretation* in its broadest sense" as that "perception" by which "one *addresses* oneself to something as something and *discusses* it as such," my point is that this account of interpretation as accompanying discussion is more properly a mode of ornamentation than it is of the interpretation of signs.[27] There is a distinctive, non-hermeneutic mode of relationship to phenomena (including language) in Heidegger, as well as in Thoreau, Dickinson, and Whitman.

To stick for the moment with Heidegger, in *Being and Time* he conceives of human beings as "alongside" and in relation to the world, rather than as apart from it or within it.[28] The sense of *Dasein* (the engaged human being) as in an attending relation to the world—neither merged into it, nor outside and looking at it—is quite different from a picture of a subject looking into the meaning of a world that lies before him. Rather than seeing appearances as representations of an absent meaning, they are ornaments that mark out, attend, and engage with a Being which underlies and encompasses all particular phenomenal appearing and experience. As it inflects Heidgger's writing, ornament characterizes a relationship of ontic phenomena to truth that is neither representational mediation, on the one hand, nor meshing of truth to appearance, on the other. At its broadest, my claim is that although Heidegger presents his understanding of the world as one comprised in the relationality of the sign, in practice his understanding of the "relational totality" comprising the world through the netted connections of human awareness and things is more properly an ornamental relationship of adorning, and responsive attending, than a representational or signifying one.[29]

The ornamental aesthetics in Thoreau, Dickinson, and Whitman encourages a more fluid relationship between the ontic and the ontological levels than that found in Heidegger. In their work, immediate experience becomes more acutely permeated by the underlying sense of Being or of all-encompassing conditions of reality; in turn, Being itself becomes unnervingly unsteady and suceptible to the impact of force. Consider the following passage in *Walden*:

> [I]n dealing with truth we are immortal, and need fear no change nor accident. The oldest Egyptian or Hindoo philosopher raised a corner of the veil from the statue of divinity; and still the trembling robe remains raised, and I gaze upon as fresh a glory as he did, since it was I in him that was then so bold, and it is he in me that now reviews the vision. No dust has settled on that robe; no time has elapsed since that divinity was revealed. That time which we really improve, or which is improvable, is neither past, present, nor future. (*W*, 99)

The veil is not just covering the divinity, or truth, but is clearly *placed* there, denoting the importance of what it obscures. The veil, rather than being simply a cover or a "representational mediation," "trembl[es]" with an eerie life. Its raising suggests the importance of the veil's presence as neither a cover, nor a representation, of truth, but as that which goes with it and which brings one to it. Dressing truth with robe and veil makes it attractive, so that one moves toward it. This drawing toward is distinct from either being blocked from truth or finding a transformed home for it. We could also consider the laces on a dress, just over a breast, in Dickinson's poem:

> The thought beneath so slight a film –
> Is more distinctly seen –

INTRODUCTION

As laces just reveal the surge –
Or Mists – the Appenine – (203)

Ornamentation can be found to have a *privileged* relationship to truth: it can point to what is unrepresentable, and indicate its presence and its value, without performing the transformative mediation of representation or the full merging of truth into the sensory and temporal (whether located ontologically or ontically). Instead, we can begin to think of what appears in our experience as, with Dickinson and Thoreau, a "trembl[ing]" adornment to truth.

At issue here is not simply a literary historical claim, but the possibility of thinking of poetry as a way of relating to the world, rather than as an expressive object. Ornament, here, is a means of being in relation to the praiseworthy and also simply to the present. Such art engages questions about human comportment in the world that are, themselves, foundational to Heidegger's philosophy. For instance, he writes in *Being and Time* that "[l]etting something be encountered is primarily *circumspective*; it is not just sensing something, or staring at it. It implies circumspective concern, and has the character of becoming affected in some way."[30] This interest in how to adjust, approach, and encounter is shared by both Heidegger and Thoreau, Dickinson, and Whitman.

In its commitment to finding the underlying condition of Being which makes possible and is the essential truth of apparent daily life, and in its understanding that objects or things do not exist in themselves but only as objects of concern, engagement, and even use for human subjects, Heidegger's work has some affinities with Marxist critiques of knowing trained on the immediate way that objects appear to an individual subject.[31] The Marxist-Hegelian tradition finds that historical processes are the ground of reality, while for Heidegger it is the temporally thrown quality of *Dasein*, but the two parallel developments of Marxist philosophy and phenomenology both stress the need to know the totality of relations through which the subject's encounter of the object is produced. Each rejects the alienated, individuated knowing of mere objects by an isolated, abstracted subject. In this regard, these two very different intellectual traditions share an ambition to redeem human experience from modern conditions of alienation and individuation by unearthing hidden conditions of connection and ongoing human processes that explain and connect the phenomena which comprise momentary life.

In the account of ornament that I develop out of Heidegger's work and out of the poetic and aesthetic projects of Thoreau, Whitman, and Dickinson, I locate a different way of thinking about the nature of immediate relations. While my thinking is imbued by Heidegger's phenomenology and distant from historicist work that aims to uncover the historical processes thought to give the immediate its true meaning, at its heart the topic of ornamentation concerns a relationship between the immediate and a sense of totality or reality that is not one of explication or expression in either a truly historicist or classically phenomenological sense. This is because an ornament adorns and draws attention to, whereas a representative sign expresses or embodies. The liveness and individually influenced peculiarity of a moment of relationship is central to ornamentation; the ornament never can become a fully explicable phenomenon with any final relation to a given understanding of a totality. It returns us to the uncertain, unfolding contingency of the immediate, and throughout the book I argue for the dignity and integrity of such immediate relationship. The immediate experience of relationship is laden with complexity, changeability, and openness in a way that is unacknowledged by both Marxist and phenomenological critiques of an individual's immediate observation, and by more recent defenses of the value of the uninvestigated appearance and facticity.[32] Ornamentation is not a gentle respite from critical interpretation but an occasion to rethink what an immediate perception is, and what it might contain. Thus, in this book I pick up the commitment to deep understanding that is central to twentieth-century criticism and seek to relocate it in the flickering life of nonessential ornamental contacts. In this return to immediate experience, I have been encouraged by a noted statement of the Buddha: "[I]t is just within this fathom-long body, with its perception and intellect, that I declare that there is the cosmos, the origination of the cosmos, the cessation of the cosmos, and the path of practice leading to the cessation of the cosmos."[33] It suggests that there are forms of immediate experience quite other than mystified transparency or blank self-evidence.

INTRODUCTION

ORNAMENTATION AND REPRESENTATION

Three sites for theorizing ornamentation have oriented its use in literary studies: Enlightenment aesthetics, poststructuralist criticism, and material culture. These disparate fields all define ornamentation in relation to the primary axis of representation, often figuring it either as empty form or utter materiality. As its status as form and matter fluctuate, in these discussions ornament remains a bit player in relation to the overriding theorizations of representation. In beginning with a representational structure, such approaches cannot illuminate the particular qualities of ornamentation and tend to dismiss it altogether unless it can be rendered into a symbolic form.

Enlightenment philosophers argued that the aesthetic experience of art or nature was valuable because it could lift a subject up from the world of personal interest and sensory experience and bring him closer to the disinterested, rational contemplation of justice and truth. "[I]t is through Beauty that man makes his way to Freedom," maintains Friedrich Schiller in *The Aesthetic Education of Man*.[34] The capacity for aesthetic appreciation, in Schiller's view, marks a transition from sheer animal being toward full humanity: "When, then, we find [in a person] traces of a disinterested and unconditional appreciation of pure semblance, we may infer that a revolution of this order has taken place in his nature, and that he has started to become truly human."[35] Schiller's is just one of a range of Enlightenment era investigations of how aesthetic experience negotiated between sensual, interested experience and the disinterested work of rational judgment.[36] This is the center of Enlightenment aesthetics: negotiations among sensual particularity and the universality of disinterested judgment.

In the broad context of Enlightenment aesthetics, ornament sometimes crops up as a version of fallen, sensual appreciation, or of aesthetics gone to seed. When the eighteenth-century painter and theorist Sir Joshua Reynolds dismisses some forms of painting as "merely ornament,"—"striving which shall produce the brightest tint, or, curiously trifling, shall give the gloss of stuffs, so as to appear real" —his point is that ornament must be kept in its place because its color, texture, and shine elicit desire rather than appreciation.[37] And for Schiller, ornament is an aesthetic practice that heads toward aesthetic elevation, but has not quite gotten there yet: "And what sort of phenomenon is it that proclaims the approach of the savage to humanity? So far as we consult history, it is the same in all races who have escaped from the slavery of the animal state: a delight in *appearance*, a disposition towards *ornament* and *play*."[38]

And yet, like an ace that can be played high or low, ornament also shows up as an art so purified that it is all empty form. In the third *Critique*, Kant wrote that "[e]ven what we call *ornament*[]... does indeed increase our taste's liking, yet it too does so only by its form, as in the case of picture frames, or drapery on statues, or colonnades around magnificent buildings."[39] The ornament that is utter "form" reappears as an example of free beauty, "according to mere form."[40] Across Enlightenment aesthetics, ornamentation slides between reprobate sensuality and pure formal interest, never striking that balance of subjective appeal and rational disinterest that made aesthetics matter.

Its very slipperiness in Enlightenment aesthetics made ornament interesting to poststructuralist critics of the aesthetic, notably Jacques Derrida and Naomi Schor. Reading the discussion of ornamentation in the third *Critique*, for instance, Derrida observes that for Kant the ornamental frame as "design," or "organization of lines" is an object of purely formal beauty, but once it is gilded, it becomes "sensory mat[ter]," appealing in its tactile reality.[41] The instability of the distinction between humanly desired materials that appeal to the senses and forms that produce disinterested contemplation is central to Derrida's deconstruction of Kantian aesthetics. And, in her discussion of Reynolds's aesthetics, Schor observes that "he implicitly reinscribes the sexual stereotypes of Western philosophy which has, since its origins, mapped gender onto the form-matter paradigm, forging a durable link between maleness and form (eidos), femaleness and formless matter."[42] In practice, however, she finds that ornamentation creeps into Reynolds's aesthetics, such that all he can do is seek "to moderate the effects produced by its indiscriminate profusion."[43] The paradigmatic separation of form from the material detail, of which ornamentation is a subset for Schor, cannot hold.[44]

INTRODUCTION

While Derrida and Schor used the case of ornament to critique the separation of form from matter, and of disinterested aesthetic appreciation from sensory desire, it is precisely that large ambition that keeps their work on ornamentation from providing a satisfying account of it. Ornamentation is more than the hairline crack in Enlightenment aesthetics' claim to negotiate between materiality and form. This whole discourse's organizing frame of the relationship of materiality to form, and of desire to aesthetic disinterest, is largely irrelevant to the topic of ornamentation. I will get at this point—that ornament is an extraneous element in Enlightenment aesthetics and in poststructuralist critiques of it—by way of an investigation of discussions of ornamentation as a language in both literary theory and the study of material culture.

In deconstructive accounts of ornamentation in literature, it again stands indifferently for materiality and for empty form. In his account of Rousseau's theft of a ribbon in the *Confessions*, De Man describes the stolen "pink and silver colored ribbon" as "in itself devoid of meaning and function," but also as capable of "circulat[ing] symbolically as a pure signifier."[45] This meaningless decorative object first serves as a signifier of Rousseau's cascade of desires; it next serves as a prefatory substitute for that other signifier, "Marion," which De Man will claim functions just as would "any other word, any other sound or noise."[46] De Man prepares us for the key claim that a word used by accident is only a noise by the discussion of how a meaninglesss decorative ribbon can signify. In crossing from ornamental object to meaningless word, De Man highlights the condition of language as matter to which meaning is added. But the choice of the ribbon is peculiar; this is not the same as a stone, a scrap of tin, or just any unremarkable piece of stuff. The ribbon is an ornament, and its comparison to a linguistic signifier (the sound or mark "Marion") metonymically bolsters the claim that the form of language, even when meaning is stripped from it, remains compelling. In their account of De Man, Steven Knapp and Walter Benn Michaels contend that there's nothing interesting about "the material condition of language," which "is inherently meaningless."[47] But by rendering that "material condition" ornamental by the metonymic connection of the sound "Marion" to the ribbon, De Man implies that the materiality *is* interesting, because it is distinct from any random instance of matter.

INTRODUCTION

To associate the material form of the signifier, stripped of its signified, with ornamentation is to say that while it does not mean, and thus does not function as language, it nevertheless has some hold or attraction. That hold is the form it shares with a signifier carrying meaning.

Susan Bernstein's discussion of Horace Walpole's *The Castle of Otranto* is a more recent example of how deconstructionist theory positions ornamentation as a formal and material phenomenon, one that lacks meaning but retains interest. She identifies the materiality of language when it can no longer be linked to any meaning (such as Walpole's neologism "sharawaggi") as a condition of "stranded matter" which is also "decorative."[48] An interest in ornament as meaningless form turns back into an interest in ornamentation as materiality; here ornamentation is a way to talk about the attraction of materially inscribed forms that have no meaning. Still, exploring ornamentation as form drained of meaning takes us into a cul-de-sac in which ornamentation flips between form and materiality.

The Grammar of Ornament is one of the first texts in modern industrial design, written by Owen Jones, the designer of the 1851 London Crystal Palace. Jones's title claims that ornamentation has the same form as a language, and that it can be learned as a structure or system akin to a language. Unlike the comparisons of language to ornament in deconstructive criticism, in Jones the point of calling ornament a language was to imply that one can learn it and apply it in different contexts. Hence, Egyptian style might be used in Victorian parlors, as long as its rules were followed properly. For the art historian Gülru Neçipoglu, such approaches to ornamentation as a language in the sense of a learnable formal structure that can be applied anywhere failed to understand their subject.[49] In her argument, the formalism of nineteenth-century industrial design was linked to an imperialist view of the decorative styles of foreign and historical cultures as a set of meaningless forms that could be transferred onto Western manufactured goods. (Jones's work abstracted designs from their historical and cultural meanings, making them available for industrial manufacture.) Like Neçipoglu, many design historians and scholars of material culture resist framing ornament as an empty linguistic form.[50] They reject the idea that ornamentation is just a formal structure through which one might say anything or nothing. Instead, they argue that ornamentation is a language in use, and one needs to be able to read it in its contextual situation.[51]

Art and design historians' views that ornamentation is not a language in the sense of an empty, usable form but in the sense of a semiotic carrier of historically and culturally situated meaning is essentially that of material culture scholars. A major early scholar in the field, Henry Glassie, approvingly observes that "scholars ... have begun to view objects as books that, no matter how pretty the bindings, are worthless until read."[52] In the words of Jules David Prown, another scholar of material culture, "The methodology of material culture is also concerned with *semiotics* in its conviction that artifacts transmit signals which elucidate mental patterns or structures."[53] To do so, the study of material culture works in the terrain of cultural studies, focusing on how historical and cultural meanings are conveyed in objects. For example, in his groundbreaking reading of Victorian America's decorative arts, Kenneth L. Ames offers this interpretation of decorative sideboards bearing carvings of freshly killed game: "[T]hese objects celebrate a predatory impulse that was at the very heart of nineteenth-century society ... [which also] was incorporated into a social structure and a culture that allowed powerful people to prey, not only on the animal world, but on members of their own species."[54] Here, material culture is made legible by being compared to a language, but unlike language it seems only to carry the meaning of its culture. These decorative objects directly express their context without the need for or interference of any particular human agent, artist, or speaker.

Katherine C. Grier has pointed to the limits of taking language as the master-semiotic system on which to model the study of material culture. She writes that "a fully developed semiotics of material culture is going to look much different than linguistic models and ... it will try to take into account ways of knowing for which language is but a translation."[55] Part of what a linguistically based approach can't accommodate is what distinguishes ornamentation from language, which is what would make it ornamental rather than representative. In the very act of declaring that "objects are books," for instance, Glassie invoked the irrelevance of the decorative—"no matter how pretty the bindings"—as if the validation of decorative objects as a topic of study depended on their being taken

INTRODUCTION

as not decorative. And even though Neçipoglu sets out to dismantle the opposition "'meaningful' versus 'decorative,'" she herself argues for the central meaningfulness—the semiotic force—of ornamentation.[56] As rich as the work done under the ægis of material culture is, insofar as it depends on a semiotic model in which the meaningfulness or representativeness of ornamentation is what is worth studying, it tends to bracket ornamentality as a problematic quality standing in the way of the ability to understand ornament.

Deconstruction's sense of ornamentation as the materiality or the form of language drained of meaning is far from the core belief of both art history and material culture studies that ornamentation is materially embodied form that conveys meaning, particularly cultural and historical meaning. And yet, these two broad approaches do understand ornamentation through the terms of representation, for they both consider how sensible objects, which are shaped into forms, can convey meaning. They take different positions, but they agree on the terms of the debate: Where does ornamentation fall on the semiotic grid in which matter is formed into shapes that convey meaning? The shortcoming of the discussion is that it is grounded in signification at all, let alone linguistic signification. Looking across aesthetics, literary theory, and the study of design and material culture, no coherent theory or definition of ornamentation emerges; instead, it moves around on a nexus of matter/form/meaning. This is not because ornamentation reveals the collapse of models of signification, or aesthetics, in which an idea or truth is made available through a material signifier; it's that it just does not work in them, because an ornament is not about the use of an audible, sensible, or legible signifier to communicate meaning, and hence not about the play between meaning and materially sensible form. And, insofar as ornament *does* become a bearer of meaning, it does so not because it is a pure material signifier that acquires meaning, as does any other signifier. Instead, the ornament is an already complex entity involving more than a materially sensible form, which then becomes a signifier. My point is comparable to that Roland Barthes made regarding ideological signification in *Mythologies*. As Barthes argued, a sign already composed of a signifier and a signified can then itself become the signifier of an ideology. Similarly, an ornament, as an already complex form calling attention to and conveying value upon something other than itself, might then be taken as a signifier of a cultural meaning. But this is not because ornament is at root another name for a signifier, a materially sensible form bearing meaning.

The major treatments of ornament in aesthetics, deconstruction, and material culture I have just sketched are oriented around a structure of meaning and of representation carried through materially embodied form.[57] In contrast, I will contend that ornamentation is about how one object rests upon and in relation to another; how an object carries and even carries out human attention (one approaches and touches something by ornamenting it, which is quite different from expressing an idea about it); how both writers and readers work with and among objects of attention; and how objects both shed and receive notice, light, and value. Particularly crucial is the use of ornamentation to confer and mark value, without containing an account or representation of what it is that is thereby valued. Also critical is the way that ornamental art adorns and moves within the temporal world, rather than transcending it as pure form or being grounded within it as utter materiality.

Thus the account of ornamentation that this book develops differs from those with which most literary criticism has been engaged. And in reaching that account, I depart from some basic principles of cultural studies and historicism about the relationship of thought to not simply the material signifier that carries it, but to the materiality of the culture from which it springs. In *Culture and Society*, Raymond Williams articulated an early version of a core principle of cultural studies: that literature and philosophy are the expressions of the cultural conditions out of which they are formed. Williams studied this idea in the work of nineteenth-century theorists of culture such as Samuel Taylor Coleridge and Matthew Arnold, whose arguments that cultural practice is also a form of social being were, in Williams's view, responses to the individual alienation and cultural division wrought by the Industrial Revolution. But it is also an idea central to Williams's work, as to any Marxist-influenced account of culture in which the material conditions of production are the real cause and meaning of cultural practice (although even

INTRODUCTION

Williams gives a quite subtle account of this relationship). In Williams's words,

> An essential hypothesis in the development of the idea of culture is that the art of a period is closely and necessarily related to the generally prevalent "way of life," and further that, in consequence, aesthetic, moral, and social judgements are closely interrelated. Such a hypothesis is now so generally accepted, as a matter of intellectual habit, that it is not always easy to remember that it is, essentially, a product of the intellectual history of the nineteenth century.[58]

While this view is clearly indebted to Marx, Williams observes that it also emerges out of ninteenth-century discussions about design and decorative art "in which the important names are [A. W.] Pugin, [John] Ruskin, and [William] Morris."[59] For these theorists and practitioners of architecture, design, and ornamentation, the essential aspiration was to produce ornamentation grounded in meaningful, humane, and nonexploitative life. They contrasted the ethos of the craftsman and artisan working by hand to the grotesque factory-made ornamentation that the Industrial Revolution had unleashed, and the alienated, inhuman conditions of life of both the factory workers who produced such objects and the consumers of such mass-market luxuries.

In this exemplary section of Williams's work, we can see the logic of a critical tradition in which grounding in history is linked to grounding in material production, and of an intellectual history in which ornamentation is a nexus for considering the alienation of capitalist production and attempts to return to material conditions to redeem it. In other words, critical principles about the ethical and political value of locating art as a product of material cultural conditions in the nineteenth century are here identified with arguments for the importance of ornamentation as a handcrafted, material object, rather than as an ungrounded factory-produced commodity. And yet, in the work of Thoreau, Dickinson, and Whitman, ornamentation rarely, if ever, functions in meaningful relationship to this framework; it is rarely (perhaps only in Thoreau) a sign of capitalist alienation, and almost never a sign of materially grounded cultural being. In their work, ornamentation functions in terms more akin to those of a poetic tradition with origins in archaic Greece, as I discuss in the next section. Thus, even in a methodological sense, understanding ornamentation in these writers' work requires departing from critical principles about how meaning is embedded in its material form—be it the material form of historical context or the material form of ornamental objects (of which there are no images in this book). At stake in the account of ornamentation I offer is, then, the need for a critical practice that departs from the long-standing "intellectual habit" of grounding ourselves in materiality, whether it be the materiality of the signifier or of historical conditions in a particular period.

ARCHAIC POETRY: ORNAMENTS AND OBJECTS

Key aspects of ornament that concern Thoreau, Dickinson, and Whitman have connections as far back as the song of archaic Greek *kleos* poets. Archaic poetic song was often identified with ornamental objects and aligned with the exchange of treasures including crowns, trophies, and other decorative objects. This tradition was supplanted in the fifth century by what would become a modern understanding of literature as a materially and linguistically fixed object representing something not present to the poet or the poem. According to Anne Carson, the poet "Simonides's inscriptional verse is the first poetry in the ancient Greek tradition about which we can certainly say, these are texts written to be read: literature."[60] In Carson's account, this form of literature was largely the result of the invention of technologies of inscription, which enabled poetry to be written upon stones and sold. She observes that "[t]he difference is physical: Simonides' poem has to fit on the stone bought for it"; "only an inscriptional poet has to measure his inspiration against the size of his writing surface."[61] The poem as a crafted object with a significant material presence was also the poem as representation. In Andrew Ford's consideration in *The Origins of Criticism*, in the fifth century one finds "a new word for 'likeness': *eikōn*, from a root meaning 'to resemble,' is used both for crafted 'likenesses' and for verbal 'images.'"[62] Out of this emergent account of literature as a representative work, Plato developed his definition of art as "giv[ing] a particular kind of pleasure without necessarily embodying or expressing philosophical truth."[63] Then, "with a further revision of the concept, Aristotle installed *mimēsis* at the center of his theory of poetry as 'representation.'"[64] As both Carson and Ford have it, much of the subsequent history of Western poetics has worked from this basic concept that a poem is a voice's expression in and through a material object. Poetry's identification with an inscribed object in turn enabled its stability as a linguistic artifact: a written-down poem is the same every time one reads it. According to Ford, this stabilization of the text by means of its material fixity made possible the first formalist criticism, which identified genres and judged the qualities of texts apart from the contexts at which they were sung or the persons who performed them. From this perspective, it is ironic that contemporary criticism has thought of the turn to material objecthood as a way of rejecting formalist analysis, for if the perceived stability of texts written on stone, papyrus, or paper made it possible to think of a poem as a stable and autonomous linguistic object, emphasizing material objecthood is necessary to, not an attack upon, the text's status as formal linguistic object.[65]

Thoreau, Dickinson, and Whitman were writers, not singers or performers. And yet their writing is not framed around the presumed identity or stability of the material text. Even at the level of the made artifact, Thoreau's massive journals have no endpoint, only the limit at which he dies. Dickinson's frequently revised, rearranged, and recopied poems evince writing as something different from the production of singular material objects or finite textual entities. Whitman's identification of *Leaves of Grass* with his ongoing life and his willingness to expand, cut, retitle, and otherwise rework his writing together suggest a cognate understanding that writing continually *happens*. Such writings are objects of relation and engagement for their authors, and then in turn for their readers, rather than fully independent objects that stand apart from their engagement by persons. The difficulties of editing such large, unstable texts underscores that they are not created as independent things in themselves but as occasions for human involvement.

As Ford argues, before the advent of the literature of objects and representations, Greek poets were considered divinely inspired persons who could summon up both religious and philosophical truths through song. These are the poets whom Marcel Detienne called "masters of truth."[66] But if Detienne's phrase stresses the singer's access to a mystically apprehended truth, Ford's work focuses upon the occasionality of such singing and the categories of the appropriate and the graceful. Archaic songs were not seen as independent works, solidly existing apart from the speaker or context; rather, they were performed at symposia, or ceremonial feasts, and they were judged in terms of their appropriateness to the occasion. Ford observes, "There is no *literary* criticism in the archaic period because 'the appropriate' and its congeners (*to prepon, metron, kairos*) always involved social and religious values."[67] This appropriateness was part of a process by which the singing of a song joined together the men in attendance with a "combination of ritual and social decorum."[68] And "[s]ymposiasts evaluated singing as a symbolic form of behavior in which the performer's observance of *to prepon, metron*, and *kairos* revealed his commitment to an order, *kosmos*, that was social and political as well as aesthetic."[69]

Carson writes that "[t]he Greek word *kosmos* can denote many kinds of order—planetary, governmental, social, sartorial, linguistic—as if all the different strands of human and natural complication in the world were woven out of one texture, extending over both space and time."[70] *Kosmos* also has another, related meaning: ornamentation that marks the completion of what is right.[71] Ford observes that the "notion of order in *kosmeō* . . . can denote a neat, effective arrangement and also an elegant, decorative one."[72] In the change from archaic to classical (and, in the classical scholars' sense, modern) concepts of poetry, the meaning of *kosmos* "was loosened from political and social order to signify ornamental arrangement, decoration."[73] An archaic tradition of occasional song performed in relation to a social moment, to mark and give value to an ordered world, moved into a way of thinking about the appropriate order of words and form in a poem, and on into the rhetorical approach to thinking about what figurative ornaments were appropriate or not. Through such routes, ornamentation survives into nineteenth-century literature as a trace of a premodern sense of poetry as song, linked to the decorous and occasion-based behavior of the poet. In this vein, far from being an especially material entity, ornamentation is antithetical to the poem as independent object. And such poetry is not grounded in the way material objects represent an absent human meaning; rather, it is an intense form of persons' relationship to their immediate world. The stakes of this distinction are not simply literary-historical, or even ones of genre definition; at issue in the difference between the two ways of thinking of poetics are two different realms of belief about how human beings exist in the world.

In Carson's reading, Simonides is central to the initiation of Western poetry, especially its terms of boundedness and representation in compensation for loss. She observes of a poem in which Simonides complains of his patron's stinginess, "Delay, disappointment and hunger are experiences catalytic for poets. When Simonides went to dine with Hieron, he had to complain of hare and snow withheld."[74] This local deprivation can be linked to Simonides' career as a writer of epitaphs and memorial poetry, which depended on the idea that poetic representation is a remedy for the loss endemic to the human realm. "The purpose of the monument is to insert a dead and vanished past into the living present,"[75] to carry over the lost person and lost time into the current moment. But these forms of loss and deprivation within the world—not having the dead with us, not having the "hare" to feed on we would like—are brilliantly linked in Carson's reading to a sense of loss endemic to the distinction between the physical and metaphysical worlds. She offers what she calls an "overtranslat[ion]" of a line in Simonides: "It is in fact upon the world of things needing to be uncovered that the world of merely visible things keeps exerting its pressure."[76] In Carson's words, "Simonides is interested in rendering the fact that ἀλήθεια (truth) cannot be seen in this world, no matter how tyrannical the pressure exerted on it by τὸ δοκεῖν (appearances)."[77] Poetry comes into being in the separation of lived experience from a metaphysical fullness and truth that can be intuited but not inhabited. And so the poem becomes a bounded object, a work of accepting and moving within a world of limits. Carson offers a powerful example of a major modern critical account of poetry as a work of representation and limitation in the face of the loss of presence, and as a bounded remedy for the condition of subjects living in time.

Andrew Ford reads Simonides differently than Carson, arguing against the classification of Simonides as an initial figure of Western literature. He writes, "it is anachronistic to read Simonides as the first of the *mimēsis* theorists rather than as one of the last of the *kleos* theorists."⁷⁸ His Simonides is a poet of the tradition of divinely inspired singing in socially appropriate modes, facing and objecting to the advancing formalist sense of the poem as a fixed artifact representing, rather than participating in, human life:

> As a poet of civic celebration and commemoration, [Simonides'] interest in artifacts was less the aesthetic one of how to marry truth to representation than the traditional singer's concern to confer wide and enduring praise on notable exploits. Simonides will be seen to argue that no physical object—even stones on which songs may be inscribed—can broadcast fame so widely as or so long as performance.⁷⁹

The objection to the poem-as-artifact is vividly conveyed in Ford's account of a poem in which Simonides all but trash-talks a memorial inscribed in stone. The poem in question is carved "on the tomb of the Phyrgian Midas" and quoted by Plato in *Phaedrus* 264:

> A maid of bronze, on Midas' tomb I stand.
> As long as waters flow and trees grow grand,
> Waiting here, on tomb wet by many a tear,
> I'll tell the passer-by: Midas is buried here.⁸⁰

In Ford's gloss: the poem's "implication is that, though men may come and go with the seasons, the fame of Midas has found a solid, permanent form. What makes the boast possible is that fame—Midas' name—has been written down."⁸¹ Simonides will have none of this; he rages back that since "all things are weaker than the gods; and stone / even mortal hands can shatter," the inscribed poem is surely "the devising of a fool."⁸²

The dispute between Simonides and the inscribed epitaph is, as Ford explains, over a new idea of permanence. The poem claims that stones (things of the material world) and poems (things written by persons) can last, whereas Simonides' view is that, as Ford puts it, nothing "humans might make can remain fixed in a nature that is constantly changing."⁸³ To drive the point home, Simonides imagines "breaking *stone*,"

INTRODUCTION

"shatter[ing]" this object that is reputed to be magnificently "durable."[84] Simonides believes that what *is* lasting has capacities of both flow and flux, which characterize the reiterated, re-performed song of the *kleos* poet: his "[i]nsist[ence] on the unique value of living, moving, and sounding song reasserted its connection to the life of a just and happy city."[85] The song that participates in this "flux" is ornamental: "The memorial that will never be defeated by time . . . is no physical construct but the memory, praise, and glory (*doxa*) of their deeds. This is summed up at the end as the 'great ornament to virtue and fame that is ever-flowing.'"[86] What's particularly surprising about this is that ornamentation as fluid praise appropriate to a particular social occasion is antithetical to the poem as the artfully crafted linguistic and material object.

Following the work of Deborah Steiner and Leslie Kurke, Ford argues that Pindar also saw poetry as an ornamental and social process. Pindar's poetry is almost entirely in the genre of *epinikion*, poetry that is, in Kurke's words, "written on commission for victors at athletic games and usually performed at the site of the games or at the victor's home in the context of a victory celebration."[87] Pindar frequently references ornamental objects, including the crowns and other ornaments received as the reward for victory at the games, and treasures exchanged by aristocrats to identify their social solidarity.[88] He often figures his own poetry as an ornamental object associated with ritual displays and exchanges. Ford argues that while modern critics have often taken Pindar's comparisons of poetry to ornamental objects as a means to stress poetry's material objecthood, Kurke's analysis shows that ornamental objects, treasures, and fancy gifts, including Pindar's poetry, mattered less for their objecthood and more for the way that they could be given, received, and moved between and across persons and places. Again, at stake is not just a shift in types of poetry, but different beliefs about how human beings relate to the world. Is the experience of the world captured and isolated in linguistic representation? Or is the world experienced as and through our way of speaking and acting in relation to it? Is language something brittle and apart from experience, or is it a part of it, moving in relation to life?

Like Simonides, Pindar resisted the transition to writtenness and literary objecthood. In one of Thoreau's translations of Pindar, the immobile statue is contrasted to the *kleos* poet's fluctuating praise in terms similar to those in Simonides' poem about Midas's tomb:

> No image-maker am I, who being still make statues
> Standing on the same base. But on every
> Merchant-ship, and in every boat, sweet song,
> Go from Ægina to announce that Lampo's son,
> Mighty Pytheas,
> Has conquered the pancratian crown at the Nemean games.[89]

"[S]weet song" far outpaces the immobile "statue" of the denigrated "image-maker." As an instance of Pindar's hostility to the emergent form of object-poetry, Ford brings up Kurke's discussion of the Lydian headband in Pindar. (In one translation, the passage reads: "A suppliant of Aiakos / on behalf of his city and his people here, / I touch his sacred knees, bringing / a crown of Lydian fabric, intertwined / with whistling strains of the flute, / to adorn / Deinis and his father Megas, winners / in the double race at Nemea.")[90] This headband, in Ford's summation, has often been read as an example of the emerging idea of a poem as crafted artifact. But, following Kurke, he points out that the headband is a "gesture[] toward the tradition of elites exchanging 'top-rank' objects," which "shows the victor how to convert his wealth and momentary success into the lasting esteem of his city."[91] "[N]ot only embroidered but 'tinkling,'" this headband and other such objects are, as Ford quotes Steiner, "'clamorous things'" rather than solid, material objects.[92] As in Simonides, this ornamental tradition emphasizes a flowing, changeable art that is more lasting than stone's shatterable rigidity. Pindar's "[v]egetal imagery presents fame not as uneroding solidity but as perpetually recurrent flowering; it places song's 'force' in 'its movement, its liveliness.' Such metaphors are often complemented with images of fame as liquid and flowing."[93] Here we are touching again on the role of ornamentation as a "recurrent flowering," which is the antidote to a poetry of stone and limitation.

Ford, like Carson, does emphasize the fifth-century emergence of concepts of the poem as a written text with a fixed form located in a material object rather than a social occasion. He also shows us how much this emergence of the poem as formed thing is identified with the emergence of Platonic and Aristotelian concepts of the centrality of mimesis to art, and the transition in Athens from an aristocratic to a democratic society which led to a new emphasis on representation rather than decorum. But Ford also offers us a window into the way that even as this enormously influential idea of poetry was emerging, it was in conflictual dialogue with an ornamental poetics aligned with fluid bestowing and a strong sense of the world's impermanence and instability. Despite the dominance of the twinned traditions of thinking about poetry as bounded written texts and as fixed, physical objects, the different sense of a poetry of ornamental fluctuation, aligned with social relations and conceptions of the decorous, the appropriate, and the praiseworthy, survives as an intermittent counter-poetics all the way into the work of Thoreau, Dickinson, and Whitman.

My purpose is not simply to point out that the archaic Greek *kleos* poets' ideas of ornamentation have a long, if little-noticed, extension into literature written in English. There is an intrinsic interest in ornamental poetics' way of maintaining a relation to what is praiseworthy and even what is simply present. It contains a proposal that literature may exist primarily as a relation to the present, rather than as an object which carries a meaning about an absent, displaced presence. It engages less with what humans make than with how they comport themselves—appropriately, gracefully, or even shamefully—in the world. Such questions are foundational to Heidegger's philosophy, in which comportment, bearing, and engagement are more primary than objects taken as things existing in themselves, apart from our relation to them. Heidegger was himself deeply engaged with the poetry of Pindar and archaic Greek philosophical thought as found in, for instance, the enigmatic writing of Parmenides. On one level, the permutating impact of classical education in English (of the kind that Thoreau and Emerson received) is accountable for the appearance of archaic Greek ideas of ornamentation in nineteenth-century American literature, where they could be found even by writers lacking such classical education themselves. But on a more important level, in their own terms, Thoreau, Dickinson, and Whitman adopt ornamentation's power to evoke a mode of relating to the world quite unlike that offered by the literary image-object with which most modern literature has been identified. And in this regard they share with Heidegger—as I will argue—a sense of the philosophical and human stakes in shifting from a representative to an ornamental poetic and aesthetic practice. What comes of thinking of literature as a way of connecting and relating to life, rather than as a way of framing and recalling it?

OVERVIEW OF *ORNAMENTAL AESTHETICS*

The rest of this book develops a theory of ornamental aesthetics and poetics through extended readings of onamentation in Thoreau, Dickinson, and Whitman. Chapter One, "Beautiful Thoreau," lays out the terms for a consideration of ornamentation's relationship to both poetry and the world through discussions of Heidegger and Thoreau, with reference to work on poetics by Elisa New and Susan Stewart. I argue for the centrality of the beautiful to Thoreau, and analyze his identification of natural beauty with ornament. Abandoning the attempt to interpret nature's meaning or to frame it in symbolic form, in the prose of his *Journal* Thoreau developed a contrasting poetic form, grounded in ornamental notation rather than symbolism or verse. Thoreau's accounts of ornamental beauty in the *Journal* and also in *Walden* and other writings offer a poetics of touch, and an aesthetics in which beauty is a matter of both doubt and reactivity. Ornamentation, for Thoreau, names and locates the refracting relationships that characterize the temporary contacts which constitute nature, the mind, and the relationship between them. This chapter also argues against a major strain of Thoreau scholarship that has emphasized his attempts to minimize the human presence in relationship to nature, and argues for the importance of his sensitivity to and interest in the way that the mind and body of the person impact and are impacted by natural phenomena.

Chapter Two, "Dickinson's Ornamental Form," expands the concerns about poetry's relation to the world and the investigation of a specifically ornamental poetics set forth in Chapter One. I argue that Dickinson engages with ornamentation to evoke a sense of human existence as a buoyant series of flickering contacts among mental and physical phenomena. Cicero's rhetorical theory presents ornamentation as a means of responding to the waywardness of an audience's attention, and Dickinson's poetry reveals a comparable view of ornamentation's link to the temporary quality of noticing. Poems notice things only to lose interest in them or fall apart, as a landscape might briefly be adorned by raindrops that Dickinson likens to pearl necklaces. In this regard, her poetry does not abide by the central logic of representation in the face of loss that is central to much poetic theory. Instead, it is a transitive mode of ornamenting the Open, a claim I use to locate the seeds of an account of an ornamental aesthetics in Heidegger. Here, ornamentation becomes a name for form in the light of the Open: form as an emergent, fluttering distinction rather than necessary structure or abstract rule. This part of the book also argues against a major strain of Dickinson criticism that emphasizes the materiality of her manuscripts and views the human mind as a problematic intrusion upon objects. Taken together, the first two chapters lay out ornamental aesthetics as a set of poetic practices and philosophical concerns that emphasize a reacting and impressing attention to the changing qualities of phenomena. Ornament stands as a mode of attending to the world, in which the human mind partakes of the world's basic condition of both transition and responsiveness; this is an alternative to critical theories in which the person stands as a problematic other to a world he seeks, always with sacrifice, to represent.

Chapter Three, "Whitman and the Distinction of Ornament," considers how ornamental objects and ornamental poetry mark the esteemed and distinguished. I first contend that Whitman's poetry is essentially ornamental, a point I make through comparison to George Puttenham's *Art of English Poesy* and its significant discussion of ornament. The ornamentation in Whitman turns on his sense of poetry as a bestowed object, his commitment to the excessively drawn-out line and the swollen poem, and his gestures of draping and weighing upon. Out of such practices and figures, he develops a poetry that lays praise and even a candid brilliance across the world. I argue that although Whitman's poetry has long been seen as analogous to the universal suffrage, and as engaging tensions in democratic representation between the claim of the universal and the particular, his poetry abjures representation for a practice of ornamental bestowing of praise. Unlike previous accounts of Whitman's politics, which consider how democratic ideals might be practiced, I argue that the work's politics concerns proper behavior, or the appropriate and decorous. Rather than being a poet of democratic harmony, Whitman uses the associations of ornamentation with brilliant outshining and aristocratic elevation to bring a sense of torqued contention into his work, and to highlight the forceful made-ness of the world. Throughout the book, even as ornamentation enables a sense of living connection among persons and world, one saturated in terms of praise and honor, it also moves into a sense of the impressed, made quality of the world. Thus in Thoreau, Dickinson, and Whitman, ornamental aesthetics lacks the underlying sense of rightness in the cosmos with which ornamentation in the archaic Greek period was identified. And, because its sense of the intimate, immediate presence lacks the redemptive image of grounding found in materialist accounts of ornamentation, it poses the possibility that to be in close contact with reality would necessitate abandoning attempts to see the world as right or wrong, and unraveling the very premise of judgment that is initially at stake in ornamentation as a marker of appropriate or well-set.

What motivates the connections I make between the work of Thoreau, Dickinson, and Whitman and texts on ornamentation from other cultural contexts? I locate intellectual and formal connections that are not motivated or explained by historical connections, but by the substantive identity of the artistic and philosophical commitments at stake. Ornamental aesthetics operates as does the aleatory materialism of Louis Althusser or the infidel poetics that Daniel Tiffany has recently considered: a set of ideas and practices which are available to and engaged by writers in any period or context. Tiffany argues that the long discredited idea of connections formed between and across texts from different time periods and even different cultures, rather than in physical and temporal contexts, is a powerful means to find alternatives to what a given culture insists upon as inevitably true. He writes that "the transitivity of the verbal enigma ... reminds us of the possibility of communities that defy the seemingly inexorable logic of transparency and continuity implicit in the social imaginary of the Internet. In contrast to the new ethos of instant accessibility and universality (i.e., the dogma of translation), the poetics of obscurity offers a blueprint for monadic communities which are at once inscrutable and reflective, discontinuous and harmonious, solipsistic and expressive."[94] The possibility of reading and responding to texts, ideas, and ways of understanding life other than those of our context might be the most salient feature of his account of alternative poetic traditions. For instance, he observes that "[t]he verbal spring of the canting song passes through literary history like a river in a desert, running beneath ground for long stretches, then transforming the landscape briefly in colorful and unexpected ways."[95] I think of ornamental aesthetics in a similar fashion: it is not a cultural logic but a recurring set of beliefs, practices, and possibilities which are sustained through relations between texts, authors, and readers that are more finely grained and intuitive than direct links of influence could locate. I also intend my own work to participate in sustaining such a tradition by calling attention to it and theorizing it.

Finally, in these readings I experiment with a more individual, if not personal, way of writing, partly in resistance to the new models of knowledge production that permeate contemporary universities,[96] and partly out of a commitment to retaining the individual element of reading. It is the life of criticism to allow specific persons' experiences of texts to become not only legible but persuasive enough to be meaningful to and usable by others. Discussing the degradation of persons' appearance in neoliberal culture, Jacques Rancière writes, "The utopia of postdemocracy is that of an uninterrupted count that presents the total of 'public opinion' as identical to the body of the people. What in actual fact is this identification of democratic opinion with the system of polls and simulations? It is the absolute removal of the sphere of the appearance of the people."[97] Describing the degradation of appearance under the pressure of technology and global capitalism, Jonathan Crary's 24/7 describes "a contemporary imaginary in which a state of permanent illumination is inseparable from the non-stop operation of global exchange and circulation." In such a world, ongoing illumination supports "an institutional intolerance of whatever obscures or prevents an instrumentalized and unending condition of visibility."[98] The incessant glare of global capitalism is, he argues, a corrosion of the structure of society. For in Hannah Arendt's work, he recalls, "[f]or an individual to have political effectiveness, there needed to be a balance, a moving back and forth between the bright, even harsh exposure of public activity and the protected, shielded sphere of domestic or private life, of what she calls 'the darkness of sheltered existence.'"[99] This movement between light and dark, the covered and uncovered, is itself implicitly indebted to Heidegger's understanding of truth as a careful uncovering and sheltering, rather than a bare presentation.

As I observed earlier in this Introduction, phenomenology does share with the Marxist-historicist tradition an intention to reject the modern, rational idea that the immediate encounter of an object by a subject is a source of truth or real knowledge. I return to this point to emphasize that although this is not a historicist book, neither is it a book which imagines that one person's reading yields a translucent, empirical glimpse of these texts. My readings will look utterly unmediated to historicist scholars, but they are concerned with the mediation that produces any one moment of contact between a mind and an object. This project seeks to restore to what we loosely call the immediate—the way one mind engages a text, a flower, or a rosette—its unsettled, negotiated, and even fraught qualities. The immediate moment is, as ornamental contacts reveal, far other than the reified image of individual-immediate knowing for which phenomenology, Marxist-influenced historicism, and ongoing critical accounts of close reading take it.

What most troubles me about the position that an influenced, individual mind has no valuable experiences to share—as in Fredric Jameson's famous objection that we must historicize because we "never really confront a text immediately"—is its view that the subjection of persons to influence, force, or conditions renders their experiences and ideas not only meaningless but dangerous.[100] I intend my investigation of ornamentation and my departure from familiar forms of historicist scholarship as a departure from and alternative to a culturally and intellectually ingrained lack of interest in, and inability to contact, immediate experience as it unfolds in the present.[101] This book was written with a sense that in the particularity of the person's experience is held the impermanence and unreliability, even the volatility, of every appearance in or at a condition. Thus the paradox of this book is that its commitment to offering an alternative to representational poetics is conjoined to a deep commitment to how both literature and criticism can bring out the person. While Allen Grossman contends that "[p]oetry is language in which the eidetic function is prior to all other functions," ornamental aesthetics and poetics are not concerned with this form of bringing up the form of the person.[102] And yet, its primary concern *is* the particular human experience of life, and in that concern lies its basic humanism. In their own ways, Thoreau, Dickinson, and Whitman pursue an ornamental poetics precisely as an alternative to eidetic poetics, and its humanism grounded in representation of the person. But it does not mean that their poetry is, in the end, not as committed to poetry as a manifestation of human existence.

Here it may be useful to look to the words of a scholar and teacher of Tibetan Buddhist meditation, Reginald Ray. Ray is discussing the importance of describing individual experiences of meditative practice:

> As Georges Bataille, the French philosopher, has pointed out, the affirmation of individual human experience as of supreme and unique value (sui generis) is automatically destabilizing of any kind of conservatism, including that of cultural standardization, institutionalized religious authority, or social control. When a person speaks out of the depths of his experience, he is, in effect, saying, "This unique experience of mine is important. It is sacred. It is worth speaking. What I am expressing has importance for our collective life." To speak of individual experience is to affirm the category of the unique and individual. It is, implicitly at least, to call into question the assumption that the ultimate authority is found somewhere outside, in the collective.[103]

In Buddhist understanding, as Ray continues, this personal experience is not about a subject. In Ray's words,

> our unique and ultimately individual self is, at the same time, an entirely impersonal event in the universe ... we are nothing more than custodians of this unique life and are being called to our full embodiment to inhabit, to experience, and to communicate it fully, not as a personal thing at all, but as a moment in the unfolding of being itself.[104]

INTRODUCTION

My view in writing this book has been that in the grain of particular critical observation, and of particular aesthetic practices, we can get closer to the life of experience, and hence the life of persons. But in this experience is also, as in the quotation from the Rohitassa Sutta earlier in this Introduction, the range of the cosmos and that which goes beyond the person. This is to state in terms of Buddhism what is also at issue for Heidegger: an intimate inquiry into the life of persons will take us into qualities quite other than what we at first blush expect existence to entail.

Ornamentation, an aesthetic practice that has been marginal to literary criticism and literature for centuries, is an avenue to understanding and experiencing human existence which offers fresh contact with reality. For ornament encourages us to pay attention to the nature of the human mind and its flexibility and reactivity alike. Because ornamentation is never a self-enclosed textual object or even art object, it continually pushes one back on the centrality of the experience of human thought, attention, and feeling. Ultimately, ornamentation and interest in it are intertwined: ornamental objects are often a means to draw attention, and they engage a form of attracted, but not always conceptually focused, attention, which is distinct from the attention it takes to interpret the meaning of a representation. Moreover, because ornaments are used, plied, and pursued, they are caught up in the current of the mind that is drawn to them, using them, or distracted by them. The fundamental connection of ornamentation to attending thought is compactly suggested in a sentence quoted by Grabar: "A mind settled on an intelligent thought is like the stucco decoration on the wall of a colonnade."[105] How a mind might relate to its own thought is here analogized to how an ornament relates to what it ornaments; the suggestion is that ornamentation has a quality shared with a mode of thinking. However, if the saying analogizes internal, mental processes to external, physical objects, what we will see increasingly is how fully thinking ornament entails abandoning the notion that thinking is an internal process always opposed to, and apart from, the world of things, objects, or others.

Ornamentation as a mode of praise leads into investigations of the relationship between a total praise of Being itself, and the ability of the human being to love and open to all that exists, not only to what

INTRODUCTION

is identified with or preferred. But ornamentation's use to mark special bonds of love or comradeship, and its mode of appearance as what gives value to one thing over another, also makes it a means of speaking about the uneven distribution of value or love. The relationship between these two registers—the total and the particular, the all-encompassing and the preferred—is one of the most compelling things that ornamentation can show us. And, as ornamentation moves through a wide-open world of change, it finds a way to locally point out and adorn such change as beautiful and worth one person's notice, at this spot and not another.

Chapter 1

Beautiful Thoreau

An Ornament to Nature

INTRODUCTION

Over and over, Thoreau's *Journal* takes pleasure in the beauty of nature, singling out particular aspects for their loveliness and their "effect upon the beholder":

> It has a singular but pleasant effect on the beholder to see considerable sheets of water standing at different levels— Pleasant to see lakes like platters full of water. (J, 5:6)

> Then when I turned I saw in the east just over the woods the modest pale cloud like moon 2/3 full-looking spirit like on these daylight scenes. Such a sight excites me. (J, 5:12)

> The white pine left here and there over the sprout land—is never more beautiful than with the morning light— (J, 5:20)

Thoreau describes "all very beautiful & exhilarating sights—a sort of diet drink to heal our winter discontent" (J, 6:4), or "[t]he beauty of some butterflies — dark steel blue with a light blue edge" (J, 6:250). Nature is beautiful and affecting to Thoreau, but he is especially attentive to the exceptional beauty of distinct elements of it: "Is it not the handsomest & most striking & brilliant flower since roses & lilies began?" (J, 6:262); "Our most beautiful fern—& most suitable for wreathes or garlands"

(*J*, 6:281). Beauty is located in specifically remarkable items, as when Thoreau "[s]aw a tanager in Sleepy hollow—It most takes the eye of any bird.... It flies through the green foliage as if it would ignite the leaves" (*J*, 6:138–39). The singularity of beautiful flowers, ferns, and birds is not purely about the object's singularity: it also includes how they are seen, and where and when they show best. For example, Thoreau's remark that "[t]he birds are heard through the pleasant dashing wind which enlivens every thing" (*J*, 6:141) pinpoints how the sound of the birds comes through a wind apparently felt on the skin and face, forming a composition of sensory objects and responses that excites him.

Thoreau tends to make such assessments of beauty in passing and then to proceed without further comment. As a result, the beauty in the *Journal* has an unusual limitation: it goes only so far. For instance, Thoreau writes, "A singular effect produced by a mass of ferns at a little distance—some rods square—their light yel-green tops seen above the dark masses of their fruit— At—first one is puzzled to account for it. Wht ash fully in bloom" (*J*, 6:135). Considering the "singular effect" of "ferns at a little distance" cedes first to bewilderment, and then to the memo, "Wht ash fully in bloom." Such "a singular effect" is highly valued, but it draws Thoreau in without promise of further interest or reward.

Thoreau's *Journal* is so strange a piece of writing that, as Sharon Cameron has written, it "prohibits the use of many interpretive procedures ordinarily taken for granted."[1] Its strangeness includes its overpowering length, the fluctuating ideas of its purpose that Thoreau records within it, and its combination of factual notations of natural phenomena and outbursts of reflection without explanation of their relationship to one another. The strangeness of the *Journal* makes it already a compelling and recalcitrant piece of writing, and thus it prompts one to ask about both the nature of Thoreau's interest in his topic, and of one's own interest in his writing. This can sometimes be as simple as finding oneself wondering, is there anything in or to this text? But it can also be a matter of finding that fascinating passages appear with no warning, only to be dropped almost before they've gotten under way. Or a concern keeps cropping up across an entry, several entries, even several years: it becomes hard to know if there's any relation between one thought and those noted near it in the text, and where the boundaries of a particular image or concern actually are.

Dizzyingly, one comes to feel that it might not matter where in the *Journal* one read, or if one read all of it, and as if there would be no purpose in seeking an account of it as a distinct entity. But even if the *Journal* isn't calibrated to arouse and sustain interest, it shows that intense interest—both ours and Thoreau's—can be evoked exactly under such uncertain conditions. The very recalcitrance of the *Journal* to adequate comprehension encourages its reader to risk appreciation and absorption without certainty of where they will end. What are we reading for, how do we read, if we aren't leaning toward getting a true account of the object of our study? What is the force of interest, if it isn't geared toward a full knowing of the meaning or structure of an object?

The *Journal*'s elusiveness makes it a particularly rewarding occasion to read more aesthetically—more openly, that is—than for an interpretation. I put it that way initially, but what is at issue is the nature of interpretation: it seems fruitless to read the *Journal* for a definitive account of its meaning, or an interpretation that aims to package or finish it. But it encourages one to practice an interpretation that is able to hesitate, to doubt at times, and to leave time for noticing and perceiving the text before or alongside the demand to say why, or what that contact produces. This is the kind of reading that the *Journal* itself pursues, although there it is a way of reading nature rather than a way of reading a text. Cameron finds that Thoreau's "attendance to the landscape . . . is an effort to read it,"[2] and although I will take issue with her contention that the *Journal* is not concerned with aesthetics, I try to unfold further her claim that the *Journal* is an act of reading as attending. The *Journal* observes, enjoys, analyzes, and is fundamentally preoccupied by something other than itself, and by the experience of something other than itself and the way that the mind works upon that condition. It is both a work of art and a critical work, which combine into an unprecedented art of seeing, being affected, and knowing. An essential part of this critical art is the way that observing, being affected, and judging or considering the world are understood in the *Journal* to themselves leave traces upon the world. However delicate and responsive a critical art, this is a way of engaging nature that affects it.

Thoreau's *Journal* is courageous in its willingness to attend to nature without a defined project, to pursue an investigation without yet knowing its end, without even knowing in what direction it is tending. It is also courageous in its honesty about the way that things both attract and engage the mind, even when an account of the value or the meaning of such attraction and engagement is not forthcoming. I think, here, of Anne-Lise François's suggestions about passing up the role of "the paranoid, penetrating, critical, or 'spiritual' reader who 'earns' her prized insights by tunneling below the surface of the letter."[3] Although she does not expand upon this point, François indicates that one inspiration for her consideration of "self-quieting, recessive speech acts and hardly emitted announcements" and an "ethos of nonappropriative contentment" was "the strange value accorded to 'doing nothing' or 'as little as possible' within popularly inspired Thoreauvian environmentalist discourse."[4] This identification of Thoreau with an environmentalism concerned with limiting the impact of the human presence has been a significant thread in Thoreau criticism. For example, Laurence Buell writes about Thoreau to explore the question of how literature might speak for nature without anthropomorphizing it or turning it into something that exists for human ends. While part of Buell's environmentalist criticism is a defense of the value of an aesthetic appreciation of nature and a tendency to read it as a set of symbols of divine or human meaning, the fact that he calls such practices "double-edged tools" indicates his primary view that the human presence in and use of nature are innately troubling.[5] Thus Buell reads one passage in *Walden* as evincing, in a manner he clearly endorses, how "Thoreau's colonization of his surroundings . . . gives way, when he relaxes and makes himself receptive, to the feeling of being constituted—lock, stock, and barrel—by the forms of nature. Ecocentrism replaces egocentrism."[6] Thoreau is to be praised when he writes a literature in which the person is effaced, and the "physical world" and "the nonhuman environment" come to the foreground.[7]

In contrast, my contention is that, notwithstanding his diffuse, interpretation-parrying writing in the *Journal*, Thoreau's ornamental aesthetics point to his utter commitment to the effects of observation, and to the effected and responsive qualities of the natural world itself.

His sense that there is something beautiful in how his mind relates to the moon and to the woods—"Then when I turned I saw in the east just over the woods the modest pale cloud like moon 2/3 full-looking spirit like on these day-light scenes"—is intensely relational and responsive. Thoreau hangs back much less than critical habits and environmentalist ethics suggest; what might happen in and to nature, and to himself within it, matter more than its pure isolation. It is in this commitment to touching and affecting nature, and in going with and attending it, that I locate the ornamental and poetic qualities of Thoreau's aesthetics.

THE FLOWER OF THE MIND

Thoreau's words on Anacreon's poetry, from *A Week on the Concord and Merrimack Rivers*, describe an ornamental reading of an ornamental text:

> His odes are like gems of pure ivory. They possess an ethereal and evanescent beauty like summer evenings, ὅ χρή σε νοεῖν νόου ἄνθει, *which you must perceive with the flower of the mind,*—and show how slight a beauty could be expressed. You have to consider them, as the stars of lesser magnitude, with the side of the eye, and look aside from them to behold them. They charm us ... by a certain flower-like beauty, which does not propose itself, but must be approached and studied like a natural object.[8]

Rather than posing the interpretation of poetry as an attempt to decipher the intention of the author, Thoreau finds the poems all but meaningless; they show "how slight a beauty could be expressed." Nor is the point to savor the detail of the language's sound, its figuration, or any of its identifiable linguistic features, which barely rate a mention. Instead, the poems are understood to be a kind of ornament: "like gems of pure ivory." And these ornamental gems are to be "consider[ed]" with a sidling, askance attention, found in looking near them rather than at them.

If the odes are like ornamental ivory gems, that ornamental property also applies to the mind that perceives them, which is specified as *"the flower of the mind."* What does that mean? Apparently, it is some apprehending or thinking that is a beautiful expansion, and perhaps an achievement or special display of the mind, rather than a paraphrase of the poem's meaning or an account of its relevance. Emerson had used the phrase five years earlier in "The Poet," where it figures as part of his discussion of the poet's "suffering the ethereal tides to roll and circulate through him."[9] At such times,

> he speaks somewhat wildly, or, "with the flower of the mind"; not with the intellect, used as an organ, but with the intellect released from all service, and suffered to take its direction from its celestial life; or, as the ancients were wont to express themselves, not with the intellect alone, but with the intellect inebriated by nectar.[10]

Emerson's comments convey a sense that the flower of the mind is not the controlled intellectual mind, but a more released activity. He continues by describing this mind as like that of "the traveller who has lost his way, [and] throws his reins on his horse's neck."[11] But the wildness and intensity with which Emerson describes such mental being is different from the quiet with which Thoreau characterizes "the flower of the mind" reading Anacreon's poetry.

Like Emerson, Thoreau is working out an understanding of the Greek phrase ὃ χρή σε νοεῖν νόου ἄνθει, from the *Chaldean Oracles*, a collection of fragments of unknown origin, which were once associated with Zoroaster.[12] The translation of νοεῖν that Thoreau gives is "perceive," but it is helpful to bring in Heidegger's investigation of the term in *What Is Called Thinking?* In Heidegger's reading, the word contains qualities of both perceiving and of thinking, suggesting a thought that is more receptive than shaping. Still, it is not fully recessive: "In νοεῖν, what is perceived concerns us in such a way that we take it up specifically, do something with it. . . . We take it to heart. What is taken to heart, however, is left to be exactly as it is. This taking-to-heart does not make over what [it] takes. Taking to heart is: to keep at heart."[13] To be "left to be exactly as it is" is almost a disingenuous phrase here, for the thing has also been "take[n]," and the connection of leaving with taking and "keep[ing]" adds up to a perception that is something more than noninterfering, even if it is not grasping or containing.

Like Heidegger, Thoreau characterizes νοεῖν as a perception, which in its cautious care tends to blossom near and resonate with what concerns it. This mental flowering dignifies Anacreon's poetry, and even mimics it in becoming a flower to go with the poem's "gem"- or "flower-like beauty." Here, "mind" as νόος refers to the mind not as a personal or individual being, but as a set of functions and actions. Thus, according the Liddell-Scott Lexicon, "mind" as νόος includes usages such as "to have one's mind directed to something," "mind, more widely, as employed in feeling, deciding, etc., heart," and even "resolve, purpose."[14] This is the sense of mind that means to carefully attend to, as in the word *mindful*. It's about notice and thought that are tied to a quality of caring direction toward the object. The flower of the mind, then, indicates the refined manifestation of an impersonal mental activity, which is characterized by an appreciative and attending perception. In "Walking," Thoreau again quotes the *Chaldean Oracles* on the topic of knowing: "'You will not perceive that as perceiving a particular thing,' say the Chaldean Oracles." Instead, perception will be, in Thoreau's own words, like "the lighting up of the mist by the sun."[15]

Thoreau exhibits such illuminating and flowering perception in many of his observations of natural beauty throughout the *Journal*. However, in the *Journal*, it can feel somewhat more complicated and less placid than in the passage regarding Anacreon's poetry. In 1853, Thoreau overheard his Aunt Maria complaining that "he stood haf an hour today to hear the frogs croak" (*J*, 6:41). He also recalled "standing perfectly still some 10 minutes looking at a willow which had just blossomed," only to realize "two men" were watching him watch the tree (*J*, 6:71). Such moments don't trouble Thoreau much, but they do indicate his slight self-consciousness about being observed while engaged in a seemingly pointless attentiveness. That uncertainty about his purposelessness is, in much of the *Journal*, central to his attention to nature. In particular, observations about beauty are concurrent with expressions of doubt and uncertainty. Beauty is, of course, definitely connected with purposelessness in Kant's third *Critique*, which argues that "[b]eauty is an object's form of *purposiveness* insofar as it is perceived in the object *without the presentation of a purpose*."¹⁶ But in Kant's formation, the beautiful object lacks an instrumental purpose, or even a definite meaning, while yet maintaining a distinct "*purposiveness*" to the subject who perceives it, which Kant calls the "the subjective purposiveness of the beholder."¹⁷ Thoreau's way of linking doubt about purpose or direction to beauty is, in contrast, more genuinely disoriented and uncertain.

Sometimes, Thoreau's doubt simply concerns his identifications, particularly of birds: "Have I seen the least bittern?" (*J*, 6:89); "in some uncertainty about whether I do not confound several kinds under the name of the downy-w[oodpecker]" (*J*, 6:45); "Could that have been a jay?" (*J*, 6:92). But there is further tentativeness in the *Journal* about whether he is observing nature or himself, as when he writes:

> Hark did I not hear the note of some bird then—? Methinks it could not have been my own breathing through my nose. No— there it is again a robin . . . There were one or two more fine bird like tinkling sounds—I could not trace home not to be referred to my breathing—. (*J*, 6:13)

Here, the closeness inside the mind of the sound of a bird and the breath cast Thoreau into doubt over what is part of him and what is part of his world. In other places, Thoreau expresses concern about the state of his own mind in relation to the objects it is seeking to observe. "I feel that I am dissipated by so many observations I should be the magnet in the midst of all this dust & filings—. . . I have almost a slight dry head ache as the result of all this observing" (*J*, 6:30). Although "[i]t is affecting to see a distant mt top—" (*J*, 6:58), the effect is not only of pleasure but also of a disintegration of the mind, as its focus on the individual grains of the world disperses thought. "The more I study willows the more I am confused—" (*J*, 6:81).

This confusion is, in the *Journal*, at times expressed as a frustration on Thoreau's part with his faltering ability to take nature as a symbol of inner experience. In such moods, Thoreau writes as if his purpose were to find in nature a set of phenomena to serve as symbols for a spiritual experience which he is not having, or which he cannot fit to those phenomena.

> He is the richest who has most use for nature as raw material of tropes & symbols with which to describe his life— If these gates of golden willows affect me they correspond to the beauty & promise of some experience on which I am entering. If I am overflowing with life—am rich in experience for which I lack expression—then nature will be my language full of poetry—all nature will *fable* & every natural phenomenon be a myth—The man of Science who is not seeking for expression but for a fact to be expressed merely—studies nature as a dead language—I pray for such inward experience as will make nature significant. (*J*, 6:105)

The uncertainty that we have seen thus far could, under the sign of this passage, be that of a faltering writer who couldn't find the "inward experience" to "make nature significant," to turn the mass of observations he continued to record into the "tropes & symbols" of his own life.

Of course, Thoreau shortly did succeed in turning natural experience into "tropes & symbols" in *Walden*, published in 1854, just a year after the *Journal* entries I have been considering. In *Walden* he writes that he farmed "for the sake of tropes and expression," cheerfully bragging about turning the bean-field into a metaphor (*W*, 162). Both Sherman Paul and Frederick Garber praised Thoreau for this success. Paul found that the *Journal* was mostly a tool for Thoreau to "perform this symbolizing process," yielding images such as *Walden*'s "hawk," which "symbolized his ultimate liberation from the senses."[18] Garber also saw Thoreau as engaged in this transformation of the natural world into an expression of the mind, as "[w]hen consciousness redeems nature, it transforms the world into itself."[19] From such perspectives, the doubts that we have already seen in Thoreau constitute true falterings: thus, Paul wrote that in the years following *Walden*'s publication, Thoreau "became an inspector of phenomena . . . instead of his former rhapsodies over the cricket he merely noted in the *Journal*, in a kind of shorthand, the barest fact: 'Have heard the alder *cricket* some days.'"[20] This bare noting was "the sign of his lapse and his failure."[21]

This somewhat creaky narrative of Thoreau's career, in which the symbol-making genius dropped off into a barren note-taker, is worth recalling in order to emphasize the prominence of self-doubt and faltering in the *Journal*: "The night of the year is approaching, what have we done with our talent" (*J*, 6:306). This isn't something I read in terms of either failure or triumph, though Thoreau sometimes does. At issue is Thoreau's realization that his mind is changing. It is, first, aging, as he exclaims, "Ah those youthful days! Are they never to return? When the walker does not too curiously observe particulars" (*J*, 6:56). But it also is just changing, depending on mood, the day, or whatever other factors are impinging on Thoreau. Thoreau's *Journal* is a powerful document of the alterations of an investigating mind, as it can become interested in, and even delight in, something while shot through with doubt and "confusion."[22] An author who would elucidate "the flower of the mind" is also alert to many other qualities of mental activity.

The changeability and the affectedness of the mind are evident in the *Journal* even on a quite basic level. In many of the quotations I have been touching upon, the physical location and the attitude of the observer are as much at issue as is the element that is observed. For instance: "Then when I turned"; "heard through the pleasant dashing wind"; "ferns at a little distance ... one is puzzled to account for it"; "standing perfectly still." Thoreau's notations of the season's alterations are also notations of changes in his own attire—"First hear toads (& take off coat—)" (*J*, 6:85). His looking can be almost intrusive, as he confides "by looking very carefully in the most favored & warmest localities you may find most flowers out some weeks even in advance" (*J*, 6:135). In June he not only finds a nighthawk's nest filled with eggs, but "advanced and put my hand on them—and while I stooped seeing a shadow on the ground looked up & saw the bird which had fluttered down the hill so blind & helpless circling low & swiftly past over my head ... suddenly descending it dashed at me within 10 feet of my head" (*J*, 6:171). A few days later, Thoreau finds two woodchucks fighting in a hole and grabs one by the tail "& though I had to pull very hard indeed I drew him out ... and tossed him a little way down the hill" (*J*, 6:208). These are obvious examples of what is elsewhere subtler: an interest as much in where and how Thoreau is looking as in what he is looking at. If some of these anecdotes appear to show us only his willingness to put his hand on an egg or a tail, or to look from a distance and also to look very closely, they actually reveal the way that the moods and mind of the observer are undergoing alterations of attitude, location, and disposition.

Moods was the title Louisa May Alcott gave to an 1864 novel in which she modeled her two main characters on Thoreau and Emerson. Alcott's focus on the notion of moods points up the way that Transcendentalists emphasize the experience of mental transience (they did, after all, believe that a new era in human nature was dawning). Alcott's novel bears as its epigraph a quotation from Emerson: "Life is a train of moods like a string of beads; and as we pass through them they prove to be many colored lenses, which paint the world their own hue, and each shows us only what lies in its own focus."[23] In that quotation from "Experience," Emerson's "train of moods" gives a sense of being subjected to a series of frames of mind and heart, which become a disorienting parade of "colored lenses which paint the world *their* own hue," not *our* own.[24] One might also point out his observation, in "Circles," that "[o]ur moods do not believe in each other. . . . I am God in nature; I am a weed by the wall."[25] Thoreau's careful attention to the shifts in his exhilaration, his doubt, his fastening on of attention, and his sense of aimlessness and occasional dullness are all part of this understanding that to perceive life demands contradictory and unpredictable surges of thought and feeling.

A major shift in Thoreau studies was the turn away from a focus on *Walden*'s artistic achievement to a serious focus on the *Journal* as his central endeavor. This shift was produced largely by the otherwise quite contradictory work of Sharon Cameron and Laura Dassow Walls. For Cameron, the *Journal*'s abiding commitment was to an intimate relationship with, and knowledge of, nature. In her reading, Thoreau's deepest project of observing was compromised by its transformation into the literary and legible *Walden*. Cameron's *Writing Nature* emphasizes not Thoreau's waning artistry but his "progressive refusal to interpret the observations recorded, as if the significance of the description of a tree were the description of the tree."[26] Thus Cameron "understand[s] the sustained documentation of the *Journal* as the strategy for writing about nature that resists being symbolic."²⁷ Far from failing to find a way to make nature meaningful, the *Journal* became Thoreau's primary work, consumed by "a passion for nature divorced from social meaning." ²⁸ In the *Journal*, Cameron writes, Thoreau's "lists and calculations" are redolent of "exhilaration" and "intima[cy]."²⁹

Where Cameron presses the asocial quality of Thoreau's passion for natural detail, Walls argues that Thoreau's "ultimate aim . . . was to communicate his findings to others," for he "conceived of himself as part of the community of knowing."³⁰ However, Walls does concur with Cameron that *Walden* had been a compromise for Thoreau.

> Making *Walden* socially available had meant cutting corners to create a rounded, shapely, fictional entity. . . . This is the paradigmatic aesthetic act, rendering nature into an "organic" whole. But Thoreau was alert to the consequences: first, the artist's tendency to read the shapely whole back into nature, smooth out anomaly, demand conformity. This act denied his fundamental belief in nature's vital lack of completion; so in the *Journal* he would follow nature beyond the rounded whole he had made of her in *Walden*.³¹

In turning more and more to notations, Walls argues, Thoreau sought to join in a community of emerging natural historians and biologists, and to know nature on terms more true to it than those of "aesthetic[s]." Not only was the attempt to present nature as a whole a compromise to art—notice the scare quotes around "'organic' whole"—but even the symbol-making was a betrayal: Walls asserts that "[w]hat [Thoreau] wanted, finally, was to declare that burdock and wood thrushes had an absolute reality, beyond symbolic construction."³² The *Journal* emerges from the status of midlife dissipation to principled achievement, and as in Buell's reading, not making art of nature is linked to leaving nature alone in its innate integrity.

My demurral from these readings concerns their view that because the *Journal* is not primarily concerned with the creation of symbolic meaning or with completion, it is therefore not concerned with aesthetics. The passages I began with emphasize Thoreau's commitment to beauty, and both his doubt in and the waning of his own symbolizing faculty can be seen as an *increase* in his interest in that lack of purpose identified with the domain of the aesthetic. For Thoreau, not using nature to make symbols is to allow nature to play in and on his own mind, indulging in an undirected aesthetic encounter that may well leave his aunt or those two men watching in perplexity. Thoreau's doubting aesthetics shows that things can be intensely, ravishingly beautiful without having any meaning at all. They can also command attention (roses are found "[n]ot only beautiful but rightfully commanding attention" [J, 5:150]) to an extent that is unjustifiable (serving no end that the human mind can see as reasonable, useful, or purposive) and yet inextinguishable. The beautiful can be found apart from the symbolic, the meaningful, or the finely shaped whole. In fact, finding the beautiful is for Thoreau often an interruption or an accident—it suddenly happens, and cannot be reliably reproduced or located in either himself or even in a particular tree or flower.

Rowing a boat in 1853, Thoreau and his sister Sophia "heard a singular note of distress," which turns out to be "a little dot of a kitten" (J, 6:143). Thoreau lauds the kitten for, although "almost infinitely small—, Yet it had hailed a boat—its life being in danger & sailed itself" (J, 6:144). He repeats, "It saved itself & hailed a boat!—" (J, 6:145). Calling attention often features in Thoreau's appraisals of beautiful trees and flowers in the 1853 *Journal*: "the catkin is so large & conspicuous" (J, 6:116); the tanager "most takes the eye" (J, 6:138); "the grass to which the rain has given such a start conspicuously waves showing its lighter underside" (J, 6:136); "[t]hat exceedingly neat & interesting little flower blue-eyed grass now claims our attention" (J, 6:159). Such phrasings, in which natural objects are "conspicuous," "take[] the eye," or "claim[]" the "attention" all have some of the quality of the kitten's hailing.

Thoreau writes, still in 1853, "Might not my journal be called 'Field Notes'" (J, 6:20). But the kind of notes Thoreau is making are distinct from a scientist's carefully observed particulars being freed from the shaping of aesthetic interest, as Walls encourages us to think of them. The noting is itself an aesthetic engagement. I use the word *engagement* here to denote a relationship distinct from the alienated contemplation of spectatorship; Thoreau is caught up with, and often altering in relation to, natural objects in ways that are too emotionally and physically agitating to count as detached aesthetic contemplation or spectatorship. I also use the word *engagement* for its somewhat limited quality, to denote an occasional, partial latching-on that begins and ends.

Elisa New argues that while there is a strain of American literature consumed by the ability of the sovereign mind to dictate a world on its own terms (this "genius of American originality is prior to any experience"), there is a contrary tradition of American writing that privileges "the snagged and implicated sensation of living deeply *in* the world—rather than prior to it as a detached subject, or driven ahead of it as mere vassal to deterministic force."[33] She argues that this focus on individual, located perception is the province of poetry, and in particular of the poetic line: "The poet's line, a more sapient eye, recalls mind to its mutuality with nature, and desire to its fertile source in relation."[34] The idea of the *line* as the finite spot of contact lives on in Thoreau's notations of beauty. The very curtailing of those notations—which is so unlike the proliferation of Thoreau's great paragraphs in *Walden*—has the particularizing punctuality of the poetic line. The notes in the *Journal* of natural beauty, although not in any recognized poetic form, are at heart following out the logic of the line, albeit in a more glancing and less assured manner than the "living deeply *in* the world" that New describes. This is an aesthetic but also a poetic project, precisely for the specificity and locality with which the mind contacts beauty. Poetry and beauty are not encompassed by the ambition of symbolizing or completion; an incessant work of turning and hearing the call *to be noticed* is, in Thoreau, another mode of poetic practice. "One of the most beautiful things to me now is the reddish ash—" (J, 6:140). The simplicity of such a confession reveals a mind susceptible to life, including its own moods and the phenomena which it encounters.

ORNAMENTAL ATTENDING

Attending to what calls for notice and snagging briefly onto a beautiful object are, then, ways that Thoreau's *Journal* is a poetic work. These are also aspects of the *Journal* which Thoreau explicitly identifies with ornamentation. A reconsideration of his doubts about nature will help to bring out this contention. In the *Journal*, Thoreau's aesthetic judgments come in as an accoutrement to a mind that is weakened and drawn to something it does not entirely grasp. Beauty becomes something that happens to and in the mind, when it is softened and lacks the capacity to interpret and shape. Sometimes that's quite obvious, as in this passage:

> The sunset was uncommonly fair. Some long amber clouds in the horizon, all on fire with gold, were more glittering than any jewelry. An Orient city to adorn the plates of an annual could not be contrived or imagined more gorgeous. And when you looked with head inverted the effect was increased tenfold. . . . We only regretted that it had not a due moral effect on us scapegraces. (*Jo*, 11:166)

If there is some humor here about how the glorious view has no "effect on us scapegraces," this tries to shrug off the real perplexity about the ever-increasing, somehow excessive beauty of the landscape. The passage continues:

> Nevertheless, when, turning my head, I looked at the willowy edge of Cyanean Meadow and onward to the sober-colored but fine-grained Clamshell Hills, about which there was no glitter, I was inclined to think that the truest beauty was that . . . which we failed to discern, that the forms and colors which adorn our daily life, not seen afar in the horizon, are our fairest jewelry. (*Jo*, 11:166)

Perplexed by how alien he feels to the sunset of glittering gold, Thoreau turns again (for this is the second turning of the head; first it is turned upside down, and now it is turned aside) to find some beauty that he feels connected to. But all he can get is the possibility of a beauty "we failed to discern": so, a distant beauty is dazzling but unrelated to one, and close beauty is indiscernible. In each case, what persists is a tendency to find beauty in both literal and intellectual head-turnings, with the result that beauty never seems to quite fit or to make sense. In exactly that place, Thoreau finds beauty particularly ornamental, as he imagines it as a "jewelry" that "adorn[s] our daily life."

ORNAMENTAL AESTHETICS

In the *Journal* beauty is frequently being turned to, catching the attention, and eliding attempts to lock into relation with it. This snagged quality of beauty is like the work of the poetic line as New characterizes it, but it is also presented in the *Journal* as a form of ornamentation. Consider another string of passages, now from 1855:

> Saw in the pool at Hemlocks what I at first thought was a brighter leaf moved by the zephyr on the surface of the smooth dark water, but it was a splendid male summer duck, which allowed us to approach within seven or eight rods, sailing up close to the shore, and then rose and flew up the curving stream. We soon overhauled it again, and got a fair and long view of it. It was a splendid bird, a perfect floating gem, and Blake, who had never seen the like, was greatly surprised, not knowing that so splendid a bird was found in this part of the world. There it was, constantly moving back and forth by invisible means and wheeling on the smooth surface, showing now its breast, now its side, now its rear. It had a large, rich, flowing, green burnished crest, —a most ample head-dress,—two crescents of dazzling white on the side of the head and the black neck, a pinkish (?)-red bill (with black tip) and similar irides, and a long white mark under and at wing point on sides; the side, as if the form of wing at this distance, light bronze or greenish brown; but, above all, its breast, when it turns into the right light, all aglow with the splendid purple (?) or ruby (?) reflections, *like the throat of the hummingbird*. It might not appear so close at hand. This was the most surprising to me. What an ornament to a river to see that glowing gem floating in contact with its waters! As if the hummingbird should recline its ruby throat and its breast on the water. Like dipping a glowing coal in water! It so affected me. (*Jo*, 8:16–17)

The description of the duck persists for almost as long again as what I have quoted, at which point the entry detours into finding "a good stone jug" floating in the river. Subsequently, Thoreau offers an account of some firewood, and then returns to the duck:

That duck was all jewels combined, showing different lustres as it
turned on the unrippled element in various lights, now brilliantly
glossy green, now dusky violet, now a rich bronze, now the reflections that sleep in the ruby's grain. (*Jo*, 8:19)

The heart of the matter is how the duck turns: "as it turned on the
unrippled element"; "showing now its breast, now its side, now its rear";
"when it turns into the right light." But the duck's turning motion is also
a placement "on the unrippled element," so that it turns in place as it is
"floating in contact with" the river, "its breast on the water." The image is
one of glinting and moving, but also of applied contact, brought out still
more with the simile, "Like dipping a glowing coal in water!"

That simile suggests that the duck is put into the water, as if he has
somehow been managed, and some force animates his resting and turning. We might wonder if this force is related to the different ways that
Thoreau and his companion have adjusted themselves in relation to
the duck. For they are seeking to "overhaul[]" it when it has flown off,
and trying to get the right distance—not too "close at hand," but close
enough. Thoreau also writes of how "[a]t length we went by it, and it
flew back low a few rods to where we roused it" (*Jo*, 8:17), as they have
startled up the bird and set it in motion by trying to steal close to it.
As Thoreau first thinks the duck is only a leaf, then draws in tight and
notes its colors as might an ornithologist, reaches back to note "[w]hat
an ornament to a river" the bird was, toys with seeing it as a coal dipped
in water, turns away to discuss the jug and the firewood, and then lets
the bird seep back into the attention, his mental turnings of attention
mimic the turning in the water of the duck he is considering. He is, at
any rate, himself "so affected" by the sight.

With such turnings of both duck and Thoreau, it could seem that
this *Journal* passage works like one of those famous passages in *Walden*
where natural detail and personal meaning are set into ringing counterpoint. Cameron takes the following passage as an example of *Walden*'s
metaphoric form:[35]

> The night-hawk circled overhead in the sunny afternoons—for
> I sometimes made a day of it—like a mote in the eye, or in heaven's

eye, falling from time to time with a swoop and a sound as if the heavens were rent, torn at last to very rags and tatters, and yet a seamless cope remained; small imps that fill the air and lay their eggs on the ground on bare sand or rocks on the top of hills, where few have found them; graceful and slender like ripples caught up from the pond, as leaves are raised by the wind to float in the heavens; such kindredship is in Nature. The hawk is aerial brother of the wave which he sails over and surveys, those his perfect air-inflated wings answering to the elemental unfledged pinions of the sea. (W, 159)

Seeing the two quotations together, it is evident that the beauty of the passage in *Walden* is qualitatively different from that of the *Journal* entry. In contrast to the *Walden* passage, each turning in the *Journal* entry has its own rhythm—they do not fall into sync, and the way that Thoreau's mind moves in, toward, and away from the duck, only to then turn around it and consider the duck's own turning and its "different lustres" suggests a fascination with the way they slip into and out of relation, in contrast to the "kindredship" found in the other passage. If there is altogether too much activity, and too little in the way of conclusions drawn ("It so affected me" is more a concession than a conclusion) for the duck passage to work like the one from *Walden*, this is because Thoreau's attention to the beautiful emerges in the *Journal* entry when nothing all that important is actually being worked out. It is the lack of meaning to this duck's beauty that lets it be so "splendid"—simply there, turning about with a lustre.

When Thoreau refers to the bird as "an ornament to a river" he uses a conception of ornament theorized by Ananda Coomaraswamy. Coomaraswamy observes that whereas "in modern usage" ornament often means a nonessential, trivial addition, in ancient Western and Islamic cultures alike to "'decorate' an object or person originally meant to endow the object or persons with its or his 'necessary accidents,'"; an ornament would be "whatever was originally necessary to the completion of anything, and thus proper to it."[36] He gives a number of examples of this view, some of them from Greek and Latin, others from Sanskrit. In Sanskrit, he writes, one of the words for ornament is *alaṃkāra*, a word "composed of *alaṃ*, 'sufficient,' or 'enough,' and *kṛ* to 'make,'" casting ornamentation as a making-sufficient of something other than itself.³⁷ Ornamentation was, according to Coomaraswamy, a matter of "the furnishing of anything essential to the validity of whatever is 'adorned,' or enhances its effect, empowering it."³⁸ Another Sanskrit word, *upa-kṛ*, means "'to assist, furnish, ornament," which entails completion by means of an extending accessory. Still another term for ornament is *bhūṣaṇa*, "the provision of whatever properties or means increase the efficacy of this thing or person" that is ornamented. Here ornamentation is an outfitting of an object or person to "empower[] it" and "enhance[] its effect," as "the mind is adorned . . . by learning." ³⁹

Although he did not read Sanskrit himself, Thoreau's interest in reading translations of ancient Indian texts has been well-documented.⁴⁰ And he explicitly identified the language in one of them, *The Laws of Manu*, with ornamentation. Having asserted that the book "wears the English and the Sanscrit dress indifferently"—a point he was in no position to make—Thoreau writes that its "sentences open, as we read them, unexpensively, and, at first, almost unmeaningly, as the petals of a flower," and "are the ornament of the parlor and the cabinet."⁴¹ Of course, Thoreau *was* fluent in ancient Greek, another language Coomaraswamy uses to unfold the ancient sense of ornament as necessary addition. Here he points to the multiple meanings of the Greek verb *cosmeo*: "to 'order or arrange,' and secondarily, to equip, adorn, or dress.' "⁴² In Latin, "*Ornare* is primarily to 'fit out, furnish, provide necessaries . . . and only secondarily to 'embellish.' "⁴³

Bearing Coomaraswamy in mind, it is clear why Thoreau should be so interested in considering a duck to be a jewel resting upon a river and in calling that duck's coloring a "head-dress." If the duck is an ornament, it is not an emblem or a symbol of Thoreau's mind. Rather, the duck is added to the river in a way that increases and enhances it, making the scene not different but greater and more fully itself. Nature is kitted out, so to speak, by its ornaments. Another *Journal* passage similarly emphasizes beauty as an accoutrement to nature: "How much it enhances the wildness & richness of the forest to see in it some beautiful bird which you never detected before" (*J*, 6:198). And in *Walden*, Thoreau called the pond "a gem of the first water which Concord wears in her coronet" (*W*, 179).

But what of the doubt and restlessness in Thoreau's accounts of beauty? How do they relate to perfecting and enhancing? They lend his ornamental references a quality of open-ended increase more than of completed perfection. Coomaraswamy is useful even here, for he observes that still another Sanskrit term for ornamentation is "ābharaṇa, in which the root is combined with a self-referent *a*, towards. *Ābharaṇa* is generally rendered by 'ornament,' but is more literally 'assumption' or 'attribute.'"[44] The idea here is that ornamentation has a quality of going-toward, as would an attribute that accompanies an object. This quality is present in the story of the duck revolving its breast upon the water and being dipped into it like a coal being applied, and in Thoreau's darting after the duck, scaring it up, and revolving it in his mind. Similarly, enraptured by some "little striped breams," Thoreau writes that he "can only poise my thought there by its side and try to think like a bream for a moment. I can only think of precious jewels, of music, poetry, beauty, and the mystery of life" (*Jo*, 11:358–59). To be adequate to "the beauty of the fish" (*Jo*, 11:360) takes a certain placement of thought by the side of the fish, which bespeaks the beauty of arts including the ornamental ones of "precious jewels." And yet, unlike the sense of completeness that Coomaraswamy's work accords to ornament, in Thoreau beauty is attended by constant motion, a sense of the mind's failure to grasp its world, and by immersion in the alterability of both mind and nature. His movement toward the world, and application of attention to it, partakes of the classical form of ornamentation without yielding completion or a sense of rightness.

Thoreau proliferates comparisons of beautiful elements in nature to ornaments throughout the entirety of the *Journal*, but with particular frequency in the early 1850s. I will quote a large number in order to give a sense of the frequency of these comparisons across the 1853 *Journal*:

> The pines are as white as a counterpane with raised embroidery & white tassels & fringes. (*J*, 5:416)
>
> The birches droop over in all directions like ostrich feathers. (*J*, 5:418)

Sometimes I was in doubt about a birch whose vest was buttoned smooth & dark—till I came nearer & saw the yellow gleaming through as where a button was off. (J, 5:425)

It is glorious to behold the life & joy of this ribbon of water sparkling in the sun—The wind blows eastward over the opaque ice . . . . all watered or waved like a tessellated floor—a figured carpet— (J, 6:17)

The Alders are almost generally in full bloom & a very handsome and interesting shew they make with their graceful tawny pendants—inclining to yellow. They shake like ear drops in the wind—almost? Perhaps—the first completed ornaments with which the new year decks herself— (J, 6:29)

The late pipes (limosum?) now nearly a foot high are very handsom like oriental work—Their encircled columns of some precious wood or gem. or like small bamboos—from oriental jungles. very much like art. (J, 6:112)

Now is the time to walk in low damp maple copses & see the tender luxuriant foliage that has pushed up mushroom like—before the sun has come to harden it—the ferns of various species & in various stages—some now in their most perfect & beautiful condition completely unfolded tender & delicate but perfect in all their details—far more than any lace work—the most elaborate leaf we have. So flat just from the laundry as if pressed by some invisible flatiron in the air. Unfolding with such mathematical precision in the free air—green starched & pressed—might they not be transferred—patterns for Mechlin & Brussels. (J, 6:151)

Its great plaited leaves look like a green shirt bossom— (J, 6:154)

In fact the flower is all green both leaves & corolla— The leaves alone—& many have no scape—would detain the walker— Its berries are its flower— A single plant is a great ornament in a vase—from the beauty of its form—& the rich unspotted green of its leaves. (J, 6:175)

> Visited my night hawk on her nest.... A fanciful work in bronze to ornament a mantel. It was enough to fill one with awe. (*J*, 6:184–85)
>
> What shall I name that small cloud that attends the sun's rising, that hangs over the portals of the day like an embroidered banner & heralds his coming. (*J*, 6:207)
>
> The late or river rose spots the copses over the water. a great ornament to the river's brink now. (*J*, 6:256)[45]

A number of these quotations do, of course, contain similes: the cloud is "like an embroidered banner," leaves are "like" a green shirtfront, and water on the ice is "like a tessellated floor—or figured carpet." But such similes are fundamentally different from the kind of symbol-making discussed earlier: these propose a similarity that has no apparent expressive benefit. In the symbolic passages ice, clouds, or a hawk became carriers of a thought or emotion. In contrast, to say the ice looks like a carpet is a way to not have to tell us what the ice means. Saying the leaves on a tree "shake like ear drops in the wind" does not explain why shaking leaves on a tree are compelling, it just transports that same question to another domain: Why are shaking earrings on a person compelling? Likening a natural object to a decorative one reiterates the vacant interest of, for instance, how something hangs off of something else, rather than making it meaningful.

This desire for extension is implicit in Thoreau's note on "small fruits." He entertains the idea that he, like them, is "maturing," but what really interests him is their lack of change:

> This is the season of small fruits. I trust too that I am maturing some small fruit as palatable in these months, which will communicate my flavor to my kind. Here they hang for many weeks unchanged—in dense clusters half a dozen touching each other.— (*J*, 6:293)

It's important that "for many weeks" the berries persist, "unchanged." But, in contrast to such an interest in sheer uninflected duration, the *Journal* also concerns itself with how things begin, how they last, and when they die. Even in that quotation about the berries, he has homed in on how "[t]his is the season of small fruits"—their time of appearing—and on the way that they endure, hanging in their clusters. This focus upon not just what is noticed, but on how it endures, is accompanied by concern about exactly how long his own attention to the thing lasts. It is for this reason that the question about his own fruiting of the mind crops up just there—how long am I interested in an unchanging cluster of berries? What will my interest turn into over time?

In an 1858 passage, Thoreau writes that "[e]ach humblest plant, or weed, as we call it, stands there to express some thought or mood of ours, and yet how long it stands in vain!" (*Jo*, 11:126–27). We find the shell, here, of the idea that natural forms are meant as signs of human (or divine) thoughts, and that sense of Thoreau wanting to find the thought to complete the symbolic expression of each leaf or weed. That notion, in itself, produces an exhausting image of just how many thoughts and moods it would take to match up with all of nature. But here, too, the failure to find the thought that nature means gets diverted into the interest in natural forms' meaninglessness and their vain waiting. That's what really interests Thoreau here: forms that are waiting, tending toward the human and even moving toward meaning, but which may never arrive at either. For even though at this moment Thoreau is exclaiming over a day when his mind does feel like it is attuned correctly—"Wherever I walk this afternoon the purple-fingered grass stands like a guide-board and points my thoughts to more poetic paths than they have lately travelled" (*Jo*, 11:126)—this attunement never produces the right interpretation of the purple grass. The grasses just guide the motion of thoughts, and let Thoreau be "overcome by their beauty" (*Jo*, 11:126) because he has learned to "favorably attend to them" (*Jo*, 11:126). In such attending, the problem of interpretation has been let go.

Similarly, Thoreau's images of natural objects as man-made ornaments (leaves as earrings, limosum like "encircled columns of some precious wood or gem," a hawk as a bronze "ornament" upon "a mantel") are not accompanied by pained musings upon whether his mind will find some way to make sense of what has been seen. This is because through such ornamental images Thoreau's thinking proliferates, from hawk to mantel ornament or from cloud to banner, and making the comparisons becomes a way of inducing enough variety or mental activity to sustain the extent of his interest in a beauty that brooks no real fruiting of thought.

Thoreau writes, in one of the examples quoted earlier, that "lace-work" ferns' forms might be "transferred" into "patterns for Mechlin & Brussels." It is in this spirit of transfer that Thoreau makes many of his comparisons of nature to crafted ornamentation. To write that a leaf is like an earring, that is, transfers and thus extends the beauty of a hanging, fluttering thing, rather than making it into something meaningful. "[A]ll over the town within an hour or 2 have come out little black 2 winged gnats with plumed or fuzzy shoulders— When I catch one on my hands it looks like a bit of black silk ravelling" (*J*, 6:12). The appearance of "plumed" gnats, covering "over the town," resembles another decoration—"a bit of black silk ravelling." Such comparisons as of gnat to silk string draw out the rumination upon natural objects without transforming it into an interpretation of them. It's as if his mind glides from interest in a dangling leaf to a dangling earring, persisting in being interested in dangling, even if giving a nod to variety by transferring the dangling from tree to ear.

If ornamentation is a way merely to extend apprehension, it can also commemorate moments of beginning, changing, and ending, which characterize nature and Thoreau's mind alike. In this spirit, he writes that the clouds are "like an embroidered banner" which "heralds" the "coming" of "the day" (*J*, 6:207). The earrings/leaves are "[p]erhaps— the first completed ornaments with which the new year decks herself" (*J*, 6:29), a comment in which being bedecked is a way to commemorate a change, this time of the seasons. The observation about ferns like lace-work comes quick on the heels of the claim that "[n]ow is the time to walk in the low damp maple copses & see the tender luxuriant foliage" (*J*, 6:151), where ornamentation appears at a distinct break point in time. Speaking of the "river rose," Thoreau finds it "a great ornament to the river's brink now" (*J*, 6:256). All these ornaments, in sum, show us how beautiful objects' commanding of attention marks out finite spans of time. They call attention to what is not lasting; their calling-attention has precisely the quality of "don't miss this," the kind of underscoring that we need when what is being considered is on the wing. Indeed, at one spot in the *Journal* Thoreau comments that the poke plant's "death is an ornament to nature—" (*J*, 7:15). If this returns us to the role of ornament as that which completes something, it is also to underscore how in Thoreau's usage ornament is caught up with a world taken to be a place of entities broken off or extended more often than they are perfectly completed.[46]

The pace of Thoreau's ornament is one of enduring extention marked out by sharp transitions and highlighted points. The temporality of such aesthetic notice and reflection is not that of long-crafted achievement but of stilled duration and occasional punctuation. Ornaments for Thoreau also accede to the inherent changeability of the mind by highlighting moments of beginning, changing, and ending within a process of attention that is, on a deeper level, ended only by Thoreau's death. Ornament to Thoreau is also a way of marking out a beauty that happens to and upon the mind: beauty will suddenly dawn in the mind in a way that ornaments it. Finally, it is a mode of thinking as aesthetic experience in which considering, valuing, and both rendering and finding beautiful are encompassed in a gesture of crowning attention.

The poke plant's death could ornament nature, according to Thoreau, in part because its death was not "not premature." He prays, "May I mature as perfectly root & branch as the poke" (*J*, 7:15). And yet, as Emerson's funeral address on Thoreau reckoned all too painfully, Thoreau died prematurely:

> The scale on which his studies proceeded was so large as to require longevity, and we were the less prepared for his sudden disappearance.... It seems an injury that he should leave in the midst of his broken task, which none else can finish,—a kind of indignity to so noble a soul, that it should depart out of Nature before yet he has been really shown to his peers for what he is.[47]

But perhaps Emerson hit closer to home when he observed, in the same oration, that however incomplete Thoreau's life might be, "[h]is study of Nature was a perpetual ornament to him."[48] He did not need to complete his study of nature, as its function was this adorning of the mind engaged in it. We could even say that the work of the *Journal* is to increase and to mark out the essentially valuable nature of Thoreau's own mind. This value, moreover, includes rather than excludes mortality, doubt, and weakness. We assume that a life must yield some fruit, that it has a finished end or narrative arc, but Thoreau's work shows that thinking is not so much about completion as it is about attending, as Thoreau's study of nature is said, by Emerson, to "ornament" his mind.[49] Even in this case, the use of ornamentation to honor Thoreau entails a sense of Thoreau's incompleteness, as a "broken" or imperfect life is crowned by its study of nature.

Heidegger writes, in *What Is Called Thinking?*, that "[w]hen we judge something—as when we say: 'That tree is blossoming'—our idea must maintain the direction toward the object, the blossoming tree."[50] But to consider the possible conformity of that idea to its object—a conformity that "has long since been equated with truth"—we should also consider "what is this anyway—to form an idea, a representation?"[51] Speaking rather ironically, Heidegger sums up this view as follows:

> When we form an idea of something—of a text if we are philologists, a work of art if we are art historians, a combustion process if we are chemists—we have a representational idea of those objects. Where do we have those ideas? We have them in our head. We have them in our consciousness. We have them in our soul. We have the ideas inside ourselves, these ideas of objects.[52]

But Heidegger will suggest that this understanding of ideas (as representations "inside ourselves" of external objects) is a superficial account of what an idea entails. Having an idea, far from being a representation of something outside oneself, is a kind of meeting or confrontation:

> The word "idea" comes from the Greek εἴδω which means to see, face, meet, be face-to-face.... we stand before a tree in bloom, for example—and the tree stands before us. The tree faces us. The tree and we meet one another, as the tree stands there and we stand face to face with it. As we are in this relation of one to the other and before the other, the tree and we *are*. This face-to-face meeting is not, then, one of these "ideas" buzzing about in our heads.[53]

Here, having an idea has been turned from having a mental, internal representation of an external object to a meeting of a human being and a tree: "the face-to-face, the meeting, the seeing, the forming of the idea, in which the tree presents itself and man comes to stand face-to-face with the tree."[54] Heidegger continues,

> When we think through what this is, that a tree in bloom presents itself to us so that we can come and stand face-to-face with it, the thing that matters first and foremost, and finally, is not to drop the tree in bloom, but for once let it stand where it stands. Why do we say "finally"? Because to this day, thought has never let the tree stand where it stands.[55]

When standing "haf an hour" to watch a tree or otherwise dallying in nature, Thoreau seeks a comparable knowing of the tree through something other than conceptual grasping.

Further on in *What Is Called Thinking?*, Heidegger writes that true thought, rather than the possession of opinions and beliefs, or the pursuit of systematic logical thought with its series of propositions, is a giving of thanks:

> The Old English *thencan*, to think, and *thancian*, to thank, are closely related; the Old English noun for thought is *thanc* or *thonc*—a thought, a grateful thought, and the expression of such a thought.[56]

This aspect of thinking as thanking suggests a gentle acknowledging and gracing of that which is thought about, rather than a seizing of it or even a constitution of it.

> The originary word "thanc" is imbued with the original nature of memory: the gathering of the constant intention of everything that the heart holds in present being. Intention here is understood in this sense: the inclination with which the inmost meditation of the heart turns toward all that is in being—the inclination that is not within its own control and therefore also need not necessarily be first enacted as such.[57]

Rather than seizing on the world and shaping it, this intentionality opens toward a world that has reached out to it. Heidegger understands intention as a leaning-toward that has the quality of heartfelt concern or care.

Heidegger would go beneath the division of "subject and object" and the problem of the subject's internal, representational thinking (formed in conscious, cognitive intentionality) to locate a world of "thing[s]" which we find "touch[] us." These things are "gathered *toward* us beforehand. In a certain manner ... we ourselves are that gathering."[58] Heidegger transforms the problem of how a subject's thinking relates to the objects it is about into a process of gathering and inclining which includes in it both things and human beings. This gathering is not an identity but a state of being "in contiguity,"[59] a phrase in which one can already hear a resemblance to ornament's attentive, completing relation to what it ornaments. Indeed, this sense of the human being as going with the world through its care is already present in *Being and Time*: "[H]aving to do with something, producing something, attending to something and looking after it, making use of something, giving something up and letting it go, undertaking, accomplishing, evincing, interrogating, considering, discussing, determining.... All these ways of Being-in have *concern* as their kind of Being."[60] This concerned engagement is, for Heidegger, the basic reality of humanity: "Dasein, when understood *ontologically*, is care.... [I]ts Being towards the world [Sein zur Welt] is essentially concern."[61]

For Heidegger, thinking is a combination of letting what is thought about lay before one, while also cradling it or taking it to heart. It concerns the apparent form of what is seen, but this form is wrapped up with and in a relationship to the activities of the person. In his elaborate interpretation of a sentence from Parmenides, he writes of how the Greek term for saying means "[t]o lay before, to lay out, lay to": "the Greeks understand stating in the light of laying out, laying before, laying to, and *for this reason* call that 'laying' λέγειν."[62] This saying that is also a laying before is engaged with a perceiving in which taking-up emerges as a "taking-to-heart."[63] So, bringing the laying and the taking to heart together,

[t]he conjunction of λέγειν and νοεῖν is the fundamental characteristic of thinking which here moves into its essential nature. Thinking, then, is not a grasping, neither the grasp of what lies before us, nor an attack upon it. In λέγειν and νοεῖν, what lies before us is not manipulated by means of grasping. Thinking is not a grasping or a prehending.[64]

By means of gestures of laying and taking, Heidegger describes understanding as relationship. Such understanding is an intimacy consisting in a play of noninterference and curiosity, of being affected and grazing, rather than a contact between two distinct entities resulting in either identification or manipulation.

Thoreau thinks of both his relationship to nature, and nature's relationship to itself, in terms like those of Heidegger. Knowing is an adorning contact, which, while it touches and cradles and comes toward the world, does not grasp it or create a representation of it that can be isolated from the relationship itself. And yet the relationality in Heidegger has a peculiar status, for his commitment to the ontology beneath existence means that although he mentions gestures such as "attending to something," actual cases of attending or the particular experience of looking recede from view. This displacement of the feel of experience, together with the overriding commitment to unseating the philosophical sense of the subject outside of a world of objects to stare at, can lead Heidegger to write as if there were no difference at all between human beings and the things with which they are concerned. Heidegger writes, "For the Greeks . . . [t]o be present is to come close by, to be here in contrast and conflict with to be away. But whence does the presence come closer—and closer to what?"[65] Heidegger describes this closeness as having the quality of "a luminous appearance in the sense of illumined, radiant self-manifestation."[66] Thus, "the coming into present being and being present, does not mean that what is present comes *toward us* men as an object." It means, instead, "nearness, in the sense of the radiance issuing from unconcealedness into unconcealedness."[67] Nearness or closeness is not a nearing of two things, nor again of object and subject, but a self-sufficient illumination. Nearness is so suffusing, however, that the tree and mind are all but lit into invisibility by its overpowering brightness.

In contrast, while Thoreau attends to the world and rests alongside it with Heideggerian concern, he never seems to lose the distinguishability of items in the world, from himself to a poke plant. Thoreau knows, like Heidegger, how critically different some kinds of intention are from others (such as the intention to take nature as a symbol for spirit, to give scientific labels to one's findings, or to bring "the side of the mind" to an object). But Thoreau's sense of the primacy of cultivating a relationship of attentiveness to the world also has a quality of doubt, affectedness, and disappointment, which seems absent from Heidegger's work. Of course, for the early Heidegger at least, fallenness and anxiety are constitutive parts of human existence. A sense of loss in superficial talk and alienation from the condition of Being, which Steiner captures as "frenetic inertia" and "flail[ing] about emptily," is necessary to *Dasein* even if it also is the condition which urges us back to a more authentic, concernful connection to the world.[68] The care which Heidegger characterizes as *Dasein*'s ontological condition is less an a priori condition than a response to the frightening sense that human beings are thrown into the world—that we exist in and among things which we have little control over and which are not, in themselves, in any way "for" human beings. In response to this unnerving, depersonalized sense of accidental coming into being, *Dasein* either looks to things on the surface for comfort, or searches for a deeper connected relation to things.

If this is not quite immanent, deep belonging, it is still the case that the issue, in Heidegger, has to do with a basic way of being (at the level of ontic existence or of ontological care) and in this sense has little ability to engage with the way a person's individual experience might fluctuate or relate to distinctions. In contrast, Thoreau's investigation of forms of knowing that aim at uncovering Being occurs right at the level of ontic experience; thus his observation of a reddish ash looking beautiful carries with it a profound sense of the thrownness of Thoreau's mind. While Heidegger pushes majestically toward Being, which appears in yet is not found in what is extant or ontic, Thoreau brings before us that which has the qualities of Being that Heidegger identifies (a relationship with human knowing, a power found only in careful attending, thinking as a gesture of grateful relationship), but which is still found in the transient, sensually available things of daily dealings, and even in moods and passing thoughts. To speak of the "flower of the mind," in this context, betokens a beautiful adornment of thought to the world, or to a poem or bird, as well as a recognition of a person's states of wilting and decay.

Elisa New, whose discussion of the line I considered earlier in this chapter, argues that mortality, and hence human partiality, is central to American poetry. Accepting the fallenness of human life "adds to our tally of losses," but also "bestows a certain salutary friction—tactility, amplitude, nap—that wakens perception to itself."[69] This means that good "poetry finds its subject where something has happened, and the poet her calling among hearers who know she will spare them 'All' to impart more pertinent news, to wit, 'how it is,' and not merely with her, but 'with us' as well."[70] New's investigation into the centrality of mortality to a sense of human life, and of the way that poetic form depends upon its inability to be or speak of All indicates another reason that the *Journal* can be read as a form of poetry. For this is a text about partial moments and the fragile reality of one man seeing a bird in the forest. And yet in Thoreau the partiality of what poetry, a person, or a form can do or be is not separated from a sense of the All. The point of connecting Thoreau's work to Heidegger is to emphasize the former's sense of the availability of Being to a sensitive, resonant human presence—to an individual, that is, in a more realized and ontic sense than in Heidegger's own work. If Heidegger's philosophy aims to connect the seemingly partial, fleeting quality of experience to philosophy, locating Being within experience, it does so through an ironing away of the particularity of experience. In Thoreau, in contrast, concernful connection to Being occurs through emphasizing the particular, accidental, gracing presence of that particular person, an ornament to the world to which he responds.

THE TOUCH OF ORNAMENT

Thoreau is utterly at ease comparing natural phenomena to decorative ones, as when he observes that a bluejay is "a neat and delicately ornamented creature, finer than any work of art in a lady's boudoir" (*Jo*, 11: 319). He is far from alone in thus leaping from nature to decorative ornament; the great American naturalist William Bartram observes "the large expanded flowers, that so ornament" a plant, and describes how "Nature unfolded her joyfull Vernall carpet displaying a lovely scene of vegitable gayity, crouds of vegitable beauties dres't in their richest flower Mantles."[71] Kant clusters natural and decorative beauty together just as comfortably: "No one can use reasons or principles to talk us into a judgment on whether some garment, house, or flower is beautiful."[72] And analyzing free beauty, Kant writes that

> [m]any birds (the parrot, the humming-bird, the bird of paradise) and a lot of crustaceans in the sea are [free] beauties themselves [and] belong to no object determined by concepts as to its purpose, but we like them freely and on their own account. Thus designs *à la grecque*, the foliage on borders or on wallpaper, etc., mean nothing on their own: they represent [*vorstellen*] nothing, no object under a determinate concept, and are free beauties.[73]

Kant's passage aligns natural beauty with ornament because both appear to have no meaning or content. They are lovely, empty forms.

Thoreau can seem to transfer forms from nature to ornament on the same principle, that they are both examples of empty formal beauty. "What pretty wreathes the *mt* cranberry makes ... [the leaves] are of such a shape as might fitly be copied in word or stone—or architectural foliages" (*J*, 8:33); "The great green acorns in broad shallow cups— How attractive these forms! No wonder they are imitated on pumps—fence—& bed posts" (*J*, 8:299). Natural beauty, in such passages, seems weirdly incidental to nature. Far from a crowning adornment to nature, beautiful forms are somewhat randomly located in nature and might just as well be pasted onto bedposts. One could hazard a guess that nature is so easily seen as a form of decorative art because both nature and ornamentation lack intentionality: they are both cases of meaningless formal beauty.

But even in the case of free beauty, Kant's aesthetics is concerned with the question of intentionality. Jonathan Loesberg maintains that Kant's primary concern in the *Critique of Judgment*

> was to indicate the coherence of apprehending the natural world as purposive, even though one had no basis for concluding that it was actually designed according to a purpose. By apprehending an object as having a purposiveness without a purpose, one was both attributing to it a design on its surface and recognizing that that design did not come from any external purpose, and might not even be a feature of the object.[74]

For Loesberg, then, Kant's attention to nature in the *Critique of Judgment* is all about how we might read nature as if it were the expression of a divine intentionality, even if we could not quite assert that it was.[75] While I have previously considered Thoreau's relationship to the project of making symbolic meaning as an issue of *his* intentions, this suggests a distinct way of framing the topic. Is nature, apart from the artist's ability to make meaning of it, *in itself* meaningful, carrying the symbolic intentions of a divine intelligence?[76] Thoreau can think of Nature as a designing force that might be capable of expressing meaning through its forms. For instance, he writes in one *Journal* passage:

> Each and all such disguises & other resources remind us that not some poor worms instinct merely, as we call it, but the mind of the universe rather which we share has been intended upon each particular object— All the wit in the world was brought to bear on each case to secure its end— It was long ago in a full senate of all intellects determined how coccoons had best be suspended— — kindred mind with mine that admires & approves decided it so. (J, 8:12)

Here we see Thoreau taking a reasonably assertive stand that some "intellect[]" "determined" nature, and that nature is the product even of "inten[t]" rather than accident.

But what kind of intention really concerns Thoreau here? "[T]he mind of the universe," a mind the same as his own ("which we share") and even a corporate body's mind, such as the "senate of all intellects." The issue of nature's intentionality is not quite a question of its having a meaning to convey, in the way his language of emblem and symbol can make us think, nor even of its having some concept or purpose. Instead, bursting out from the language of the eighteenth-century aesthetic questions about whether nature is designed by God, and the language of Transcendental (even Swedenborgian) interest in nature as the symbol of both God and man's thoughts, is a fascination with natural forms as the result of causal forces: "What puny causes combine to produce such decided effects!" (*Jo*, 11:96). Here, intention is about the leveraging of a forceful power upon an object, rather than a meaning expressed by that object: "All the wit in the world was *brought to bear on* each case" (my emphasis). The idea of purposive intention as meaning-giving is superseded by an account of purposive intention which has two qualities: (1) the bearing of attention onto an object, and (2) the bringing to bear of a physical pressure upon the object. More directly, in the passage quoted in the previous paragraph, he exclaims over how "the mind . . . has been intended upon each particular object."

Intention as mentally attending and physically contacting casually coincide in one *Journal* entry, when Thoreau lavishes an embarrassment of attention upon a kitten who "looks steadily at objects far and near, first turning her gaze to this side then to that" (*Jo*, 14:314–15). That kind of attention is interlaced with the physical bearing down on the kitten betrayed in the observation that she "does not discover that her tail belongs to her till you tread on it" (*Jo*, 14:314), and a comment on "the sound that arose" when he "rock[ed] onto" the animal's "leg" (*Jo*, 14:315). As in this example, for Thoreau looking at an object almost insensibly shades into bearing down on it, and then noticing its reaction. And what interests Thoreau in what he looks toward is often how it has already been altered by a prior force, as when he writes of how "[t]he curls of the yellow-birch bark form more or less parallel straight lines up and down on all sides of the tree—like parted hair blown aside by the wind—or as when a vest bursts & blows open—" (*J*, 8:9). The interest in forms—curls arranged in parallel lines—is also an interest in how some pressure of air or body has pushed an object apart to make it react and take a new shape. If Thoreau's formulations sometimes carry the traces of the questions about how intentional content (or meaning) is seen to be lodged in form, these traces are a vocabulary that fails him as he works upon his more central concerns with how the attention of an observer is brought to bear upon ("intended upon") an object, how objects and forms are produced from applications of direct, physical force, and what the relationship might be between these two kinds of bearing-down.

> Tall feathery white pines—look like a cockerel's tail in a shower—both these & white pines their branches being inclined downward have sharpened tops—like fir & spruce trees—Thus an arctic effect is produced— Very young white & pitch pines are most changed—all their branches drooping in a compact pyramid toward the ground except a single plume in the centre. They have a singularly crest-fallen look. (J, 8:20)

Here, the shape of the pines has been "inclined downward" by the weight of snow upon them, so that the form is seen as a "change[]" resulting from the impact of the natural world upon itself. This particular passage also pursues how a force creates effects out into the implicit way that the scene affects Thoreau, either by prompting him to think of "a cockerel's tail in a shower" or "an arctic effect," or to find "a crest-fallen look" in the scene. This passage sees nature as a space of forms created by the exertions of impacts, and as a set of forms capable of further impacting the mind that is attending to them.

While Loesberg focuses on the problem of how to read intentionality into nature, Frances Ferguson argues that Kantian aesthetics is entirely about *effects*—including the effect of a person trying to read intentionality into nature. Ferguson writes that "[f]rom the moment that Kant distinguishes the sublime from the beautiful principally on account of its being natural—its not having been produced by human beings for human beings—the aesthetic appreciation of nature becomes something quite distinct from a *recognition* or *understanding* of objects." An aesthetics concerned with nature is, she writes, an "aesthetic appreciation of what was never made to be appreciated," and an appreciation that is not about the object as such but about the subject's experience of it.[77] In Ferguson's reading, that experience has to be understood as one of being affected by the aesthetic object. Aesthetics, she argues, "mak[es] effects so much more important than intentions that the aesthetic can lay claim to a pleasure that was never meant."[78]

This association of aesthetics with effects is much closer to how Thoreau writes about intentionality in nature, as a complicated set of cause-and-effect relationships. That said, unlike the focus in Kant on how nature and art affect a subject—the effect on a subject that was the focus of Enlightenment justifications of art, and even of defenses of aesthetics in our own time—Thoreau trains his attention not just on how nature affects himself, but on effects within nature. He is as interested in how nature affects itself, and how he affects nature, as he is in how nature affects himself. It adds up to an interest in *affecting in itself*, regardless of where it occurs or in what direction it tends (in nature or in Thoreau, between them, from one object to another, from the object to the mind, or from the mind back onto the object). We already saw something of this commitment to affecting in Thoreau's accounts of himself laying his hands on eggs, turning his head, and chasing the duck, and thus in the entire *Journal*'s caught-up, engaged moments of looking. This process of affecting is central to Thoreau's ornamental aesthetics. In his understanding, ornamentation consists of forms that are the effects of certain conditional applications of pressure, attending, and other forms of forceful presence.

"The snow lies handsomely on the shrub-oaks—like a coarse braiding in the air—" (J, 7:206) Thoreau writes, thinking of decoratively braided beauty as a matter of placing-upon. Snow and ice, for Thoreau, are especially powerful for their modes of ornamenting the landscape by lying upon it so as to alter it. As he writes just a few pages further on, "Why do the vast snow plains give us pleasure—the twilight of the bent & half buried woods!" (J, 7:219). Snow ornamentation bends and half-buries, breaking and altering the forest. Placing and reacting are found in another moment from the *Journal*, on Thoreau's trip to Maine: "In the course of the night got up once or 2ce & put fresh logs onto the fire making my companions curl up their legs" (*J*, 7:59). This also characterizes ornamentation for Thoreau: how placing can cause a reaction, often a bending or a curling, as when the birch's bark is made to "curl[]" in the same manner as "when a vest bursts & blows open."

This is powerfully evident in a series of passages on the appearance of a forest following a severe ice storm. Here, Thoreau observes that

> [n]o two trees wear the ice alike. The short plumes & needles of the spruce make a very pretty & peculiar figure. I see some oaks in the distance which by their branches being curved or arched downward & massed are turned into perfect elms, which suggests that this is the peculiarity of the elm— Few if any other trees are this wisp-like—the branches gracefully drooping. I mean some slender red & white oaks which have recently been left in a clearing— Just apply a weight to the end of the boughs which will cause them to droop on all sides—& to each particular twig which will mass them together & you have perfect elms. (*J*, 5:418–19)

The curiosity here is in how the form of the elm emerges through the way that oaks are "curved or arched downward," bent by the weight of the ice upon them. Beauty emerges when one has "[j]ust appl[ied] a weight to the end of the boughs," although the passage is notably vague about who or what has applied this weight. Still, this passage turns upon the fascination, for Thoreau, of nature as a set of objects reacting to applications of force.

Thoreau also finds this ice-covered forest to be ornamental: it looks "[a]s if the world were a great frosted cake with its ornaments— the boughs gleam like silver candlesticks" (*J*, 5:419), and the birch trees "fell over every way in graceful ostrich plumes all raying out from one centre" (*J*, 5:421). While here the connection between ornamentation and how form emerges from applied pressure is incidental, it elsewhere becomes clear that ornamentation is produced by the bringing to bear of forces upon objects. Thoreau remarks, for instance, that ice crystals resemble "broad fern leaves or ostrich plumes or flat fir trees with branches bent down" (*J*, 7:196).

It is a hallmark of beauty, for Thoreau, that it results from some blunted impact such as the oblique way fir branches are "bent down." One example of this is his observation,

> Those spotted maple leaves— What mean their bright colors?— Yellow with a greenish centre & a crimson border on the green leaves—as if the great chemist had dropped some strong acid by chance from a phial designed for autumnal use! Very handsome. (J, 5:89)

Beauty, here, is seen as if it were the result of a liquid being "dropped" on a leaf, burning it out in a way that recalls the duck as a glowing coal dipped into the water. Concern with what was meant (the attempt to read "What mean their bright colors") cedes to a concern with what was done, "as if the great chemist had dropped a strong acid" upon a leaf. This is the key distinction: between thinking a leaf has a meaning, to thinking a leaf had something put upon it which altered it. Under the ægis of environmental concerns with human transformations of nature, critics, including Buell, have read Thoreau as a writer concerned with how nature might be preserved from the impact of human beings upon it.[79] But Thoreau's *Journal* is consumed with the concept of touch, and how one thing affects another, rather than with respectful renunciation of the ways humans might affect nature. Thoreau's interest in nature recurs around sites at which forces are being exerted, often through placements, and yielding various responses and reactions.

What can be confusing about this is the way Thoreau enmeshes the idea that forces are at work in and upon objects with the idea of himself as a force at work in nature. Take, for instance, a passage from *A Week on the Concord and Merrimack Rivers*, in which Thoreau writes,

> I have passed down the river before sunrise on a summer morning, between fields of lilies still shut in sleep; and when at length flakes of sunlight from over the bank fell on the surface of the water, whole fields of white blossoms seemed to flash open before

me, as I floated along, like the unfolding of a banner, so sensible is this flower to the influence of the sun's rays.[80]

The flowers are like an ornamental "banner" in part because they are seen to react under the "influence" of some external force. That force is the light of the sun, but also, implicitly and adjacently, the force of Thoreau's presence among them. The passage also slightly obscures the difference between Thoreau's "floating" as a physical action and his mental action of looking at the flowers. This elision of the difference between his looking at the flowers ("seemed to flash open before me") and his possible physical jostling of them through the action of his boat is displaced onto the elision of the difference between the way sunlight would fall on a flower and the way an object would fall on it, in Thoreau's phrasing of "flakes of sunlight" which "fell on the surface of the water." This is especially so since if the sun falls on the water, the implication is that the light then makes the lilies themselves open.[81] And since light is of course that by which one sees at all, the falling of light seems as if it might enable a looking, so that the flowers' opening comes across as a response both to some touch (the deepening of the daytime) and to their being rendered visible. There's a confusion, here, about how the lilies are flashing open in response to the sun, to Thoreau's passing boat, and also, implicitly, to being attended to by Thoreau himself.

But what is confusing for us—how can the action of the sun on the lily be the same in kind as the placing of his attention onto a lily?—is not confusing to Thoreau. He seems to understand nature as engaged in a process of placings, and to see his watching it as a similar process of placing. Aligning these placings produces moments of aesthetic rapture; as he learns,

> [o]bjects are concealed from our view not so much because they are out of the course of our visual ray (continued) as because there is no intention of the mind and the eye toward them. We do not realize how far and widely, or how near and narrowly, we are to look. The greater part of the phenomena of nature are for this reason concealed to us all our lives. . . . There is just as much beauty

visible to us in the landscape as we are prepared to appreciate,—
not a grain more. (*Jo*, 11:285)

This prepared appreciation must always be attuned with the way that nature is shifting, as nature "constantly draws a curtain over this part or that. She is constantly repainting the landscape and all surfaces, dressing up some scene for our entertainment" (*Jo*, 11:296). The sense is of a nature constantly opening up different aspects of itself to view, and of a viewer who must repeatedly alter and adjust his "intention of the eye and the mind" to notice these fleeting scenes and touches.

Amid a string of entries concerned with November lights, the similarity of nature's placing and Thoreau's placings of his mind and body surfaces as a provisional principle:

> The very sunlight on the pale-brown bleached fields is an interesting object these cold days. I naturally look toward [it] as to a wood-fire. Not only different objects are presented to our attention at different seasons of the year, but we are in a frame of body and mind to appreciate different objects at different seasons. I see one thing when it is cold and another when it is warm. (*Jo*, 11:330)

The light is placed "on" the fields, and this placing of the light—on the fields, but also in the cold—draws Thoreau's mind "toward [it]." But the placing of his mind and body is also part of what brings out this engagement of mind and light, as he notes the way his physical and intellectual being are themselves shifting places "we are in" at different times. The work becomes this aligning of the placing of nature and the placing of the mind, a work that requires constant adjustments of mind and eye to respond to the constant adjustments in nature, even as these adjustments of mind and eye themselves can alter what "nature" is seen to be.

So Thoreau will notice when "[t]he polypody on the rock is much shrivelled by the late cold. The edges are curled up, and it is not nearly so fair as it was ten days ago" (*Jo*, 11:329). In that passage, he takes in how nature alters itself—cold shriveling and curling a plant—and how its beauty can alter. And he will notice how critical it is to calibrate his mind and body to attend to the beauty that is being "presented to our attention," as when "there was a perfect halo of light resting on the knoll as I moved left to right" (*Jo*, 11:331). In that phrase, not only is his attention shifting from side to side, but what is seen has a quality of slightly animated placing, as the "light [is] resting on the knoll" (*Jo*, 11:331). This kind of resting, which always seems susceptible to replacement or alteration, is often thematized as ornamentation, as when Thoreau observes some "pretty" ferns "in a recess under a shelving rock, as it were pinned on rosettewise, as if it were the head of a breastpin" (*Jo*, 11:333–34).

If nature can ornament itself by seeming to pin a rosette of ferns on its breast, or as "some evergreen shrubs are placed there to relieve the eye" (*Jo*, 11:332), Thoreau himself can pin, place, and otherwise affect nature. In a way, he is already doing so by inclining his mind toward the ferns in a recess, or marking out "spotte[d] maple leaves" with the judgment, "[v]ery handsome" (*J*, 5:89). His tendency to think of himself as engaged in making appointments with natural objects, or traveling to find them, also has this quality of picking out and placing, as when he "go[es] to look for evergreen ferns before they are covered up" (*Jo*, 11:321). And if his observations about how cranberry leaves or acorns have forms that might be taken from nature and copied into the realm of architecture or furniture are another way he thinks of himself picking nature out and up, he also quite literally picks up pieces of nature—plants, frogs, a feather—and brings them into his home. As he recommends in an early essay,

> Bring a spray from the wood, or a crystal from the brook, and place it on your mantel, and your household ornaments will seem plebeian beside its nobler fashion and bearing. It will wave superior there, as if used to a more refined and polished circle.[82]

Nature is there to be cut into, and this cutting and re-placing will let the object respond. "I am pleased to cut the small woods with my knife to see their color" (*J*, 5:470).

It has not been adequately commented that Thoreau loves to touch natural objects: "The neatly & closely folded plaited leaves of the hellebore are rather handsome objects now— As you pull them apart they emit a slightly marshy scent some what like the skunk cabbage— They are tender—& dewy within—folded fan-like" (J, 5:13). And he loves to bring pieces of nature home with him, like the frogs he puts in a box in the parlor, "peeping *on the piano*" (J, 5:17). Or,

> It is 8 days since I plucked the great Orchis—one is perfectly fresh still in my pitcher. It may be plucked when the spike is only half opened & will open completely & keep perfectly fresh in a pitcher more than a week. Do I not live in a garden—in a paradise—? I can go out each morning before breakfast—& do & gather these flowers, with which to perfume my chamber where I read & write—all day— (J, 8:202)

The flowers are curious to Thoreau because of the way he can cut them and bring them inside, and then watch the way they react to that situation, and how that affects him in turn. This might seem like a very ordinary thing, putting flowers in a pitcher or a vase. But this application of nature as ornament is on a continuum with other ways of looking at nature by singling out objects upon which to exert a force, and then watching them respond. For example, he "opened" a nest of snapping-turtle eggs and poked them, noting that his "finger left a permanent dimple" on the soft shell. "I opened one . . . The halves of the shell *immediately* as soon as emptied curled up as we as we [sic] see them where the skunks have sucked them" (J, 8:208). This is a prodding into nature, looking at how its shape alters under the pressure of his own body, and seeing the way his body affects the eggshells.

Among the most compelling of these passages about nature's beautiful reactivity is a series of descriptions of lilies Thoreau brings home.

> I have plucked a white lily-bud just ready to expand and after keeping it in water for 2 days (till July 3d) have turned back its petals with my hand and touched the lapped points of the petals when they sprang open—& rapidly expanded in my hand into a perfect blossom with the petals as perfectly disposed at equal intervals as on their native lakes— . . . I cut its stem short—& placed it in a

broad dish of water where it sailed about under the breath of the beholder with a slight undulatory motion—The breeze of his half-suppressed admiration it was that filled its sail. It was a rose-tinted one. (*J*, 5:172)

I bring home a dozen *perfect* lily buds . . . which have never yet opened— I prepare a large pan of water— I cut their stems quite short I turn back their calyx leaves with my finger, so that they may float upright I touch the points of their petals—& breathe or blow on them & toss them in. They spring open rapidly or gradually expand in the course of an hour— (*J*, 5:181)

The undulation and opening of the lilies emerges under the conditions Thoreau has brought to bear upon them in carrying them home, cutting their stems, and floating them on water. Thoreau "touch[es]" the lilies, and breathes on them, as one "sailed under the breath of the beholder." When the flowers come to "spring open rapidly or gradually expand," it is as if in evidence of their reactive excitement and self-revelation. What lilies do is flash open under pressure—except this reactivity is to an intervention of Thoreau's, as he has cut them, touched them, breathed on them, and admired them. Admiration has become aligned with affecting an object so as to make it respond by altering its form.

In his commitment to touch and its effects, Thoreau partakes of the poetic function of *deixis* as Susan Stewart has explained it. She writes of a tradition of English poetry in praise of the created world that goes back to "Cædmon's Hymn," the first known poem in English. Such poetry has, she argues, a central facet of "pointing or designating."[83] This "pointing . . . is derived from the face-to-face situation of the poet and his or her listener," as when Cædmon praises nature *to* the person who has demanded that he sing a poem to him.[84] Stewart continues,

> The rhetorical term *deixis*, signifying "to point out" or "pointing," is of great use to us in thinking through such issues. . . . Liddell and Scott's Greek lexicon gives the following as translations of *deixis*: "to show forth, point, display, bring to light, hail, exhibit, reveal, to greet by means of words or form." *The word* deixis

connotes the appearance of form in more than its visual dimensions and implies apprehension by touch or motion. Emphasizing the bringing forth of form over notions of imitation and representation per se, deixis yokes rhetoric—that is, an intention to move and a reciprocal receptivity to be moved—to visual and aural appearances. (my emphasis)[85]

In Stewart's account, praise poetry hails or marks out nature, and as in Thoreau's prose, this marking out is combined with "touch or motion" which affects both the praised world and the poet who attends it. Stewart continues,

> To be in contact with an object means to be moved by it—to have the pressure of its existence brought into a relation with the pressure of our own bodily existence. And this pressure perceived by touch involves an actual change; we are changed and so is the object. . . . Touch thereby continues its dual trajectory of going out and bringing in; in the "shuttle" of visual perception, we have a gestural enactment of the coming and going of deixis, motions that articulate the point of contact. . . . We may say in fact that visual perception becomes a mode of touching when comparisons are made and the eye is "placed upon" or "falls upon" relations between phenomena.
>
> This temporal aspect of touching also implicitly bears a notion of causality. The pressure we feel when touching a material thing—a pressure toward and against the thing and toward and against ourselves—brings about an idea of causality, of something having happened or made another thing to happen.[86]

Thoreau's fascination with ornamental and natural forms as reactive effects and his entire practice of poising himself to praise nature are signs that he did develop as a major nineteenth-century poet, if not a symbol-making one. For his writing and his living are engaged in a serious reimagination of the nature of poetic work as an act of ornamental placement. The elaborate process of meeting and touching-on the world which Stewart sees as the heart of a major strain of English poetry is reimagined without meter or line and made freshly urgent and responsive in Thoreau's *Journal*.

ORNAMENTAL REACTION

Louis Althusser traced a tradition of aleatory materialism "opposed, as a wholly different mode of thought, to the various materialisms on record, including that widely ascribed to Marx, Engels and Lenin."[87] Althusser's aleatory materialism began in Epicurus's understanding that "before the formation of the world, an infinity of atoms were falling parallel to each other in the void. They still are."[88] Form arises when "an infinitesimal *swerve*" of those atoms occurs, and "induce[s] *an encounter* with the atom next to it, and, from encounter to encounter, a pile-up and the birth of a world."[89] For Althusser, this is also an account of forms as the result of accidental occurrences among materials. Taking Heidegger as one example of aleatory materialism, Althusser writes that "*there are occurrences*," or that "'there are encounters' [*ça se rencontre*]; in Heidegger, that 'things are thrown' in an inaugural 'destining.'"[90] Such thrown encounters lead to

> the gigantic pile-up and collision-interlocking [*accrochage*] of an infinite number of atoms, from which a world is born.... Whence *the form of order* and the *form of beings* . . . whence, finally, what one must call an *affinity* and a complementarity [*complétude*] of the elements that come into play in the encounter, their "readiness to collide-interlock" [*accrochabilité*] in order that this encounter "take hold," that is to say, "take *form*," *at last give birth to Forms, and new Forms*—just as water "takes hold" when ice is there waiting for it, or milk does when it curdles, or mayonnaise when it emulsifies. Hence the primacy of "nothing" over all "form" and *of aleatory materialism over all formalism.*[91]

While the quotation ends contrasting materialism to formalism, Althusser allows that the terminology of materialism versus formalism is insufficient. He puts materialism in scare quotes and parenthetically comments, "we shall have to have some word to distinguish it as a tendency."[92] Overall, he is suggesting that form is not an abstractable property of the mind, and that materiality is not a determining, solid ground. Instead, the world as a whole is a field of materiality that is fundamentally in motion, and is occasionally impacted in ways that lead it to accidentally take a certain shape. This strain of philosophy and aesthetics imagines, with Thoreau, that form is the result of some reaction in and among the material. Form is not a transcendental or universal category, but is instead something that happens. Materiality, though, is also something that happens, insofar as atomic particles only accidentally take a certain form, becoming ground or water or body.

Working out from texts including Althusser's on aleatory materialism, Jane Bennett has written about "the capacity of things—edibles, commodities, storms, metals—not only to impede or block the will and designs of humans but also to act as quasi agents or forces with trajectories, propensities or tendencies of their own."[93] Particularly relevant here is her "Spinozist notion of affect, which refers broadly to the capacity of any body for activity and responsiveness."[94] Bennett claims "there are," in the world, "always a swarm of vitalities at play":

> To figure the generative source of effects as a swarm is to see human intentions as always in competition and confederation with many other strivings, for an intention is like a pebble thrown into a pond, or an electrical current sent through a wire or neural network: it vibrates and merges with other currects, to affect and be affected.[95]

Thinking of agency in terms of a distributive range of vitalities alters the structure of cause and effect. For, Bennett continues, "[i]nstead of an effect obedient to a determinant, one finds circuits in which effect and cause alternate position and redound on each other."[96] In Bennett, intentionality is always converging with the affective reactivity found in not only plants and animals but even metals. If nature consists of ever-widening, shifting, and unpredictable impacts between such forces, it is no longer an issue of nature being either divinely purposive or bluntly mechanistic:

> In a world of lively matter, we see that biochemical and biochemical-social systems can sometimes unexpectedly bifurcate or choose developmental paths that could not have been foreseen, for they are governed by an emergent rather than a linear or deterministic causality. And once we see this, we will need an alternative both to the idea of nature as a purposive, harmonious process and to the idea of nature as a blind mechanism.[97]

What Bennett brings up here is not just the crossability of the mental and physical worlds—such that intention is found in minds and stones—but the common *irritability*, or *reactivity*, of both minds and stones, of persons and things. Here, existing means being subject to reactivity, or unable *not* to have motions and alterations as a result of whatever conditions we, or things, are among.

Some of my contention thus far has been that Thoreau is utterly imbricated in an aesthetic engagement with nature, one that hinges upon how forces act in and on nature, and how his own mental and bodily adjustments in relation to nature are themselves affected by, and capable of affecting, nature. It is an aesthetics about modes of sporadic adjustment and engagement, of reactions and of redounding effects across persons and things. It's not hard to imagine how this might overlap with Bennett's theory: it would be a way to cast Thoreau's understanding of how mental phenomena affect external physical phenomena as a symptom of his understanding of himself as part of a world composed of affective materialities. His indifference to the difference between mental and physical intention, that is, would be evidence of his conception of the world as composed of materials that are, like himself, capable of sudden fluctuations, responses, and animations. But whereas Bennett's work opens up the field to infinite swarms of impacts, the *Journal*'s focus upon the local moments—"I see where squirrels have eaten walnuts along the wall & left the shells on the snow" (*J*, 8:9)—forces the attention onto small sites where cause and effect can be paired back up.

Some of the fruitlessness of Thoreau's noting, the way that it emits pointless observations such as "The beauty of some butterflies—dark steel blue with a light blue edge" (*J*, 6:250), serves to insist on a locatable, delimited, moment at which to pinpoint *that* one thing touches another, or *how* one thing touches and thus affects another. Such limited notes perform an action of containing, and Thoreau's ongoing tracking of his own mind's reactivity, like the reactivity of plants and animals, similarly keeps his nose to the ground. He insists that the attention stay trained on what can be seen, in a particular case, so as to shield one from the overwhelming untraceability of larger ranges of cause and effect.[98] This interest in affecting actually works, then, counter to the infinite affective networks that interest Bennett, for it focuses on specific spots of causal impact ("It so affected me!").

That is true not only in Thoreau's ornamental aesthetics, but in contemporary American writing about ornamentation. When he writes that "[i]t is no crystal palace we dwell in" (*J*, 6:267), we glimpse Thoreau's awareness of the 1851 Crystal Palace, the paradigmatic site at which the fresh glitz of mass-manufactured decorated objects was displayed and discussed.[99] Many readers are familiar with Thoreau's apparently hostile reaction to his culture's beliefs about ornamentation, as in passages from "Economy" such as the following:

> At present our houses are cluttered and defiled with [furniture], and a good housewife would sweep out the greater part into the dust hole, and not leave her morning's work undone! . . . I had three pieces of limestone on my desk, but I was terrified to find that they required to be dusted daily, when the furniture of my mind was all undusted still, and I threw them out the window in disgust. How, then, could I have furnished a house? I would rather sit in the open air, for no dust gathers on the grass, unless where man has broken ground. (*W*, 36)

That kind of language has enabled a common reading of Thoreau as a proto-modernist critic of the Victorian era's saturation with ornamentation.[100] Where his peers were lost in brocade curtains, upholstery, and knickknacks, Thoreau envisions the parlor docked of its "ottomans, and sunshades" (W, 37). And yet, as I have shown, Thoreau was in fact quite deeply committed to using ornamentation in his writing and to characterize his own relationship to nature.

The key thing in *Walden*'s denunciations of ornamentation is precisely their hostile, reactive tone. Far from being substantive departures from the thought of his time, the passages in *Walden* avow attitudes to ornamentation quite similar to those of American women writers. For instance, "Economy" inveighs against foreign fashions of interior decoration ("invented for the ladies of the harem and the effeminate natives of the Celestial Empire" [W, 37]), looks to nature for a source of decorative beauty not found in a home trumped up with costly "bawbles" bought on credit (W, 38), and objects to the excessive dusting such things require. These are all hallmarks of women's writing on interior decoration at the time. As Katherine C. Grier has shown, writers such as Caroline Kirkland, Catherine Beecher, Harriet Beecher Stowe, and Alice B. Neal themselves opposed elaborate decorations that seemed to bespeak class pretensions and required more labor to clean than the average housewife could provide.[101] Like Thoreau, they advocated decoration characterized by intimacy with nature, thrift, and ease of upkeep.

Beauty as an incidental result of activity appears in, for example, Harriet Beecher Stowe's *House and Home Papers*.[102] Stowe contends there that the worn patches on upholstered furniture are "marks and indentations which the glittering in and out of the tide of social happiness has worn in the rocks of our strand," and as such are not flaws but assets to a room.[103] Advocating the use of plants rather than expensive curios to ornament a home, Stowe confronts the prejudice that "[p]lants are always either leaking through the pots upon the carpet," and suggests that this can be remedied by replacing "flooring" with "rich earth," turning the inside space into a self-cleaning environment.[104] This idea, of a home so filled with nature that it becomes nearly self-sustaining, rubs shoulders with Thoreau's assertions in *Walden* that "the pine wood" was his "'best' room ... always ready for company" (W, 141), in which "a priceless domestic swept the floor and dusted the furniture and kept the things in order" (W, 141–42).

What Thoreau takes most from his own time's discussions about decoration is, I think, the connection of ornamentation to forms of reaction or being affected.[105] Even his militant tone, in that chapter, is in the grain of the didactic proclamations of the writers Grier studied.[106] Thoreau's intensely emotional and judgmental writing about ornament in *Walden* indicates how closely reactivity of the mind (which includes its unpredictable responses to environmenal or contextual stimuli) can be to the topic of ornamentation itself. Thoreau was exquisitely attuned to the sensitivity of his mind to conditions of all kinds: "Our moods vary from week to week with the winds & the temperature" (*J*, 5:49), he writes, or, rather sweetly, "What a salad to my spirits is this cooler dark day" (*J*, 5:314). The "tragedy" of the killing of a moose during his trip to Maine seems to poison his mind, having "affected the innocence—dstroyed [*sic*] the pleasure of my adventure" (*J*, 7:69). His engagement with domestic writing about how environments might be affected by their use, and how persons are affected by their domestic environments, informs his larger curiosity about how ornamentation engages placements of mind and object which precisely produce effects.

The restlessness, doubts, and tracing of alterations in his moods discussed earlier in this chapter clearly indicate his sense of his own mind as a site of reactivity and alteration rather than of identity. And a significant amount of his writing about slavery in the *Journal* is about his outrage and discomfort with how much what was happening around him affected his mind:

> [M]y old & worthiest pursuits have lost I cannot say how much of their attraction. and I feel that my investment in life here is worth many percent less since Massachusetts—since Massachusetts last deliberately & forcibly restored an innocent man anthony Burns to slavery. . . . Suppose you have a small library with pictures to adorn the walls—a garden laid all around—& contemplate scientific & literary pursuits &c &c & discover suddenly that your villa with all its contents is located in hell—and that the justice of the peace is one of the devil's angels has a cloven foot & a forked tail—do not these things suddenly lose their value in your eyes. I feel

that to some extent the state has fatally interfered with my just & proper business— It has not merely interrupted me in my passage through court-street on errands of trade—but it has to some extent interrupted me & every man on his onward & upward path in which he had trusted soon to leave Court street far behind— (*J*, 8:198–99)

Thoreau feels invaded by the Burns case, and the source of his anger is primarily at the way that knowledge of the injustice has rattled his brain, or "interrupted" him (something he figures as the ruin of a well "adorn[ed]" room). The frustration this sensitivity conditions continues:

> There is a fine ripple & sparkle on the pond seen through the mist— But what signifies the beauty of nature when men are base? . . . The remembrance of the baseness of politicians spoils my walks—my thoughts are murder to the state— I endeavor in vain to observe Nature—my thoughts involuntarily go plotting against the state— I trust that all just men will conspire. (*J*, 8:200)

Here, being touched by his time feels for Thoreau like being "spoil[ed]" or invaded. I say invaded because the violence of his response, even his "plotting" for revenge, has the wild reactivity of a being who feels threatened in his very core, susceptible to too many invasive influences.

This is due to Thoreau's abiding concern with how his inner life is irredeemably sensitive to the environment in which it occurs. Thoreau's *Journal* is a record precisely of how, even at its most self-enfolded, the mind is beyond control and is continually being "affected" by other things—be they trees, flowers, and birds, or critical aunts, slave-catching governments, and the people whose casual conversations drift into the *Journal*. What is revealed is a preoccupation not with how mind relates to matter, but how in each realm what is actually happening is a constant reacting, which takes forms including those of breakage, springing open, and approaching. To see Thoreau as a forward-thinking modernist is to miss how his ornamental poetics turns on thrown, unsettling moments of pressing-upon contact and encounter.

CONCLUSION

Ursula Heise has argued that environmentalist criticism must abandon its traditional focus on the intimate resonance of a human subject with a natural location. That mode of environmentalism, she observes, has claimed Thoreau and Heidegger as its intellectual founders, each with a cabin retreat. In "Building Dwelling Thinking," according to Heise's gloss,

> Heidegger holds against the "homelessness" of modern society the well-known image of the Black Forest farmhouse, which exemplifies a mode of inhabitation in which construction is not so much a mere process of turning a set of materials—stone, timber, slate—into particular objects as part of the very process of living itself. Such dwelling, for Heidegger, should ideally give expression to the essence of human existence, and should also aim to give other forms of being an occasion—or a "location"—to manifest their own presence.[107]

I have suggested, in contrast, that neither Heidegger nor Thoreau is really invested in the cultivation of an essential self through retreat to an untouched environment.[108] There is in Heidegger a sense of the world as a site of uncertainty and even accident, which is likely what led Althusser to locate Heidegger in his lineage of aleatory materialists. Nevertheless, the sense of changeability and doubt about the unpredictable wreaking of a world is surely more present in Thoreau. This has to do with the greater attention in Thoreau to the precise experience not of place, or environment, but of the ongoing contacts made between mind and phenomena. Thoreau's articulation of such a variety of relationships of attention, so many modulations of how it *feels* in his mind and body to be attending to a flower, a bird, or sunset, to be comporting in relationship with the world, include attention to the interaction of the beautiful and the delightful with the accidental and the affected in the sense of the influenced. Whereas there is in Kant some sense of a stability and a clarity to that state of playing-suspension by which he characterizes aesthetic judgment, for Thoreau aesthetic apprehension is a state of reckoning with, rather than suppressing, the mind's changeability and unreliability.

My point is not just that it is mistaken to cast Thoreau aside as the no-longer-relevant practitioner of a place-based attention to nature. It is a contention for the ongoing urgency of remaining aware of and engaged with the kind of activity that goes on within a human being. Although my investigation of Thoreau has led me to an understanding of form as effect that is, as I have discussed, in sympathy with recent work influenced by Althusser's aleatory materialism, part of what Thoreau has to offer us today is an exquisitely sensitive account of a mental climate, and its ongoing interactions with and reactivity to a wide range of stimuli. Our discipline has prided itself on seeing beyond subjectivity for some time, and recent work on new materialism continues this trend to insist on the moral power of ignoring the domain of the person.[109] If the engagements and experiences in nature that Thoreau performs often stretch our sense of the container of the person, I think it is essential to recall his commitment to the domain of individual human experience. That experience happens in and with a world, in interactions with it at times gentle, at times forceful; but never does he suggest that the most ethical thing one can do is to erase or eradicate the presence and influence of human beings. That a species confronting its power to destroy the natural world should respond with a wish to destroy itself, as in the turn to materialism, is perhaps to be expected, but it is the impulse to destroy, not the presence of the person, which is at issue.

Chapter 2

Dickinson's Ornamental Form

INTRODUCTION

Placing-upon is as central to ornamentation in Dickinson as it is in Thoreau, but for her it more frequently involves buoyancy than transformative weighing down. One instance of this is a poem about a bee who is said "Opon a Lilac Sea / To toss incessantly" (1368). Another is this little poem on joy's transience:

> Exhiliration is the Breeze
> That lifts us from the Ground
> And leaves us in another place
> Whose statement is not found –
>
> Returns us not, but after time
> We soberly descend
> A little newer for the term
> Opon Enchanted Ground – (1157)

The poem sets forth confidently to define what "Exhiliration is," but as it progresses, explaining exhilaration becomes less about defining it than seeing what it does. It "lifts us from the Ground," separating us from one base, only to leave us in "another place," which is, we find out five lines later, another "Ground." While exhilaration can lift us up, it cannot free us from grounding altogether. Instead, it partakes of a structure in which placing or grounding is characterized by uprooting and departure.

Perhaps because her sense of placement is so light, Dickinson usually spells the word "upon" as "opon," as if it were a hybrid of open. In one poem, she uses "opon" to explain a condiment's placement on food: "Surprise is like a thrilling – pungent – / Opon a tasteless meat" (1324). The logic of this displaced simile is that surprise tastes like an unexpectedly intense condiment, as if one were eating something "tasteless" that turns spicy. But it is also, somewhat differently, that being surprised is like having a pungent placed upon oneself. One is both meat and eater, so to speak, in the flexible conception of Dickinson's image.[1] The conceptual flux of that case of being upon is akin to the more literal restlessness with which Dickinson uses "opon" to characterize activities happening in a given location, such as "I cannot dance opon my Toes – " (381) or "A Spider Sewed at Night . . . Opon an Arc of White" (1163 A). In all three cases, Dickinson's "opon" pertains to cases of instability, whether of physical motion, transporting emotion, or conceptual lability.

Dickinson associates such mobile placing with ornamentation, as is implicit in an image of flowers ready to be carried away: "I will give him all the Daisies, / Which opon the hillside blow!" (95). The association appears in poems I will discuss in this chapter through images of ornaments, such as tassels, laces, or ribbons, and images often used as ornamentation (birds, bees, and flowers). This unsettled ornamental placing-upon is a thematic element of Dickinson's work, but it is also central to the way that images and ideas are posed within and across the poetry. This is a quintessentially ornamental poetry: a poetry about placing one thing upon another to respond or relate to it, and also to mark out its value.

A key instance of Dickinson's ornamental placing is the way that the bee tossing "Opon a Lilac Sea" seems to re-emerge in

Two Butterflies went out at Noon –
And waltzed opon a Farm –
Then stepped straight through the Firmament
And rested, on a Beam –

And then – together bore away
Opon a shining Sea –

> Though never yet, in any Port –
> Their coming, mentioned – be –
>
> If spoken by the distant Bird –
> If met in Ether Sea
> By Frigate, or by Merchantman –
> No notice – was – to me – (571 B)

"Two Butterflies" concerns a dancing out across a series of unsteady locations. The butterflies waltz "opon a Farm" by flying over it, and "waltz[ing]" underscores the lilting quality of that flight. Its unsteadiness is jarred and increased by the momentous "straight" step that cuts "through" the sky. This enables the butterflies to take a sunbeam as a place of rest, forming a literally light ground. They then "bore away / Opon a Shining Sea," as the poem emphasizes both the metaphorical transformation of sky into sea and the original focus upon sunlight (the "beam"), with the focus on the sea's "shining." This turning of the sky to sea brings down the air, giving it the tactile drag of water, while highlighting how the air contains light by adding the reflective quality of water. In the waltzing, resting, and bearing away, Dickinson offers a form of being-placed characterized by lightness, as it occurs in a place of weighted buoyancy and refracted light. This buoyant placement also has a quality of iteration, both within the poem and as it ties out to similar formulations in both earlier and later poems.

Although in the examples just considered Dickinson articulates delight around the premise of objects being upon things, the condition can also occasion despair. There's that slide out of exhilaration, and in "Two Butterflies," the butterflies are destroyed and lost to the attention. In "There's a certain Slant of light," the general sense of "Despair" depends on a form of being-on as departure:

> When it comes, the Landscape listens –
> Shadows – hold their breath –
> When it goes, 'tis like the Distance
> On the look of Death – (320)

The last two lines formulate "distance" as a quality that can be located "on" the expression of, by implication, a dead person's face. Except that this dead face is not present, only the abstraction of "the look of Death," so that a quality is found on an abstraction, which itself rests upon the spirited-awayness of the dead person's face. Even placement as the location of distance on death is tied to departure, because the last two lines would describe not what the slant of light is like, but what its going/having gone is like. That Dickinson does not specify "when it has gone," or "as it goes," but "when it goes" suggests as well that the light's actual presence is a form of departure, or of going.

The acuteness with which Dickinson registers joy and pain should not blind one to the extent to which her poetry contends with the complementarity of the two feelings. At its simplest, this complementarity lies in the fact that we can't stay in either state for long. "Exhiliration" is, after all, defined as a force that moves from one place to another, but cannot hold us there; it leaves us to slide back to earth. For Dickinson, as for Thoreau, the changeability of both the world and the person experiencing it are central to ornamental aesthetics. Unfolding this argument about Dickinson's ornamentation will also mean arguing against views of her work as an anti- or unpoetic project, and against the identification of her work with the objecthood and the visuality of her manuscripts, for such accounts either misunderstand or are simply opposed to Dickinson's sense of what being grounded in the world means.

ORNAMENTAL GROUNDING

Dickinson considers contingent placing-upon as an ornamentation in one of her earliest poems:

> The morns are meeker than they were –
> The nuts are getting brown –
> The berry's cheek is plumper –
> The Rose is out of town.

> The maple wears a gayer scarf –
> The field a scarlet gown –
> Lest I sh'd be old fashioned
> I'll put a trinket on! (32)

The first stanza stresses the advent of a new season, as a series of objects are changing: mornings meeker, nuts browner, berry plumper, and rose departed. While the second stanza continues, in its first two lines, by starting lines with objects (the maple, the field), it also introduces the topic of dressing. So the poem moves from transformation and departure (the nut getting brown, the rose's absence) on to wearing scarves and gowns, but that topic extends rather than departs from the original interests of the poem. Since to wear a scarf is also to be able to remove it, the decorative turn is a way of figuring the donnable and removable quality of the colors of fall. The poem ends with a twee outburst, "Lest I sh'd be old fashioned / I'll put a trinket on!" which, in its charge of sudden decision, feels like another thing "put on" the poem: it is an unexpected and unintegrated addition.

Dickinson identifies ornamentation with contingent placing-upon in another early poem:

> A Drop fell on the Apple Tree –
> Another – on the Roof –
> A Half a Dozen kissed the Eaves –
> And made the Gables laugh –
>
> A few went out to help the Brook
> That went to help the Sea –
> Myself Conjectured were they Pearls –
> What Necklaces could be –
>
> The Dust replaced, in Hoisted Roads –
> The Birds jocoser sung –
> The Sunshine threw his Hat away –
> The Bushes – spangles flung

> The Breezes brought dejected Lutes –
> And bathed them in the Glee –
> Then Orient showed a single Flag,
> And signed the Fete away – (846)

The first two lines focus on the contrast between the kind of specificity had by "the" tree and roof, and "[a]" and "[a]nother" Drops. The tree and roof are clearly distinct, yet each is touched by a falling drop that is part of the larger rain shower. The sense that what started as a single encounter can be multiplied expands with "[a] Half a Dozen" drops on "the Eaves"; the increasing number of drops is a counterpoint to the accruing of located aspects of the environment. All the contact—of tree, roof, and eaves to drops, and of tree, roof, and eaves to one another by being contacted by drops from the same shower—erupts in the pleasure of "kissing" and "laugh[ter]."

The poem continues in luxurious multiplicity, able to spare "A few" drops to feed the accruing brook and sea. A giddy sense that things fan out and multiply is brought up short by the interposed "conjecture[]" as to what might be done with the drops: "were they Pearls – / What Necklaces could be." But this fancy of raindrop necklaces is so glancing as to be abandoned almost as it's proposed. Hence, to figure the raindrops as pearls, and string them on necklaces, is part of a way of thinking about events as quickly running into increase, and as easily dispensed with. Beauty is again linked to an object to be worn when the poem suggests that "[t]he Sunshine threw his Hat away / The Bushes – spangles flung," in which a world wearing hat and spangles is also a world of throwing and flinging. This poem is another in which Dickinson's placing is linked to agitation and transitionality, as is underscored by the abrupt way the poem ceases: "signed the Fete away – ."

Robert Weisbuch writes that the apparent settings and scenarios for Dickinson's poetry "are not mimetic but illustrative, chosen, temporary, analogous." Thus, her poetry is "finally sceneless, and this scenelessness is the fully unique quality which identifies Dickinson's lyric technique."[2] In my understanding, the question of placing in Dickinson is not even that what looks placed is really placeless, or that her voice eschews place altogether. Rather, Dickinson's poetry is a far-reaching inquiry into the transience of placing, one pursued through a theme and form of ornamentation. This contention would differ not only from Weisbuch's classic image of Dickinson's poems as placeless, but also from many subsequent critical works that have sought to put her, as it were, back in place.

Dickinson's liberation from her contextual location was once her claim to literary fame. Weisbuch's discussion of her poems' placelessness is one example of that view; another can be found in Suzanne Juhasz's *The Undiscovered Continent*, an important early feminist account of the poet. Juhasz writes that Dickinson "chose to withdraw from the external world and to live her most significant life in the world of her mind."[3] But criticism of the past twenty years steadily dismantled this view of the poet, arguing that her work was not spoken from the airy reserve of a lone mind. This critique of the solitary, transcendent Dickinson has been pursued in multiple ways, among them by looking at the formal context that the fascicles provide, at the material situation of the poetry's visual qualities on the manuscript pages, or at the way the poetry is permeated by nineteenth-century American culture and history.[4] A fundamental tension between an older view of Dickinson as a transcendent poet and a newer one of her as a contextualized poet continues to orient the field of Dickinson criticism.

There is, though, some disagreement and even confusion about the status of the opposition, and about what it means to locate Dickinson. For instance, one may frame this as a question about the poet: Can a person's mind think or create in ways that go beyond the parameters of his or her economic, cultural, material, and historical context? But it is a different thing to frame it as a question about the poetry: Can a poem be cut off from other uses of language, from the paper on which it is written or the handwriting with which it is written, or from, again, the various forms of context from which it emerges? The distinction between a person and a poem's status is one that seems to be often elided in the attempt to contextualize Dickinson, but knottier still, and more germane to my discussion of Dickinson's ornament, is the topic of exactly in what sense either a person or a poem—or anything—can be said to be in, or at, any particular place, condition, or context.

Diana Fuss observes that "all of the mythologizations of Dickinson are based on the same premise: Dickinson fashioned a radical interior life by shunning a conventional exterior one."[5] In contrast, Fuss pursued what she called a phenomenological investigation "one part Martin Heidegger, one part Gaston Bachelard," in which she points out the importance of Dickinson's physical environment to her work.[6] Yet Fuss's phenomenology is essentially about seeing how thought is transformed and conditioned by material conditions. For instance, Fuss writes,

> it was precisely because the Dickinson home was anything but private that Dickinson found it necessary to carve out her own sequestered space within the extended domain of the family living quarters. That the poet was able to retreat to her bedroom at all . . . was to a large extent made possible by the hiring of the Dickinsons' first full-time domestic servant in 1855.[7]

Although Fuss calls this reading phenomenological, in practice it is much more of a straightforward account of how a poetic mind is shaped by its historical and material circumstancs. In that sense, it is more a work of materialist cultural historicism, which gives a causal priority to material and contextual locations outside the writing.

Versions of Fuss's sense that a set of historical and material conditions are the primary causes of Dickinson's thinking inform a number of readings of Dickinson, including a subset which identify this practice with ornamentation. For example, the contention that Dickinson is of, not out of, her context is the crux of Paula Bernat Bennett's reading of "A Spider sewed at Night." Bennett argues that because Dickinson "saw the artist's primary task as extracting the eternal from the matter of daily life," the poem contains a vision of "pure Emersonian transcendence" in the spider's isolated work toward "immortality."[8] But, Bennett continues, the poet also "deploys traditional images from women's handicraft that put the poem's abstract, dematerialized status in an ambiguous light," thereby dramatizing how artistic transcendence remains interlaced with what Bennett earlier refers to as "the material world of women."⁹ This is one instance of an understanding of placing in context and its relationship to decoration that appears in much of the critical field. It depends on the opposition of "daily life" to "the eternal," and of "handicraft" and "the material world" to an implicit world of poetry and "transcendence." In an important book situating Dickinson within nineteenth-century American culture, Barton Levi St. Armand suggests that her work might be a kind of "quilting."[10] Another example of this identification of decoration with material historicity is Daneen Wardrop's description of Dickinson's "multicolored wool shawl" of "multihued paisley" as a sign that Dickinson "ground[ed] herself in the material life of a culture much more complex than the white dress alone can allow."[11]

The identification of ornamentation with handcrafting and materiality also characterizes Jerome McGann's influential comment that Dickinson had a "deep interest ... in the visual aspects of her writing," for McGann's observation about Dickinson came out of his theory of the origin of modern poetics in William Morris's socialist craftsmanship. Morris's brilliance, as McGann characterized it, was his "artisanal insight" that "art and poetry" are "crafts ... practical forms of making."[12] Linking handcraft to the materiality of the object was a "return to an earlier, craft-based method of book production—an effort to step aside from the processes and products of the age of mechanical reproduction."[13] Handcrafting and its link of hand to object thereby become modes of resisting capitalism: "When the physical aspects of writing—its signifying mechanisms—are made a conscious part of the imagination's activities, writing opens up the subject (and even to a limited extent the possibility) of unalienated work."[14] The fundamental view here is that to attend to "the physical aspects of writing" is to perform an "unalienated work" that rejects capitalist economic structures. In this case, the use of ornamentation as a materially grounded craft is opposed more to capitalist alienation than to aesthetic formalism; in either case, the contention is that decorative writing is valuable because it is materially crafted writing, linked to an embodied human presence.

This cluster of convictions about ornament and materiality also characterizes Betsy Erkkila's reading of "Myself was formed – a Carpenter –" (475). She writes, "At a time when the traditional artisanal economy of craft and handwork was being reduced to wage labor, Dickinson imagines herself as an artisan whose craft is under siege by the marketplace values of speed, cost, and efficiency."[15] Erkkila continues,

> Folding, sewing, and binding four or five sheets of paper together in groupings of eighteen to twenty poems, Dickinson, in effect, converted traditional female needlework into a different kind of housework and her own form of productive economy. She appears to have been engaged in a kind of home or cottage industry, a precapitalist mode of manuscript production and circulation that avoided the commodity and use values of the commercial marketplace.[16]

As in McGann's work, here making books by hand is intertwined with decorative art—"traditional female needlework"—and a resistance to capitalism. But why exactly does making something by hand link making with materiality, and thus yield an object redolent of the historicity of its making?

The answer is that a tacit Marxism undergirds the association of ornamental art with materiality, handcrafts, and daily labor. In Marx, there are "thing[s]" which may possess a "usefulness" that is "conditioned by the physical properties of the commodity," with "no existence apart from the latter."[17] The thing's physically inherent use-value is located also in its usability by a person, so that "[u]se-values are only realized . . . in use or in consumption."[18] This inherent presence of utility is found even in natural things, which seem as far from human orientation as possible: "Air, virgin soil, natural meadows, unplanted forests" have inherent physical qualities of being appropriatable by human beings.[19] In Marx, things possess a material quality oriented to human use, and it is here that the identification of materiality with human labor, and with human needs, is located:

> So far as it is a use-value, there is nothing mysterious about it, whether we consider it from the point of view that by its properties it satisfies human needs, or that it first takes on these properties as the product of human labour. It is absolutely clear that, by his activity, man changes the forms of the materials of nature in such a way as to make them useful to him. The form of wood, for

instance, is altered if a table is made out of it. Nevertheless, the table continues to be wood, an ordinary sensuous thing.[20]

Here Marx identifies human making, such as the crafting of objects to furnish a home, with materiality and even the identity of "wood, an ordinary sensuous thing."

In Marx, materiality is even in a sense brought into being by the work of an engaged human subject. This understanding of materiality as the *made* is essential to a Marxist sense of history as the effect of human procedures and processes. Consider how deeply the historical is equated with the worked-upon in Kojéve's reading of Hegel: "The man who works recognizes his own product in the World that has actually been transformed by his work: he recognizes himself in it, he sees in it his own human reality, in it he discovers and reveals to others the objective reality of his humanity, of the originally abstract and purely subjective idea he has of himself."[21] If human history emerges, for Hegel, out of this ability to work upon the world and transform it, history is a process of revealing humanity in objective, material form. This idea, transformed in Marx's work, becomes a principle of nonalienated human labor. Material objects matter as they are worked on and used by human subjects, and thus reveal the presence and value of human beings. In Lukács's phrasing, "Marx urges us to understand 'the sensuous world,' the object, reality, as human sensuous activity."[22] Indeed, Lukács places "the handicraft" at the beginning of a historical process ending in the industrial product with little connection to the "specialised set of actions" by which it was produced.[23]

Returning to Marx, under capitalism the "ordinary sensuous thing" is hollowed out and taken over by the commodity.

> [A]s soon as it [the wood table] emerges as a commodity, it changes into a thing which transcends sensuousness. It not only stands with its feet on the ground, but, in relation to all other commodities, it stands on its head, and evolves out of its wooden brain grotesque ideas, far more wonderful than if it were to begin dancing of its own free will.[24]

Marx's vision of the commodity (whose value is abstract, without connection to the thingly nature of the use-value to which it parasitically attaches) develops "grotesque ideas" of a decorative stamp. In contrast to the handcrafted wood table, we have a table that stands on its head with an unnerving animation. Critics who have characterized Dickinson's work as a decorative art have meant to identify it as a handmade, anti-commodified, material art, but here, Marx uses ornamental imagery to emphasize the disembodied, abstracted power of the commodity.

This is a move Roland Barthes refined in *Mythologies*. "Ornamental Cookery," he observes, combines the "unbridled beautification" of food—"chiselled mushrooms, punctuation of cherries, motifs of carved lemon, shavings of truffle, silver pastilles, arabesques of glacé fruit"— into "a whole rococo cookery."[25] This cuisine performs a double mystification of the natural: "fleeing from nature thanks to a kind of frenzied baroque (sticking shrimps in a lemon, making a chicken look pink, serving grapefruit hot)," and "trying to reconstitute [nature] through an incongruous artifice (strewing meringue mushrooms and holly leaves on a traditional log-shaped Christmas cake, replacing the heads of crayfish around the sophisticated bechamel which hides their bodies)."[26] This pressure to escape nature and then to mimic it contains, Barthes finds, "the same pattern which one finds in the elaboration of petit-bourgeois trinkets (ashtrays in the shape of a saddle, lighters in the shape of a cigarette, terrines in the shape of a hare.)"[27]

If the wooden table is Marx's object carrying the presence of unalienated human being, Barthes loves the touch of wooden toys:

> [Wood] is a familiar and poetic substance, which does not sever the child from close contact with the tree, the table, the floor. Wood does not wound or break down; it does not shatter, it wears out, it can last a long time, live with the child, alter little by little the relations between the object and the hand. If it dies, it is in dwindling, not in swelling out like those mechanical toys which disappear behind the hernia of a broken spring. Wood makes essential objects, objects for all time.[28]

From Marx to Barthes and into criticism on Dickinson, ornamentation is seen to figure both as the sign of a grounded material presence (wood, handcrafted books, and decorative art) or as the sign of a dubiously twisted abstraction. As I argued in the Introduction, these two uses of ornamentation—as sign of material embodiment or untethered form—are aligned with a representational problem concerning how objects carry meaning. After all, Barthes's whole project in *Mythologies* is to reveal how seemingly innocuous cultural objects like toys and food carry ideological meaning: it is the meaningfulness, however inverted and ideologically coded, that is at issue. So too, it is the meaningfulness of decorative objects that concerns McGann: carefully printed books, like carefully penciled and sewn fascicles, mean unalienated, materially located life. The differences in how ornamentation is defined concern which kind of meaning an object carries.

In contrast, I have been arguing that ornamentation in Dickinson and Thoreau is about placement-upon and changeability, rather than the way objects carry meaning or the meanings of either wholesome grounding or haywire formal invention. Such ornamentation is concerned with a different set of questions than those it holds for criticism in the grain of Marxist poststructuralism. In particular, Dickinson's ornamentation considers a changeable and buoyant mode of being placed in the world. The opposition of a wholesome, grounded materiality to an ungrounded, transcendent formalism or even an alienated, contorted capitalism is simply irrelevant to the topic of ornamentation in Dickinson. This is not only because ornamentation's status as signifier is not central to her use of it, but also because her understanding of the terms of both transcendence and grounding are so different from that of the field of Marxism and cultural studies. This also means that the idea that one must situate either her mind or her poetry in a historical context is out of sync with the poetry's own understanding of those concerns. Dickinson's ornamentation is linked to an acute awareness of temporality as temporariness, rather than as crafted grounding or even historical contextualization. Hence a poem about an event that suddenly begins and ends itself as suddenly begins and ends. In contrast to the understanding of a world divided between transcendent art and material labor (associated with handcrafted decoration and handwritten poems), this poetry understands a world made up of objects whose very existence within the contingent is an acute example of their changeability.²⁹ To put it another way, the human-object connection of the handicraft posits a reciprocal identification of person and thing that has little presence in Dickinson.

Dickinson's understanding of grounding as fugitive characterizes the very poem that both Bennett and St. Armand read as contrasting transcendence to material situatedness:

> A Spider sewed at Night
> Without a Light
> Opon an Arc of White – (1163 A)

Here, the word "opon" has Dickinson's characteristic dual attachment: it can be both that the spider sews upon the web, and that the web has no light upon it. The former reading is the primary one, and in it sewing upon is importantly distinct from simply sewing on or working on. For sewing upon adds a sense of moving across and atop the work, which would not be implied with the simpler word "on." This spiderly sewing has some of the quality of the flight of the two butterflies who went out at noon: in each case, the concern is with a positing atop and astride that is also a transport across, and this is the quality she elucidates not only in the spider's sewing of what might be a "Ruff," but in the other poems of ornamentation I have discussed thus far.

EXPERIENCE AND OBJECTS

Hannah Arendt considered metaphor a way of "turning the mind back to the sensory world in order to illuminate the mind's non-sensory experiences for which there are no words in any language."³⁰ Such an understanding of metaphor is grounded upon an understanding of a break between the outer world of phenomenal experience, and an inner space of speculation, in which thought has no object but itself. One might extend this to an understanding of inner experience in general, and argue that emotions, whims, ruminations—all manner of internal experiences—are withdrawn from appearance, and that only by metaphor are they brought before the mind and rendered knowable as objects. In contrast, Dickinson's poetry depends upon a view of the world as encompassing both the inner and outer, and both the mental and the physical. The distinction between inner and outer, as between thought and the sensory world, does not particularly register for Dickinson. This is because it is not the task of rendering what is inwardly knowable by its embodiment in the external that concerns Dickinson, but the way in which what is noticed is characterized by a transportability betraying the indifference of the place at which it appears.[31]

> No Rose, yet felt myself a'bloom,
> No Bird – yet rode in Ether – (190)

Say the speaker felt like a rose or a bird in flight; or, that she had an experience akin to the blooming of a flower, and the flight of a bird. We can parse this approximation of the lines, but the negative iteration "No Rose . . . No Bird" insists upon the absence of the objects that would constitute the implied metaphor. Of course, the rose and bird are brought to our attention at the opening of each line—"No *Rose* . . . No *Bird*"—but they are brought to our attention to mark their near-baffling absence. The absence is near-baffling because what *is* present are feelings that had been identified with the missing rose and bird: blooming and flying. Although the effect of this is to focus upon the experience of the speaker—her sense of blooming and flying—because the lines point up the absence of the objects to which such properties were once attached, we hold our attention on not just the quality of delighted expansion, but also the missing objects from which it had been thought to be inseparable.

The two lines are marked for insertion into Dickinson's draft of the third letter addressed to "Master,"[32] immediately to follow the testimony that the speaker, after her addressee "gave her something," finally "was tired no more."[33] If we were to interpolate the lines into the letter, the double negation, "No Rose . . . No Bird," follows immediately on "no more." Then the speaker has moved from marking the termination of a physical, emotional, and mental state to marking the absence of the kind of object that she is not. If the joy these lines speak of rests upon the discovery of the non-identity of qualities of blooming and riding in ether with the objects of roses and birds, that discovery is temporally predicated upon the preceding discovery of the capacity of a subjective state (being "tired") to end. Hence, what has been discovered is a joyousness not based on identity or inseparability, but found in the transience and the indifference of objects and persons to states and qualities. So the lines—"No Rose, yet felt myself a'bloom, / No Bird – yet rode in Ether –"—do not so much identify the speaker with the rose or the bird, but bespeak her experience of qualities she had previously expected to belong to those objects.

The status of objects has been of primary importance to work on Dickinson, both as a lyric poet and as a manuscript artisan. In *Lyric Time*, Cameron's first book on Dickinson, loss is considered fundamental to both human life and language. Its opposite is presence, which, Cameron writes,

> must be defined in two senses: first, as an immediate and literal being there (the opposite of absence); second . . . as being unmediated by event or language, pure essence, and therefore pure revealed totality. It is easy enough to see how immediate being becomes confused with impossible totality of being, the lost object confused with the perfection that never was.[34]

Distinguishing the presence of an object from absolute presence (having a flower in one's hand and having an unmediated existence with that flower), Cameron also points up how magnetic the elision of that distinction is: we tend to imagine that the lost object was "the perfection that never was." For Dickinson, Cameron writes, it was out of the confusion of lost object and lost presence that "the representational gesture" emerges, such that her "speakers somehow imagined that to get the lost object back, to repossess it, is to recover that wholeness of which they will be an undifferentiated part."[35] But if we seek through representation to bring back both the object represented and the idyll of presence, we can never succeed, for to have turned to representation is to have admitted the loss of presence. In *Lyric Time*, we find not only a poet for whom loss is essential, but also a philosophy in which loss is essential to human existence and linguistic representation. Cameron writes that "presence is only a metaphysical fiction, an impossible other, a true alterity."[36] This discussion can be compared to Carson's reading of Simonides (considered in the Introduction), in which modern poetry begins with the compensatory representation of lost objects and even of lost presence.

Such poetic concerns would seem to have been superseded by the debates about the editing and the very identity of Dickinson's work that have consumed the field of Dickinson studies for over a decade. What kind of thing is "No Rose, yet felt myself a'bloom, / No Bird – yet rode in Ether –"? It has been printed in different ways: in *The Master Letters of Emily Dickinson*, it is printed as part of a letter; in Franklin's *The Poems of Emily Dickinson*, it is printed as a two-line lyric; it is not included in Thomas Johnson's *Complete Poems of Emily Dickinson*, but in his and Theodora Ward's *Letters of Emily Dickinson* it is printed as a couplet at the conclusion of the letter.[37] Since it scans metrically, it sounds like verse even if not printed as such; but as an intended addition to a letter, considering it a lyric poem is surely a stretch. These problems instance that major question in Dickinson studies about not just the editing, but the identity of what Dickinson wrote: letters, poems, letter-poems?[38] Variants, or manuscripts in progress?[39] Lyric poetry, or addresses to specific audiences?[40] Separate lyrics, or lyric sequences?[41] Writing, or visually and materially imagined artworks?[42] The debates are thick enough that, as Mitchell observed, to attempt to "read" Dickinson now entails confronting a daunting puzzle about what we even mean by "Dickinson."[43]

One reason the difficulties about editing Dickinson have become definitive critical concerns is that, as Walter Benn Michaels argues, they engage in a major intellectual swing in the last thirty years to a "commitment to the material object."[44] Michaels begins *The Shape of the Signifier*'s argument against that commitment with the case of Susan Howe's reading of Dickinson in *The Birth-Mark*: to Howe, writes Michaels, "the Dickinson text is now to be understood as a 'material object,' insofar as 'the print on the page . . . the shapes of the words . . . , the space of the paper itself' are now understood as essential elements of the work."[45] Michaels argues that the commitment to the material object is also, inevitably, a commitment to the subjective experience of the object, rather than an interest in its meaning.[46] For Michaels, the point of observing this dual commitment to material objects and subjective experience is to point out that this isn't interesting, and also that it's a misunderstanding of language's basically intentional character. But I want to say, somewhat differently, that what is lost in the commitment to material objects in and of themselves is an ability to be interested in the mind, or in human experience. In practice, the dedication to the object of Dickinson entails a resistance to anyone touching Dickinson, not unlike that we have seen in environmentalist discourse on Thoreau: thinking about nature, or about Dickinson, has a capacity to shift what is thought about—which, it is felt, the critic must guard against or, at best, know for a mistake and intrusion.

In its original form, the problem of poetic representation as a means of seeking to reconstitute objects' presence is that, by its nature, it can only re-present them and thus in some sense repeat their difference from us. The difference of representation from physical presence, that is, repeats the difference between physical presence and metaphysical presence; each form of being-present with objects is only, lamentably, a form of distance from them. This frustrated aspiration to contact objects' presence, both physical and metaphysical, by some means other than conceptual or poetic representation survives in the critique of lyric in Virginia Jackson's *Dickinson's Misery*.

Jackson adopts the same set of options as Michaels—objects you experience, or texts you interpret—so much so that she grants that the thought experiment her book opens with is only "a smashed & grabbed version" of the wave poem example from "Against Theory," the article Michaels and Steven Knapp published as an assault on the critical theory of the 1970s and 1980s. The article turns on an example of a poem that seems to wash up on the beach at random, which makes one wonder, in a line from the article that Jackson quotes and italicizes, whether *"what you're looking at is a poem"* at all.[47] Jackson's version runs as follows:

> Suppose you are sorting through the effects of a woman who has just died and you find in her bedroom a locked wooden box. You open the box and discover hundreds of folded sheets of stationary stitched together with string. Other papers in the bureau drawer are loose, or torn into small pieces, occasionally pinned

together; there is writing on a guarantee issued by the German Student Lamp Co., on memo paper advertising THE HOME INSURANCE CO. NEW YORK ("Cash Assets, over SIX MILLION DOLLARS"), on many split-open envelopes, on a single strip three-quarters of an inch wide by twenty-one inches long, on thin bits of butcher paper, on a page inscribed "*Specimen of Penmanship*" (which is then crossed out). . . . Suppose that you recognize the twined pages as sets of *poems*; you decide that the other pages may contain poems as well.[48]

In the story, the word "recognize" only appears when it comes time to address finding poems: everything else that's encountered, including writing on pieces of paper, is apparently just known, or "discovered," unproblematically. "[P]apers . . . are torn in small pieces," and there's no doubt about how we know what a piece of paper is. Only poems are dubiously "recognize[d]" rather than discovered.

Like Michaels, then, for Jackson the objects around us are indisputably just there; but for Jackson, this is why objects are valuable. Go back to the paper, the scrap, the desiccated bug skeleton: objects are obvious, without the doubts that our thinking minds produce. Hence her understanding of "sentimental poetry's stress on an unrepresentable embodiment," and, in particular, her reading of Dickinson's lines about a flower, "I found her – 'pleiad' – in the woods / and bore her safe away" (48).[49] Jackson comments that "the flower has been rescued from personification rather than delivered to it," such that "[s]he did not name the flower; by taking it from the woods, rather than killing it she seems to have rescued it from being metamorphosed into other names—or other poems."[50] The animus against poetry is fueled by a commitment to the material object, and this commitment is grounded in a view that flowers, like pieces of paper, escape the tangles of our minds. In holding or seeing objects with our hands and eyes, we are connected to reality with a direct power that is betrayed when we begin to think, speak, or read. To pose the question, "What definition of the lyric turns words on an envelope into a poem?" is to imply that knowing what a poem is differs in principle from knowing what "words on an envelope" are.[51] Otherwise, you might as well ask what definition of envelope and words help you know that some impression on your eye and mind amounts to "words on an envelope" in the first place.

But it is hardly the case that the knowing of poetic forms is a distinct epistemological problem, or that we know things other than poems in a way that needs no questioning. This is why the problem of poetic representation, in both Cameron's and Carson's work, is caught up with the problem of metaphysical knowing, and the impossible desire for metaphysical presence. Even in terms of the knowing of physical objects, how do you know you're looking at a beach, a wooden box, or a scrap of paper? All kinds of objects are, *by definition*, hooked by human thinking: the being-thought-as-an-object is what makes an object an object. Perhaps we try to take recourse in the thing—as W. J. T. Mitchell puts it: "[O]bjects are the way things appear to a subject. . . . Things, on the other hand, [signal] the moment when the object becomes the Other."[52] But we are cautioned against what Jane Bennett envisions as the "moment of independence (from subjectivity) possessed by things"[53] by Bill Brown's reminder: "[W]e want things to come before ideas, before theory, before the word, whereas they seem to persist in coming after: as the alternative to ideas, the limit to theory, victims of the word."[54] Brown's words shore us up against the fantasy of an object that has been pared back down to an essential scrap: even looking at a scrap of paper, we're knowing scrap, paper, objects.

Jackson's book centers on its understanding of "the pathos of life's appropriation by literature" and its wish to hold on to that pathos.[55] This view seems driven by a hunger for a real that preexists not just literature or literary reading, but the mind itself. To put it another way, it seems driven by a fundamental aversion to minds, specifically an aversion to the mind that interprets. (When she says that Domhnall Mitchell is commited to "the existence of literary criticism," that appears to count as an insult.)[56] Perhaps the disdain for a thinking mind is explicable as a desire for presence, even at the cost of the mental experience: just a desire to be one with the world, even if the death of one's own being is the cost. But the mind, even the reading mind, is one of the objects in the world; it exists. A form of skepticism that takes the created nature of knowledge as an inescapable, lamentable error which we can at least know we are making and might even cease making is simply a rejection of the reality that the world includes persons and their thoughts. That concepts are themselves phenomenal is not an observation that invalidates them; it just describes what they are.

Jackson's work is just one example of an overarching trend in the humanities to perceive the existence of human thought and perception as an interference in the world. The premise would appear to be that the presence of the human in the world is a problem because it is not identical to objects. In almost the same breath that he warns us that things are never pristinely ahead of our minds, Brown takes up the mantle of the thing *after* the word, as if things might at long last be unbuckled from the subjects who think them. In that spirit he looks at Claes Oldenburg's sculptures, "sink[ing] into themselves, weary of form," and "tired of us."[57] Despite his awareness that the object as such is a human creation—construed by, as Heidegger puts it, "subjectivizing beings into mere objects"—Brown, too, reaches for an access to things in which they show themselves for what they really are.[58] In a later article, he strikes a plaintive note of wanting to feel wanted by Brian Jungen's sculpture:

> [the sculpture] allows us to imagine, I think, a world where the material around us—the denim of your jeans, the glass of your watch crystal, the wood of your chair seat—has, as the object of its desire, perhaps, the desire to be some other object. It is as though Jungen's work begins to expose a newly animate world, a secret life of things that is irreducible to the object forms with which we have constructed and constricted our world.[59]

Brown understands that objects are still functions of the mind (hence the idea of "the object forms with which we have constructed and constricted our world"), but entertains a world of "things" all around us, which we can access without our mind's shaping. And yet the world that eludes us is an "animate" world which "desire[s]" that we frame it as "object." Brown's language acknowledges that this is a fantasy: "allows us to imagine" admits as much, as do the qualifications "I think" (twice), "perhaps," "by my light . . . . their thingness emerges from a kind of oscillation," and a footnote, quoting the artist: "It was kind of like looking at an optical illusion."[60] In a consciously crafted fantasy, the mind's presence in the world is redeemed as the "object of" an object's "desire," and it is meant to endow the critical presence with the authority to voice its sense of itself thinking what it sees.

Silverman aims to redeem critical vision still more ardently than Brown. Beginning with the psychoanalytic proposition that "[t]he basic drive in the human subject is to see once more what has been seen before," Silverman thinks that all of our looking has a quality of appropriation, but figures this may be in some sense acceptable:

> We cannot confer Being upon the world without appropriating it, carrying it away from itself, conferring upon it a supplemental value. The world "knows" this. It does not circumscribe in any way that meaning which we can give to it. All it asks us to do is to look at it first.[61]

The argument draws on Arendt's discussion in *The Life of the Mind*. In Arendt's words: "Dead matter, natural and artificial, changing and unchanging, depends in its being, that is, in its appearingness, on the presence of living creatures."[62] Going further, with respect now to "living beings," Arendt proposes that "everything that is alive ... has an *urge to appear*."[63] Inspired by Arendt, Silverman writes,

> When we look, in the most profound and creative sense of the word, we are always responding to a prior solicitation from other creatures and things. This solicitation is aesthetic in nature: the world addresses us through its formal parameters. However, in displaying their colours, shapes, patterns, and movements to us, things do not merely request us to turn our eyes toward them, or even to answer in kind. What the world of phenomenal forms solicits from us is our desire.[64]

As does Brown, Silverman sees the mind's relation to things as one of a subject appropriating objects. And for Silverman, as for Brown, that dynamic is refigured as answering an impulse that springs out of the world, which asks to be appropriated and transformed, even against its own best interests.

The work of Brown, Silverman, and Jackson, despite its differences, evinces a belief that the relationship of minds to objects is a problem that must be fixed, unveiled, or apologized for. In this regard, they all aspire to something like that lost presence out of which the classic project of representational poetry springs. At one time the world was not split between subjects and the objects through which they seek to contact a reality that their very presence ruins. This is the ongoing Western concept that the presence of the human mind is a blot that interferes with a reality it tries to know through the objects by which it (mis)represents reality to itself. That is the heart of Jackson's argument, after all: poetics is wrong or even unreal because it is something someone thought or imagined, unlike a bug skeleton. Of course, skeletons are thought, too, but more important, thoughts also exist and are part of reality. The mind doesn't need to be abolished or redeemed, because its presence in the world not only isn't a problem, it isn't up to us. It does not matter if objects want us or not, for we are here anyway.

In contrast to the critical view I have been discussing, both Thoreau's and Dickinson's ornamental aesthetics are based in a sense that mental phenomena are part of reality.[65] For this reason, the differences between material and mental phenomena, or between inner and outer phenomena, do not greatly concern either of them. The relationships among such phenomena, and the way that they affect one another, are much more important to them. So Dickinson's ornamental poems begin to find an agitated placing of notice upon objects, in which each notice and thing is a fluttering particular, appearing and disappearing in multiple relations. Part of the joy in Dickinson's lines "No Rose, but felt myself a'bloom, / No Bird – yet rode in Ether –" is of making contact with qualities that are not parsable along the lines of inner/outer, nor even of cognitive/sensible. The real concern, I want to say, is not the relation of inner to outer, nor even self to other. It is rather of waking up amidst it all—amidst the mind, amidst emotions, amidst external objects and persons. Dickinson finds, over and over, that what is touched is also lost, as when she tells us not only that she bloomed and rode in ether, but that such a state has also come and gone. But the move is so quick—touch and distance, appearance and disappearance—that the momentous distinction between them begins to totter and to lose its axiomatic status.

Dickinson's ornamentality can be taken as a way of abandoning the "pathos" of the difference between representation and its presence, between a flower and a poem about a flower, and even between Being and the partiality of subjective human experience. While criticism still circles on the inadequacy of human experience and human thought to reality, and on the divide between material objects and our conceptual representations of them, Dickinson can remind us that this divide has its limits. As I observed at the end of Chapter One, Elisa New argues that poetry comes into being in recognition of the limitation of human life, or human life's separation from prelapsarian presence.[66] In this regard, it makes sense that arguments against believing in the poetic nature of Dickinson's writing are also arguments against the lapsarian, imperfect but real, nature of human experience. And yet, unlike in New's account of American poetry, I shall go on to argue in the subsequent sections that Dickinson's ornamentation looks past the centrality of loss to representation that has been critical not only to Christianity but also to Western culture and poetic history.

ORNAMENTAL NOTICE

Elizabeth Petrino observes that, "[s]temming from the popular portrayal of women's writing as natural and spontaneous, women's poems and flowers were often considered interchangeable" in nineteenth-century America.[67] Petrino illustrates the point with a list of "titles of some popular literary works," such as "Laura Greenwood's *The Rural Wreath; or, Life Among the Flowers* (1853), [and] Lydia Sigourney's *The Voice of Flowers* (1846)."[68] Petrino also notes that "these literary works are imbued with textual and visual puns on 'leaves' as pages of a book and on 'flowery' or 'gemmy' prose as metaphorical."[69] This understanding of poetry as flowers and gems drew upon a classical understanding that "figurative language is ornate and decorative."[70] Petrino points out that the word "fascicle" "derives from floral rhetoric"—it refers to a bundle of petals or leaves—and that even the word "anthology" derives from the Greek word for "a collection of flowers."[71] What is at stake in this "close connection between flowers and rhetoric" is, I will argue, the brevity of the connection of thought to either linguistic formulations or to other objects.[72]

My proposal leads back to a classical understanding of figurative language as the ornaments to thought. Rhetoric is one of the genres into which the archaic poet's sense of fluctuating ornament migrated after the rise of the modern idea of the fixed formal poem in the fifth century. In Cicero's *De Oratore*, it falls to Crassus to delineate the principle of "the embellishment of oratory."[73] Crassus describes figuration as a matter of thought, rather than of thought's manner of being expressed:

> [I]n order to embellish [rhetoric] with flowers of language and gems of thought, it is not necessary for this ornamentation to be spread evenly over the entire speech, but it must be so distributed as that there may be brilliant jewels placed at various points as a sort of decoration. Consequently it is needed to choose the style of oratory best calculated to hold the attention of the audience, and not merely to give them pleasure but also to do so without giving them too much of it.[74]

The use of ornamental rhetoric is calculated less as a relationship of form to content (is this ornament the best way to embody this thought?) and more as a relationship of thought to itself. Central to this consideration is how the mind of the audience is likely to wax and wane in its attention, because ornament must be "calculated to hold the attention of the audience." This holding of the attention pertains to an economy of pleasure, allotting some but not too much: "For it is hard to say why exactly it is that the things which most strongly gratify our senses and excite them most vigorously at their first appearance, are the ones from which we are most speedily estranged by a feeling of disgust and satiety."[75]

As Crassus continues, ornamental rhetoric continues to be about duration and interest:

> In singing, how much more delightful and charming are trills and flourishes than notes firmly held! and yet the former meet with protest not only from persons of severe taste but, if used too often, even from the general public. This may be observed in the case of the rest of the senses.... Thus in all things the greatest pleasures are only narrowly separated from disgust; which makes this less surprising in the case of language, in which we can judge from either the poets or the orators that a style which is symmetrical, decorated, ornate and attractive, but that lacks relief or check or variety, cannot continue to give pleasure for long, however brilliantly coloured the poem or speech may be. And what makes the curls and rouge of the orator or the poet jar upon us all the more quickly is, that whereas with the senses satiety in the case of excessive pleasure is an instinctive and not a deliberate reaction, in the case of writings and speeches faults of over-colouring are detected not only by the verdict of the ears but even more by that of the mind.[76]

One of the most familiar things you can say about rhetorical ornament is that it is an appeal to the materiality of language, and we can see roots of that view in this passage—the entire discussion takes up food, perfume, and makeup.[77] But more salient than the link of such things to materiality is that they prompt pleasures susceptible to alteration. The materiality of "curls and rouge" and "trills and flourishes" is overshadowed by the unstable relation of pleasure to any form of object. The passage is about the fact that attention reaches "satiety," and thus requires "relief or check or variety." It is a statement about the nature of pleasure, specifically but not exclusively the pleasure of a mind attending to another's language, which is to say the pleasure of the critical mind. To maintain it requires regular alteration in the identity and quality of the object to which it is fastened. This problem, while it entails the limits of physical sensation, ultimately depends on the limits of the mind's responsiveness, for the faults of rhetoric are "detected not only by the verdict of the ears but even more by that of the mind."

Here ornamental rhetoric is language attuned to the mind's changeability, and how what the mind takes notice of—even what it enjoys or craves—it will also leave. According to Marcel Detienne, rhetoric emerged in ancient Greece along with a conception of truth as part of "a world of change and movement," and a discourse of changing opinions, which "run away and escape."[78] Cicero's response to this is to seek to control the mind, feeding it the images and turns of object that keep it near-satisfied. But Dickinson all but abandons her poetry to the fugitive nature of mind and object, as figured in posed images of ornamental flowers and gems.

Dickinson's flower poetry, for example, is primarily concerned with the relationship of attention, rather than meaning, to objects.[79]

> Frequently the woods are pink –
> Frequently, are brown.
> Frequently the hills undress
> Behind my native town.
> Oft a head is crested
> I was wont to see –
> And as oft a cranny
> Where it used to be –
> And the Earth – they tell me –
> On it's axis turned!
> Wonderful Rotation!
> By but *twelve* performed! (24)

There's a basic sense of order to this poem, insofar as it concludes with a focus on "rotation" across the year, and even in the sense of a comforting back and forth motion between dressing and undressing, crest and cranny. The clear rhymes add to this—"brown/town," "see/be," as does the regularity of the rhythm. But the end of the poem is so unsatisfying: it bursts out in admiration at the "wonderful rotation," to the extent that the admiration feels like a loss of investment in what has been presented. It's as if the poem has noticed something but doesn't know what to do with it, so it throws up the hands in praise. Here praise is a form of disengagement, for the attribution of the "rotation" to "twelve" months has a similar quality of washing the hands of the ideas presented.

That turn away of the attention is another instance of Dickinson's poems' tendency to fall off rather than conclude. As an empirical observation about the poems, that's hardly a new point, but I want to add that it is a sign of Dickinson's alertness to the way that attention drifts and subsides. When do we, as readers, turn away from poems? When are we done reading? These poems already ask this question, and show us that insofar as a poem is a kind of paying attention, it can't last. The poem's strange falling off, therefore, is of a piece with the falling off of leaves that it depicts, and with the alteration from "pink" to "brown" of flowers and leaves. Dickinson's poems not only notice temporary appearances, as in "A Drop fell on the Apple Tree," they are also themselves temporary noticings. Some poems end with an abruptness which acknowledges that the noticing which constituted a poem has passed before the poem had time to conclude. In addition, the way that Dickinson will propose an image only to withdraw it manifests this temporariness of noticing: something leaps into view, only to be whisked aside.

I take the term "noticing" from another poem of Dickinson's, in which it is directly linked to ornamentation:

> The Grass so little has to do,
> A Sphere of simple Green –
> With only Butterflies, to brood –
> And Bees, to entertain –
>
> And stir all day to pretty tunes
> The Breezes fetch along,
> And hold the Sunshine, in it's lap
> And bow to everything,
>
> And thread the Dews, all night, like Pearl,
> And make itself so fine
> A Duchess, were too common
> For such a noticing,
>
> And even when it die, to pass
> In odors so divine –
> As lowly spices, gone to sleep –
> Or Amulets of Pine –

> And then to dwell in Sovreign Barns,
> And dream the Days away,
> The Grass so little has to do,
> I wish I were a Hay – (379 B)

The grass's wearing of the necklace of pearl-like dew is linked to the way, in the first stanza, multiple but distinct entities (butterflies and bees) are disposed across it. In this sense, we'd be tempted to call it a ground, except that for all its inactivity ("so little has to do") it is still *doing*: "brood[ing]," "entertain[ing]," "stir[ring]," "fetch[ing]," and "mak[ing]." The image is another of an agitated sea with multiple ornamental objects borne upon it, but here this dynamic is directly called "a noticing." By that word, Dickinson brings out the way that placing ornamentation upon an object is a mode of marking it out for notice. Moreover, the thematic of ornamental notice extends to a poetic practice of agitated placing of image, ideas, lines, or words across the poem.

Dickinson writes in "The Grass so little has to do – " that, once dead, the grass "dwell[s] in Sovreign Barns," in lines that evoke a state of being that continues after finitude should have been found ("when it die"). This continuation past the end is similar to the formulation in "My Life had stood – a Loaded Gun," in which once the speaker/gun has been "carried . . . away," "now We roam in Sovreign Woods" (764). I mean that Dickinson's writing allows a formulation such as that of continuous action (dwelling, roaming) in a privileged, plural location ("Sovreign Barns," "Sovreign Woods") to reappear in multiple locations (two distinct poems) in a way that makes it seem as if the idea itself has a life-in-death continuation across distinct spaces. Dickinson's work is characterized by concepts and linguistic formulations that appear in multiple locations, which gives a particular emphasis not to the rightness or meaning of any single location, but rather to the way concepts and phrases come into the sphere of attention, occupy it for a time, and disappear, sometimes to return.

The focus on the shiftability of attention can underscore an understanding of the tenuousness of the object/mind link from still another angle. It is not only that things themselves are movable, temporary, or finite, but that the same is true of the mind as well. Attention is, on the one hand, a mode of selection and placing: we place our attention somewhere, and the attention can also be drawn from one site to another. As our attention wanders, we could become aware of the way in which the mind is capable of alighting onto an idea or topic, and of flitting away from it. To consider the quality of attention is to consider how the mind is capable both of calling forth attention to, almost with, an object, but just as capable of dropping it, and this is true of any kind of object—internal or external.

Dickinson's poetry is constitutively about the ways that thought and things are each continually changing in relation to one another. This does not mean that they become a field without distinctions, like the raining of atoms in Epicurus that interested Althusser; it means that both thinking and acting entail streaks of contact that possess duration but also cease. The poetry is characterized by its refusal to stave off the way that not only things, but thoughts and feelings about them, are found to be temporary. It is even that the poetry seems to be, itself, a changeable *noticing*. For example, the last line of "The Grass so little has to do," "I wish I were a Hay – " has a quality of neither declaration nor wish, but rather of dangling. It's there, at the poem's end, but in such a way that we feel it might just as soon not be there. The line seems about to fall off the poem; in addition, the thought in that line is about the almost loose tooth or (to quote Emerson) "caducous" quality of interest in a supposition.[80]

There's a way that in reading Dickinson a phrase, such as the spider's "Arc of White," will stand out from the poem it is—part of? in? on? The poems do not just describe situations in which an object agitatedly rests on a sunbeam or a wave, but themselves function as fields upon which images and ideas pass. Consider how that line, "I wish I were a Hay – " depends from "The Grass so little has to do"; it is the most memorable line of the poem, but for all that it is the most tentative line in it. Just as the line lets off a wish that, in its infamous agrammaticality, grants its impossibility and even incomprehensibility (what would it mean to be "a Hay," not "hay" or "a piece of hay"?), the line also draws toward itself a going forward of the mind that it cannot fully support or sustain. It hovers at the end of the poem, drawing attention without offering it a place to rest or to fasten. The line's inherent instability (due to its agrammaticality, its somewhat random quality, and its emotional oddity as a wish collapsing into a regret), together with the way it stakes out its presence at the poem's end without fully inhabiting it, elicit what I can best call a dissociated presence. The instability of the line itself is such that, trying to hold it in our critical focus, we find that it won't fully stay put, and we become aware of the adjustments and reconsiderations we make to try and stay with the line.

These effects of flickering may resemble the shimmering that Brown located in Jungen's sculptures, but they are in Dickinson the disintegrating rhythm of thinking and feeling upon an object. The flickering is not a sign of the verge of contacting something more real than perception; instead, flickering is what we really see when we're attending, a somewhat delicate terror of the instability of perception and thinking. This is an intimation of human knowing's mortality—not its ability to control and appropriate the world, but its lack of ability to hold onto the world. Such mortality is, unlike the eventual end to life, a pervasive phenomenon of impermanence. In the understanding of Buddhism, the scholar Francisco J. Varela observes, impermanence

> is not just the leaves-fall, maidens-wither, and kings-are-forgotten type of impermanence (typically called gross impermanence) with which all people are hauntingly familiar but a personal penetrating impermanence of the mind itself. Moment by moment new experiences happen and they are gone. It is a rapidly shifting stream of momentary mental occurrences. Furthermore, the shiftiness includes the perceiver as much as the perceptions.[81]

This "penetrating impermanence," which includes both mind and object, is the kind of change that Dickinson's ornamental aesthetics is concerned with. I would also say that in relation to Dickinson, there can be a terror of the mortality of the reading itself: What poet so brings up short the wish of the reader to feel she has held onto, even satisfactorily seen and been done with, a reading? Contacting her words is fraught with the need for adjustment, as disorientation seems to follow fast on the heels of moments of comfort with what we think a particular poem means. This is what it means to consider a poetry floral, and ornamental: it grants the brevity with which a thought is touched by a linguistic formulation, and conceives of images as things that are not united with thought, or which embody thought, but rather which can be smattered in relation to thinking that is itself in flux.

DICKINSON, HEIDEGGER, AND THE ORNAMENT OF BEING

> When on a summer's day the butterfly
> settles on the flower and, wings
> closed, sways with it in the
> meadow-breeze . . . [82]

In the above lines Heidegger describes a butterfly "sway[ing]" on a "flower," at once in motion and at rest. It is an image of thinking, for Heidegger continues,

> All our heart's courage is the
>   echoing response to the
>   first call of Being which
>   gathers our thinking into the
>   play of the world.
>
> In thinking all things
>   become solitary and slow.
>
> Patience nurtures magnanimity.
>
> He who thinks greatly must
>   err greatly.[83]

The butterfly reminds us that even if "[i]n thinking all things / become solitary and slow," slowness isn't the complete absence of movement. Susan Bernstein observes that the philosopher senses that "*Dasein* [is] in a state of suspension—a quivering or hovering."[84] The place of *Dasein* is, Bernstein argues, not the solid ground of the home or the cleared space but a "quaking and quivering ground," such that "the '*da*' and the '*in*' are only fleeting instants of incision."[85] As a result, Heidegger's butterfly has a ripple of similarity to Dickinson's bee tossing on a lilac sea, and a similar understanding of being-placed characterized by ongoing motion. I would like to draw this connection out to develop my suggestion that Dickinson's poetry is ornamental because it is a poetry of temporary notice. Her poems include images of ornamental objects (lace, tassels, jewelry); her poems' images are like ornaments in that they seem placed on, but not united with, the poems (as in the agitated fields with ornaments upon them); and, finally, her poems are ornamental because they show that the noticing that poems consist of is, in its essence, a dappled and temporary placement.

Heidegger figures in Dickinson scholarship at the crux of a discussion between Allen Grossman and Sharon Cameron. At issue is Grossman's understanding of poetic framing in "Summa Lyrica":

> The frame of the poem (its prosody or closure) is coterminous with the whole poem, and must be conceived as bounding the poem both circumferentially (the outer juncture with *all* being) and internally (the inner juncture, produced syllable by syllable, with its *own* being). The minimal function of closure is to fence the poem off from all other statements, and most strenuously from alternative statements of the same kind.[86]

Grossman also locates this understanding of the framed poem in Heidegger's "The Origin of the Work of Art," which he cites:

> A work, by being a work, makes space for that spaciousness. "To make space for" means here especially to liberate the Open and to establish it in its structure. This installing occurs through the erecting mentioned earlier. The work as work sets up a world.[87]

Having thus quoted Heidegger, Grossman observes,

> The metaphor of "frame" propagates itself throughout the theory of perception. . . . What should be emphasized is that *frame* is

established through reduction by differentiation and is thus post-catastrophic, the "formal feeling" which succeeds upon "great pain."[88]

As Cameron discusses, Grossman invokes Dickinson ("After great pain, a formal feeling comes –" [372]) as both example of and evidence for an understanding of poetry as that which must begin by setting up boundaries within and around the work.[89]

In overt contrast to Grossman's understanding of the boundedness of the lyric and of Dickinson, Cameron argues that Dickinson's poetry does not "demarcate 'interior' and 'exterior,' either with respect to the margins of a poem when it is marked by variants, or with respect to the boundaries of an utterance which is often 'continued'" across poems.[90] Dickinson's poetry, she writes, "attempt[s] to contest the presumption of boundaries ... which lies at the heart of our understanding of the satisfactions of poetic utterance."[91] Instead, "[t]he single most prominent feature of Dickinson's poetry ... is the opening up of spaces. It is the opening up of spaces allowed to remain open."[92] In this regard, Dickinson's poems "manifest[]" Heidegger's Open, "that objectless place where innerness is discovered, is 'found' in and for itself. Hence its designation as 'pure existence.' It is objectless because it has no goal except simply to be."[93] To touch the Open requires

> the exchange of one way of discerning completion or perfection (in and through discrete entities, which are seen and coveted) for the perfection of mere being, in which nothing can be owned because nothing is bounded, hence nothing is discrete. . . . Precisely because in Dickinson's poetry objects and subjects are not in fact discrete—are not, that is, bounded—the relation between them and, significantly, the ways of measuring relation dispute conventional designation. Objects and subjects, like variant poems, or like words and variants to words, are not greater than, nor less than, nor even equal to each other—these being terms of measurement to which Dickinson's speech initially seems confined, but from which it is ultimately released.[94]

Although *Choosing Not Choosing* both performs and urges careful, rigorous reading of the poems, there is a sense in which the Open manifested in the poems is larger than the aspects of the poems that have been attended to. Cameron turns to the "philosophical problem that emerges from the[ ] characteristics" of the poetry which her readings "have described," stating that

> [t]he importance of identifying what specifically is revealed by identifying the features of a given body of poetry ... is in some sense only preliminary—that which helps us to see what set of problems is being worked out; the terms in which these problems are understood and negotiated; and the grounds of their appeal to us. To say less is to mistake why linguistic questions interest us.[95]

Linguistic questions matter, finally, for the ideas to which they bring us, rather than in themselves.

If saying linguistic questions are "preliminary" is not to say they are incidental to the ideas they confer, in the case of Heidegger phenomenological description is largely indifferent to formal qualities. Heidegger observes in "The Origin of the Work of Art" that the kind of "knowledge" about art that matters to him "is far removed from that merely aestheticizing connoisseurship of the work's formal aspects, its qualities and charms." [96] Concern with Being is, for Heidegger, precisely not concern with beings—making the formal qualities of artworks irrelevant in the face of undifferentiated Being. And, because Heidegger characterizes "formal aspects" of the work as superficial additions and "charms," his view of art takes shape around a tacit account of form *as* ornament. One can take this to highlight the pointlessness of formal interest in light of the Open, as all distinct aspects of objects, subjects, and language cease to have value. But, it is also to find that a commitment to the possibility of Being and the Open is entwined with a vision of form as ornament. In this sense, ornamentation is the name for the form that attends the Open.

That suggestion runs against the grain of Heidegger's more familiar view of language as "the clearing-concealing advent of Being itself."[97] Nothing could be further from an understanding of language as solely a medium for communication, or as "a dualistic thing composed of a material and a psychic part."⁹⁸ And yet, Heidegger's view of language carries in its wake that discarded understanding of language as, in Bernstein's word, an "instrumental" means of trucking thought back and forth. That instrumental view funds the sense that language apart from its content is ornamental. Bernstein quotes Heidegger: "'The talk about the house of Being is no transfer [*keine übertragung*] of the image 'house' to Being. But one day we will, by thinking the essence of Being in a way appropriate to its matter, more readily be able to think of what 'house' and 'to dwell' are."⁹⁹ And then she notes: "'*Keine übertragung*': no poetic ornament or metaphoric substitution."¹⁰⁰ Over against this understanding of language—medium for communication that can become dressed up, call too much attention to itself, play around or move when it needn't or when it can't be justified—we have the more mystical understanding of language as the way in which Being may approach but "never [. . .] settle definitively."

Here Heidegger uses an account of linguistic form as the dress to thought in order to define precisely what he does not believe in. But this rejection of ornamental language does not stay in its place as the negated view, against which language emerges as the place where Being blooms. It is both entertained and negated because Heidegger has been wondering if his use of language actually is "adornment":

> The same reference in the 1836 essay on Hölderlin's verse, "Full of merit, yet poetically, man dwells on this earth," is no adornment of a thinking that rescues itself from science by means of poetry. The talk about the house of Being is no transfer of the image "house" to Being.¹⁰¹

In defending against the possibility that his quotation from Hölderlin might be just an ornament to his thought, Heidegger names ontic form ornament. The passage indicates, almost by accident, that form looks ornamental in light of Being. Such ornament is not the house of Being, but it recognizes its unhousable, unrepresentable nature. Rather than aiming to embody Being in form, it poses form as an ornament to Being.

Susan Howe writes that Dickinson "scouts alone and alert in her clearing."¹⁰² This clearing is essentially a cognate of the Open, one of

Heidegger's ways of describing truth as an opening up to the world. He describes the clearing as follows in *Being and Time*:

> When we talk in an ontically figurative way of the *lumen naturale* in man, we have in mind nothing other than the existential-ontological structure of this entity, that it *is* in such a way as to be its "there." To say that it is "illuminated" ["erleuchtet"] means that *as* Being-in-the-world it is cleared [gelichtet] in itself, not through any other entity, but in such a way that it *is* itself the clearing. Only for an entity which is existentially cleared in this way does that which is present-at-hand become accessible in the light or hidden in the dark.[103]

Heidegger considers truthfulness as a quality of spatiality and litness within which something may be encompassed by *Dasein*. In Mark Wrathall's analysis,

> the philosophical discussion of truth can be pursued only against the background of assumptions about the nature of mind . . . and the nature of the world (in particular, how the world can be so constituted as to be make mental states and their derivatives true). Heidegger's focus on unconcealment in his discussions of the essence of truth is intended to bring such background assumptions to the foreground. The claim that unconcealment is the essence of truth, then, is motivated by the recognition that we have to see truth in the context of a more general opening up of the world, that is, in the context of an openness to the world and comportment toward things in the world that is more fundamental than thinking and speaking about them.[104]

For Howe, Dickinson's poetry takes up this uncovered clearing of truth; Dickinson, "alone, in her clearing of Becoming, keeps on experimenting, deciphering."[105] And this requires—in a line I quoted in the Introduction—the poet to "to sweep away the pernicious idea of poetry as embroidery for woman."[106] My suggestion is that insofar as Dickinson ventures into the clearing (insofar as she, to put it in less Heideggerian terms, can drop us into a presence whose fullness and truthfulness shock us out of preoccupation with the superficial and discrete), her ornamentation accompanies and acknowledges this discovery. Far from being what must be stripped away to see presence, ornament is what we can see at all in the face of Being: it is what survives in relation to presence. In Dickinson, embroidery—decorative form—rather than being the name of images inadequately fused to Being, is the form that adorns the world of presence.

Richard Chase wrestles with what he calls Dickinson's "rococo" side, finding her flights of "decadence" to be unfortunate evasions of a truthful engagement with life.[107] He writes that "Ego Friedell ... describes [rococo] ... as issuing from a 'last craving for illusion to carry one over the gateway of death.' ... It seeks to decorate and enrich a blank or bored existence."[108] Complaining of the "uninteresting decorative effect" in one poem, Chase generally characterizes her "bad poems" as those overrun with "troublesome images" of "[b]ees, blossoms, jewels, diadems, plush, bonnets, exotic geographical names, alcohol, and so on."[109] Considering such "decorative poems," Chase concludes that "one can hardly demonstrate that Emily Dickinson's paraphernalia of phoebes, leontodons, Indian pipes, orioles, and robins ever issues in major poetic statement."[110] Unhappy as he is with Dickinson's "uneasy language of jewelry" and its ilk, Chase realizes how close this decorative side is to those poems of hers he deems serious: "A thimble, a circling butterfly will appear even in those poems most consistently and powerfully evocative of the awful, just as in a predominantly light poem ... there will be a hint of infinity."[111] Chase has seen, but not fully accepted, that Dickinson's ornamental flourishes are not signs of an aesthete's bored, decadent abandonment of reality but rather a means of acknowledging what a poem cannot fit inside, or annex to, itself.

The eerie quality in some of Dickinson's poetry is, I think, a sign of that understanding of the poem as an ornament placed upon the Open.

Safe in their Alabaster Chambers –
Untouched by Morning –
And untouched by Noon –

Lie the meek members of the Resurrection –
Rafter of Satin – and Roof of Stone!

Grand go the Years – in the Crescent – above them –
Worlds scoop their Arcs –
And Firmaments – row
Diadems – drop – and Doges – surrender
Soundless as dots – on a Disc of snow – (124 E)

The untouchable dead are ensconced in the luxury of "Alabaster" and "Satin," and above them dance the forms of "Crescent" and "Arc," of "dots" and "a Disc," together imagined as part of a world in which ornamented heads lose their status. The poem is not just about a waiting, protected, dead posed against a promenade of irrelevant temporal change. It is also about rendering the awesomeness of "meek members" buried and waiting by turning the attention to what doesn't matter: the decorative quality of the diadems and the dots on the snow. The whole world is as nothing more than points on a melting circle, but in the face of the confrontation with death, the poem turns to what is susceptible to touch and to change.

The final stanza is literally subject to touch and change, insofar as it was revised from an earlier version. In that version, the turn to lightness as a response to the chill of death is more extreme:

Light laughs the breeze
In her Castle above them –
Babbles the Bee in a stolid Ear,
Pipe the sweet Birds in ignorant cadence –
Ah, what sagacity perished here! (124 B)

Susan Dickinson had written that "the first verse is complete in itself it needs no other, and can't be coupled – Strange things always go alone."[112] But Dickinson's insistence on revising the last stanza suggests that even what "go[es] alone" demands some accompaniment. In this sense, the last stanza's turn to the world above the grave is necessarily an odd appendage, as it marks (a function the original second stanza retains, with its "here") the passing of the first stanza.

To say this poem is about the dead's indifference to human affairs is both true and irrelevant, a touch-point for the poem that, while it stands as its content, fails to be particularly central to what the poem is about. The poem is not so much *about* death and change in the sense of content, or seeking to convey an understanding of it. Rather, the poem with its ostensible content stands out against a magnificent awe, in relation to which its peculiarly luxurious images are posed. As the gratuitous glamour of such images indicates, they mark out something, rather than embody or convey it. The effect of this is not scenelessness but a pointed standing at a remove from what the poem seems most to be concerned with. Like many Dickinson poems that both excite and thwart, it draws our attention toward something it doesn't contain, and in so doing becomes ornamental.

Representative poetics, like Western metaphysics, plays between an ideal of present truth and the ways it is problematically represented to and by subjects in the form of objects. The inadequacy of subject/object representation to fully hold truth, or presence, in its grasp makes a problem of human existence, or at least makes the limitation of human knowing the core of poetics. In contrast, Dickinson's poetry does not seek to essentially house full presence *or* to give a limited representation of it: instead, it works to adorn it. In this it returns to another aspect of ornamentation that Coomaraswamy recovers: "God's creation of living beings to occupy the already created world (as decoration 'fills space') has always been called 'the work of adornment.'"[113] In Dickinson's case, the adorning holds that the human experience of phenomena is a magnificent, attending presence. Partial human life is the necessary addition to presence, like Thoreau's jewel-like duck, and it need not fuse to presence or convey it, when it can simply go along with it.

> I saw no Way – The Heavens were stitched –
> I felt the Columns close –
> The Earth reversed her Hemispheres –
> I touched the Universe –
>
> And back it slid – and I alone –
> A speck opon a Ball –

> Went out opon Circumference –
> Beyond the Dip of Bell – (633)

What, really, is made known by this poem? Helen Vendler's penetrating interpretation still ends by saying that Dickinson's "metaphors tend to create this sort of nearly unintelligible cascade, which, once understood, makes the reader a participant in the sort of vertigo transcribed in the poem." [114] But how can an "unintelligible cascade" continue to provoke "vertigo" once "understood"? There is an aspect of ornamental occupation in Dickinson which does not quite submit to this kind of interpretive practice. The poem seems to pertain to its topic, rather than to speak to it or convey it. Such literature does not house or embody meaning, then, but is set in a dislocated relation to the Open, toward which it draws our attention. Hence its awe-inspiring strangeness, as "A speck opon a Ball – / Went out opon Circumference – / Beyond the Dip of Bell –" rings through a vastness that this poem addresses rather than speaks about.

The language of the poem almost directly reproduces that of "Two Butterflies." To compare more directly:

> Two Butterflies went out at Noon –
> And waltzed opon a Farm –
> Then stepped straight through the Firmament
> And rested, on a Beam –
>
> And then – together bore away
> Opon a shining Sea – (571 B)

> . . . and I alone –
> A speck opon a Ball –
> Went out opon Circumference –
> Beyond the Dip of Bell – (633)

Each poem turns upon multiply placed trivialities susceptible to flight or disappearance, captured in the shared formulation of "Went out [. . .] opon." The overlap of the two poems is still deeper, for in a later version of "Two Butterflies," Dickinson writes that they

> ... espied Circumference
> And caught a ride with him – (571 C)

Even that line had variants, including "Then overtook – [Circumference] / and took a Bout with him." All of this shows us that the poet is fascinated by a dynamic of placing-upon that is not quite steady, as to reach it is to teeter. She would place the mind upon that outer rim of what could be identified as a phenomenon, either mental or physical. This rim is identified by a boundary that is form reduced to its essence: a distinction without characteristics. Circumference is the ultimate state of form, in that it is what the mind can notice as distinct from all else (or, distinct from Being). It's something the mind notices, on which it can just barely place itself—and yet that place is one that can barely be held to. Indeed, it slips out of one poem into another, as the mind slips from one iteration of the idea to another.

In Dickinson, a playful formal resonance can make a formulation seem to flit from one place to another. The butterflies leap from farm to beam to firmament; the rain from roof to tree and road: so too, being-upon as a concern or motif appears to skitter from poem to poem. Such movability suggests a liberation into a shifting, agitated way of being, a laying-across or wearing. If the poetry—as Cameron argues—abandons the frame, the fixity, and finds the undifferentiated Open, thus abandoning the work of art in a fundamental sense, it also finds agitation, placement, and contrasts that are understood as posed to be disposed, manifested, and then abandoned. There are still forms running across the Open. That is at issue in the way "The Grass so little has to do" depicts a field of grass decorated by butterflies and bees, and with dewdrops "thread[e]d ... like Pearl," or in the way that "A drop fell on the Apple Tree" observes the smattering of water across the different locations of the landscape. This is also why such poems end so abruptly, for they exist as appearing and disappearing forms that "prance" out. In contrast to the way that Rilke, in a line quoted by Cameron, observes "[t]ransiency everywhere plunges into a deep being," in Dickinson transiency is strung like a necklace across "deep being," and indicates its value and even honor.[115]

In this respect, Dickinson's poetry pursues an element of recognition as honoring which has been seen to define the lyric. Susan Stewart writes that

> [p]oetic making is an anthropomorphic project; the poet undertakes the task of recognition in time—the unending tragic Orphic task of drawing the figure of the other—the figure of the beloved who reciprocally can recognize one's own figure—out of the darkness.[116]

In Grossman's words, the project of lyric is bringing forth the "visibility of the speaking person."[117] He also writes that such rendering-visible of the person is a marking of "the honor of the world," making the poem a celebration of human visibility:

> Poems pitch persons together toward one another full of news about being, about personal life. The poem is an occasion, across vast reaches of space and time, for the performance of the ceremony of hospitality in which the stranger is greeted and the contracts of sociability are recovenanted. This is because the poem as a common place is like a festive table where persons renew their relation to the substance of being in colloquy.[118]

It's worth observing how the pitching-together of persons is deflected into the vision of a ceremonial table, because there are intimations in that image of a decorative form of honor. But for Grossman, representation is honor's critical mode, and poetry is less importantly for him a festive table than it is a means of presenting the *eidos*, a word he uses "in its Homeric sense as the form or beauty of the person," particularly the face.[119]

Grossman's account of the ethical work done by lyric rests on its capacity to represent persons to one another by bringing them into a visibility he describes as even "sunny."[120] But to read Dickinson, as Cameron has shown us, is to see how relentlessly she violates "the satisfactions of poetic utterance," and among those is the sense of having had a person made visible to us in that way. This is sometimes the case at a rather simple level, where the simplicity can make the violation all the more evident, as in one of Dickinson's very earliest poems:

> When Roses cease to bloom, Sir,
> And Violets are done –
> When Bumblebees in solemn flight
> Have passed beyond the Sun –
> The hand that paused to gather
> Opon this Summer's day
> Will idle lie – in Auburn –
> Then take my flowers – pray! (8)

This little poem begins by discussing, with "Sir," a future moment when summer and flowers have passed. It also stresses a moment of present conversation between a speaker and "Sir," in which one anticipates the death not only of the flower and seasons, but of the speaker herself, as her hand will "idle lie." This reflection, which has a quality of preparation or preamble (when the flowers and I die, *then* . . .) is jolted by "Then take my flowers – " because the "Then" which that line considers is not the future-then, when the poet and flowers are dead, but rather an intense *now*. The poem begins by telling a listener that in the future I and these flowers will die, but then reverses course to abruptly foist the flowers onto "Sir" with the exclamation, "pray!" Anticipating the death of self and flowers leads back into an urgently present need to reject both, and enacting that rejection ruptures the initial intimacy of speaker and "Sir," even in giving both flowers, and self, to him. We are left hanging—jilted, as it were—standing with both her thoughts and flowers. In such startled foistings, Dickinson's poetry resists the pitching-together of persons, and violates the notion of poetry as anything like a "ceremony of hospitality." And yet, she holds onto the sense of the "festive table" that Grossman points to. In its acute poising of ornamental flowers, as of gems and crowns, this poetry, which so rejects the idea of art as quintessentially representational, confers attention and honor by means of ornament.

Hence Dickinson's poetry does some of the work that poetic speech did in archaic Greece, prior to the classical era with its rational philosophers, democratic citizens, and literary craftsmen. Archaic Greece is characterized by a mythological order of truth, in which "masters of truth," as Detienne called them, spoke in verse of inspired visions, in a philosophical poetics that Heidegger admired. For such seer-poets, Detienne argues, speech was a mode of bringing into visibility, and truth was a matter of being brought to light and out of obscurity. Such speech begins in vision, as when "[o]ne day in Crete, the herb gatherer Epimenides fell into a sleep so deep, without beginning or end, that he had all the time in the world to speak in person with Truth."[121] Detienne continues, "the poet uses his sung speech to celebrate human exploits and actions, which thus become glorious and illuminated, endowed with vital force and fullness of being."[122] Such speech is concerned with a truth indistinguishable from praise: Detienne quotes Pindar, "'I will praise the man I love, warding away lurid blame and bringing him true glory, like a stream of water.'"[123] Dickinson's poetry participates in such poetic work, in which the labor is not to convince, nor even to represent, but to notice and thus to praise. In this regard, we can understand the underlying similarity between the poetic work being done by both Dickinson and Thoreau. Each develops the element of praising the world, which, as Susan Stewart observed, characterized "Cædmon's Hymn," the first known poem in English, and which Detienne shows to have had a long history in poetry. This work of noticing, attending, and loving what is seen marks the shared poetic project of these two figures, and makes their work at once poetic and ornamental.

I have, then, invoked Detienne's history of Greek thought, which traces a shift from truth as revealed to privileged visionaries whose speech casts a praising light, to truth as a matter of propositions to be tested, judged, and debated among persons. And I have said that aspects of Dickinson's art of noticing—her ornamental poetics—partake of both sides of this historical cleft. On the one hand, her poetry's recognition of transience links it to the ornament of the rhetorician; on the other, her poetry's use of form as the ornaments of the Open, sometimes called the "plain of truth," evokes the work of Detienne's ancient visionary singers. But Dickinson's poetry is distinct from both traditions in that she can see truth in terms of transience. Her poetry is not a retreat from the time-bound world into a timeless mental space; it is an investigation of the truth found in and through an intense sense of fugitiveness. In this sense, too, we see that Dickinson may wander further afield even from Heidegger; there is still less of a ground, just a wearing, one might say. In the way that ornamental objects rest on shifting seas and grasses, it may seem that all Being is ornamental, and that rather than that wholeness of presence there are only fluttering particles.

* * *

Although the devotion to the problem of Being can lead Heidegger to neglect particular beings, there is—as Bernstein has discussed—a way in which the form of what is around us is for Heidegger retained as a kind of imprint, like the indentation left on a pillow when we lift our head from it. Bernstein pursues the issue with regard to *Being and Time*, where, she observes, Heidegger states that "a fundamental trait of *Dasein*, *In-sein*, or Being-in" is that it "cannot be structured as the relation between two things existing side by side in the world." That is to say, "[t]he relation of Being-in is not like that of 'the water is 'in' the glass." But even as Heidegger lays out this notion that human existence is a mode of inhabiting that is *not* like the way water is in a glass, the formulation carries with it this sense of "inness"—not spatially in, and yet "in," in a way defined by its opposition to the mode of spatial being-in. The result is, Bernstein argues, one of "ghostly presence," as if the world of equipment and spatial relations wafts over into the domain of Being.[124]

Heidegger's conceptions of Being not only echo his accounts of beings, they circle around modes of situation. We can already see this in the fundamental distinction between being in a glass and being in a world; it also characterizes "The Origin of the Work of Art." The essay frames the question of the identity of art as a question of placing: "The picture hangs on the wall like a rifle or a hat."[125] As Heidegger launches his meditation on the difference between how pictures and rifles hang on the wall, his rumination on *what* a thing is gets caught up with *where* it is:

> The stone in the road is a thing, as is the clod in the field. A jug is a thing, as is the well beside the road. But what about the milk in the jug and the water in the well? These too are things if the cloud in the sky and the thistle in the field, the leaf in the autumn breeze

and the hawk over the wood, are rightly called by the name of the thing.[126]

The question of the thing is a question about *placeability*, or about how one thing inhabits another, such that we cannot entirely tell if the "thing" is "the leaf" only, or "the leaf in the autumn breeze," "the cloud" or "the cloud in the sky."

The issue of placing resurfaces in the definition of the work, much as it did in the transition from being in a glass to being in the world. For example, he asks, "where does a work belong? . . . within the realm that is opened up by itself."[127] This work, cut off from the world of mere thingly placing and cut off from its creator, is nevertheless defined by its being placed "within" a new kind of space rather than transcending placeability. In sentences Grossman quotes, "A work, by being a work, makes space for that spaciousness. 'To make space for' means here especially to liberate the Open and to establish it in its structure."[128] Thus the art itself does the work of "in-stalling"; art is made in being "set forth."[129] My point is how fully the artwork in Heidegger is a matter of placing.

A primary example of this is the Greek temple, which Heidegger calls a "setting up," a "br[inging] forth," and finally a way of framing what it is set up and brought forth against and out of.[130] Thus,

> the temple-work, in setting up a world, does not cause the material to disappear, but rather causes it to come forth for the very first time. . . . The rock comes to bear and rest and so first becomes rock; metals come to glitter and shimmer, colors to glow, tones to sing, the word to speak. All this comes forth as the work sets itself back into the massiveness and heaviness of stone, into the firmness and pliancy of wood. . . . That into which the work sets itself back and which it causes to come forth in this setting back of itself we called the earth. Earth is that which comes forth and shelters.[131]

The "temple" as work is superseded, for Heidegger, by the kind of situation the temple establishes between world and earth, such that the art becomes concerned with this resting of the temple in the world, or with its "setting." Although Grossman cites this passage as an example of the necessity of framing and fixity for the poem, it is neither fixity nor framing that seems at issue here so much as this capacity to summon up placing or setting as such.

Both setting-in and setting-against are formulations that shape Heidegger's thinking. Consider how he distinguishes between the object and the thing in "The Thing":

> As the self-supporting independence of something independent, the jug differs from an object. An independent, self-supporting thing may become an object if we place it before us, whether in immediate perception or bringing it to mind in a recollective representation. However, the thingly character of the thing does not consist in its being a represented object, nor can it be defined in any way in terms of the objectness, the over-againstness, of the object.[132]

Distinguishing thing from object concerns whether the thing or object under consideration is "place[d] . . . before us" and put in a relation of "over-againstness" or not. If the object is "that which stands before, over against, opposite us,"[133] we might imagine that the true thing is that which, in its doubled "independence of something independent" exists outside all situation and placement. And yet, in "The Thing" being-placed before us is superseded by a distinct form of "Nearness," such that "Thinging is the nearing of the world. . . . As we preserve the thing *qua* thing we inhabit nearness." Even though things "do not appear *by means of* human making," as objects do when placed before us, they still do not "appear without the vigilance of mortals," which is achieved in part by "the step back from the thinking that merely represents . . . to the thinking that responds and recalls." If this stepping-back of the mind is "no mere shift of attitude" but a step beyond "representational thinking," it is still an understanding of spatiality: placing supersedes representation.[134]

I say that, even though in "What Are Poets For?" Heidegger defines representation as a placement before consciousness: "What stands as object in the world becomes *standing* in representational production. . . .

What stands thus owes its presence to a placing whose activity belongs to the *res cogitans*, that is, to consciousness."[135] In contrast, he intimates a knowing of "the heart," which does not entail this placing-representation.[136] Nevertheless, knowing continues to have a quality of placing, both in the way that "the return from the realm of objects and their representation into the innermost region of the heart's space" has, already, a quality of placing and bringing-inside, and is then also put *"in this precinct"* of language.[137] Even Heidegger's metaphors of a way of being in language that is not caught up with signifying concepts focus on being in a place: "When we go to the well, when we go through the woods, we are always already going through the word 'well,' through the word 'woods,' even if we do not speak the words."[138] Over and over, when Heidegger wants to talk about a way of knowing that abandons focus on formal appearances, and on an objectifying mode of placing objects before the cognizing mind, we find accounts of placements of mind. This is what is at stake in Heidegger's lines quoted at the beginning of this section: thinking is someplace, in that way that Bernstein reminds us is a "quivering," not a grounding: "When on a summer's day the butterfly / settles on the flower and, wings / closed, sways with it in the / meadow-breeze."

In "The Origin of the Work of Art," placing is avowedly unfixing, like the bees' settling that is also a swaying:

> [W]e have indicated in the work rather a happening and in no sense a repose, for what is rest if not the opposite of motion? It is at any rate not an opposition that excludes motion from itself, but rather includes it. Only what is in motion can rest.... Where rest includes motion, there can exist a repose which is an inner concentration of motion, hence a highest state of agitation, assuming that the mode of motion requires such a rest.[139]

Heidegger is telling us that art is concerned with a setting-in place that is also restless and unfixed. Nothing could be further from the idea of the poem as stable, fixed, bounded entity; this is essentially the vision of being-upon as restless, ornamental placement that Dickinson has already brought us to. Heidegger and Dickinson are both deeply concerned with agitation as rest, and placing as motion, in which what would look from one perspective like a solidifying situatedness turns out to be exemplary of impermanence and contingency. The consequence of such an understanding would be that formal connections, understood as superficial and temporary, are both a consequence of and a marker of (a way of noticing) insight into the Open.

Dickinson can, therefore, help us to see that Heidegger's work contains strands of an account of art as fundamentally ornamental. I am drawing out such strands against the more overt qualities of "The Origin of the Work of Art," such as its focus upon the grandeur of the Greek temple and the artwork that reveals the historical direction of a people. In this undercurrent of his work, Heidegger points to an ornamental art concerned with what it is to be placed, and which understands placement as a matter not of foundation but of realizing the hang*ing*-in-space, the place- and replaceability of any thing that we consider, including our considering. This would be an ornamental art concerned not to embody the Open, nor even to represent it, but to notice it. Even further, such an art would be found in ways of attending that consider the volatility of where and how we look and consider. That would be the kind of work art could still do in the light of the Open, and it would name ornament's pleasure and seriousness in contrast to a long history of using it to signify triviality. Further, it would name why the seriousness of ornament is indistinguishable from its pleasure, insofar as that pleasure that seems so light, tripping, and immaterial is the lightness that comes from noting the transiency and the contingency of form.

CONCLUSION

In Elisa New's discussion of Dickinson, she reassures us that in one poem, "[t]he butterfly's resplendence" is "not merely decorative," and that in another, "[t]he 'Fuzz' on which the bee subsists is not decorative."[140] It is the heart of New's argument that the beautiful, in American literature, is not decorative or trivial but is, instead, "the face of Being itself." Beauty in American literature is not there just as it "adds a bit of grace to the world but as it expresses the Grace that supports the world." My understanding is similar, insofar as beauty does have a "philosophical prestige," and even a potentially religious standing, in this literature.[141] But it is antithetical to the idea that ornamentation names something other than this beauty of Being, and it is antithetical to that view because I don't believe, with New or with the Western tradition, that it is through representation or encapsulation in form that grace, presence, or the Open are known. In her discussion of Jonathan Edwards, New writes that "'Glory' is not a decorative attribute . . . Glory is where God graces nothingness with his light."[142] Yet such gracing is what ornamentation does: it is an activity that does not encapsulate or tell of reality, but goes toward and along with it to honor it.

Ironically, using the dismissive phrase "merely decorative" is to touch upon ornament's most important manifestation: as a way of seeing form as contingent in nature. And "merely decorative" is an appropriate phrase insofar as it uses ornamentation to make a judgment about what matters, even if it is made against ornamentation. Form is merely ornamental insofar as it is form that serves to mark attention and value rather than to embody thought. This is, again, the way that work "opon" anything—like butterflies stepping straight into the firmament, or flinging spangles on a bush—could continue to be of interest, or even just could continue at all, after having stepped straight into the unframed Open.

Chapter 3

Whitman and the Distinction of Ornament

INTRODUCTION

"I will not have in my writing any elegance or effect or originality to hang in the way between me and the rest like curtains. I will have nothing hang in the way, not the richest curtains" ("P," 717). "[L]iterature" must not be "dressed up" like "a fine gentleman" in "costumes and jewelry [which] prove how little it knows Nature."[1] Whitman's declamations against ornamented writing are indeed legion; most famously, in the 1855 "Preface" to *Leaves of Grass*, he uses ornament as a term to dismiss formal elements such as rhyme, meter, and metaphor:

> The poetic quality is not marshaled in rhyme or uniformity or abstract addresses to things nor in melancholy complaints or good precepts, but is the life of these and much else that is in the soul. The profit of rhyme is that it drops seeds of a sweeter and more luxuriant rhyme, and of uniformity that it conveys itself into its own roots in the ground out of sight. The rhyme and uniformity of perfect poems show the free growth of metrical laws and bud from them as unerringly and as loosely as lilacs or roses on a bush, and take shapes as compact as the shapes of chestnuts and oranges and melons and pears, and shed the perfume impalpable to form. The fluency and ornaments of the finest poems or music or orations or recitations are not independent but dependent. All beauty comes from beautiful blood and a beautiful brain.... but the gaggery and

gilt of a million years will not prevail. Who troubles himself about his ornaments or fluency is lost. ("P," 714)

A paraphrase of this passage would properly begin by observing that Whitman uses ornament to signify a clutter of artificial poetic conventions that ignore the real source of literary art. But the passage tolerates the very "gilt" it tells us not to "trouble[] ... about." Consider: in the assertion, "Who troubles himself about his ornaments or fluency is lost," both ornament and fluency are set aside from worry, which is not a categorical dismissal. Each is retained so far as they may occur without premeditation and anxiety.

In light of the sentence, "Most works are most beautiful without ornament," when Whitman states that "[t]he fluency and ornaments of the finest poems or music or recitations are not independent but dependent," it sounds as though "fluency and ornaments" are to be dismissed because they are dependent rather than independent. In that way of reading, the subsequent sentence would offer an alternative definition of independent, non-ornamental beauty: "All beauty comes from beautiful blood and a beautiful brain." Yet that sentence defines beauty as dependent, because it "comes from" something else (the blood and brain). Thus the proposition that "[a]ll beauty comes from beautiful blood and a beautiful brain" is not a contrast to the shallow artifice of "fluency and ornaments" but a definition of the quality of what Whitman has deemed "the finest poems or music or recitations." These sentences, taken together, articulate that "fluency and ornaments" can count as beauty, and that their beauty is dependent.

That account of beauty as dependent is in accord with Whitman's view that "[t]he rhyme and uniformity of perfect poems show the free growth of metrical laws and bud from them as unerringly and loosely as lilacs from a bush." While "free growth" must entail a form of independence (otherwise, it wouldn't be free), it too depends on its origin in "metrical laws," a dependence Whitman likens to the dependence of flowers on a plant and its roots. The organic images are of flowers which adorn the plant, as the "lilacs or roses" reside "on" the "bush[es]." The flowers' residing on bushes is akin to other relationships of outgrowth in this passage, such as the statement that "rhyme and uniformity ... take shapes as compact as the shapes of chestnuts and oranges and melons and pears." The passage opposes ornament that is made with excessive strain and artifice on the part of the maker to ornament that emerges from, and partakes in, natural processes and activities. Moreover, organically emergent form is ornamental because it rests in relationship to that from which it depends or which it may adorn.

Overall, in the 1855 "Preface, " what is encouraged about ornamentation is its relationality: it emerges from something, and rests upon or in relation to something else. This not only relational but behavioral form—a form of changing and responding—is repeated across Whitman's work and constitutes its ornamental quality. For instance, even Whitman's hand resting on his hip in the famous engraving that is the frontispiece of the 1855 edition of *Leaves of Grass* indicates the importance of a pressing-upon relationality to his project. The text often represents gestures and poses that entail resting-on, and even Whitman's grammar and lineation manifest qualities of adornment as laying-upon. These images and forms of placing adornment bespeak a basic sense in Whitman of a behavioral aesthetics, or (as Heidegger would put it) a manner of comportment within the world.

Stephen Cushman argues that Whitman, despite reiterated contentions about "the secondary importance of formal or aesthetic concerns," had a significant investment in poetic form:

> Whitman's repeated claim that he succeeded at last in leaving stock poetical touches out of *Leaves of Grass* . . . does not correspond to reality. Regular rhyme and meter may be gone, but, for example, alliteration, anaphora, assonance, apostrophe, parallelism, and personification are all stock poetical touches and all prominent features of Whitman's verse.[2]

Among these "stock poetical touches" are those of ornamentation. In the 1855 "Preface," for instance, this "poet who continually renounces stylistic ornamentation, along with 'the smooth walks, trimm'd hedges, poseys and nightingales of the English poets,'" actually "link[s] his verse to the carefully cultivated[,] . . . and even . . . ornamental, products of gardens, groves and orchards."[3] Considering the skepticism

Cushman and other critics have cast on Whitman's claims to abandon poetic form, it is not entirely peculiar that while Whitman announces his stripping away of the false ornamentation of Western poetry, he is still deeply invested in ornamental poetics.[4] In arguing that Whitman remains invested in poetic ornamentation, I further explore how ornamental poetics unfolds an understanding of human beings' relation to the world through terms other than those of the subject's representation of an external, object world to himself through linguistically framed concepts and images. Uncovering this aspect of Whitman leads me to argue against a critical tradition in which his poetic work is seen as a form of representation homologous to that of liberal democratic politics, and to look instead at the disequilibrium in his sense of poetry as honorific lighting. For in addition to focusing on ornament as relational and dependent, Whitman sees it as a form of gloryifying light ("the daylight is lit with more volatile light" by poetry ["P," 721]), and as a mode of praising song (the poet's "thoughts are the hymns of the praise of things" ("P," 713). And in "Song of Myself" this lighting, singing poet also "come[s]" "[m]agnifying and applying," approaching and impacting the world. Whitman evokes a sense of the world as appropriately celebrated and ornamented and yet, at the same time, continually and even unjustly impressed and effected.[5] This experience of reality through ornamental aesthetics is radical not in proposing ideal solutions to suffering and injustice, but in beginning to explore what it would mean to praise an existence that is clearly seen as basically lacking in justice or right. The problem of praise which ornament confers—as a weighing-down, skewing adornment—is the reason for its centrality to Whitman's poetics.

THE ORNAMENTAL POETICS OF "SONG OF MYSELF"

The first stanza of "Song of Myself" presents a poet moving gently across the world: "I lean and loafe at my ease observing a spear of summer grass" ("S," 5). Like the revolving duck that captivated Thoreau, or Dickinson's butterflies dancing across a sunbeam, Whitman's shifting between "lean and loafe" poses a being-in-place that is in unsettled motion.

WHITMAN AND THE DISTINCTION OF ORNAMENT

> I am there, I help, I came stretch'd atop of the load,
> I felt its soft jolts, one leg reclined on the other,
> I jump from the cross-beams and seize the clover and timothy,
> And roll head over heels and tangle my hair full of wisps.
> ("S," 171–74)

Body "atop" a wagonload of grass, leg atop another leg, Whitman then turns this layering into a rolling that apparently covers the whole body ("head over heels") with the implied ornamentation of "wisps" of "clover and timothy." In another instance of the recurrent theme and form of laying-over and across, Whitman writes of "[a] few light kisses, a few embraces, a reaching around of arms" ("S," 26). There is a casual and temporary way that bodies brush against each other, one arm on or "around another," and the syntax has a lovely light hold on these images: "A few ... a few ..." like two loosely tied bundles. The singular "reaching around" is cut out from any particular scene or story, like a little piece in a collage balanced at the edge of those bunches of caresses.

The line about kisses and embraces is immediately followed by one about aesthetic pleasure:

> A few light kisses, a few embraces, a reaching around of arms,
> The play of shine and shade on the trees as the supple boughs wag.
> ("S," 26–27)

Interest in how an arm reaches or a kiss weighs skips into a comparable interest in light and shade's "play," forming an undirected engagement upon a natural object. Trees "wag," their limbs at once flexible and strong, as "shine" and darkness play across them. As the line speaks of two kinds of undirected motion (play and wagging) superimposed upon each other, it and the line above it superimpose different cases of contact (light on tree, arm or mouth on body) on one another.

There's been so much attention to the inclusiveness of Whitman's syntax and his line that perhaps we haven't seen clearly enough the effect of layering that he also achieves: long lines laid on the page in an accretive piling.

> I mind how once we lay such a transparent summer morning,
> How you settled your head athwart my hips and gently turn'd over upon me,
> And parted the shirt from my bosom-bone, and plunged your tongue to my bare-stript heart,
> And reach'd till you felt my beard, and reach'd till you held my feet. ("S," 87–90)

The passage begins simply with "how once we lay," but the specificity of Whitman's wording—here, and especially in the lines to follow—keeps one from taking it as simply a term for having sex. There is something odd about "once we lay such a transparent summer morning," in part because the phrase "a transparent summer morning" names a particular time but also names that morning as a see-through non-place, without location. The line emphasizes not simply the tryst, but the "I mind" of it: the formality of the act of bearing-in-mind that this occurred. That formality, by which Whitman is marking out how in some emptied space the two of us "lay," makes what one first takes as a slightly vaguely worded but sexually specific passage into one that marks out a relaxed placing together with an air of the remarkable or the salient. That is to say that there is something differently literal, differently explicit, about this part of the poem: the distinctive specification of a set of activities whose eroticism does not reside in their reference to displaced sexual acts.

The next lines stress careful, slow-motion placing: "you settled your head athwart my hips" might, again, seem to refer to some obvious sexual act, but it also just describes placing one's head on someone else's pelvis. Whitman writes that "you settled"—slowly let your head come, over time, to rest—"athwart" his body, in a compositional riding. The parting of "the shirt from my breast-bone" has a dance-like quality, as if the lover is performing actions, now not of resting upon, but of separating. One might think of the shirt being parted as an unbuttoning, but the specificity in the line is of the shirt being parted "from my bosom-bone," which is a distinct motion of un-placing or peeling off of Whitman. The tongue that "plunged . . . to my bare-stript heart" is in the vicinity of penetration, but is more in line with the moving up and down, along the front of the speaker's body, that is then named in the line, "And reach'd till you felt my beard, and reach'd till you held my feet." That line does evoke the speaker's being licked all over his body—but then it clearly speaks of "reach[ing]," which is distinct. Kissing is also associated with reaching in the 1855 "Preface," where Whitman speaks of "the reached kisses of the soul" ("P," 724). The point of this is the distinctiveness of making "reaching," a somewhat generic gesture, central to the sexualized activities in the poem. This passage creates a mode of activity that is at once strikingly formal while also being in itself sexualized.[6] Rather than working as displaced depictions of sexual encounters, these passages sexualize forms of encounter such as laying-on and reaching, which might be indifferently located in the field of the body or of writing, and which are also foundational to human engagement with the world in any form.

Ornamentation has stood at times as an art form that fails (or refuses) to lift desire into the disinterested realm of aesthetic experience, or which pulls aesthetic pleasure back into the realm of desire.[7] Drawing attention is, after all, a form of attracting, and that makes a link between ornamentation and desire. Similarly, in Whitman the reason for linking ornamentation to sexuality is not in ornament's materiality or its appeal to sensory pleasure, but in its relational and applied quality. It is the very impressing, laying-on and across quality of *both* the depicted physical activity and the poetic language itself which carries that quality; it isn't clearly located either in one place or the other but in the activity that is associated with each. All these gestures involving reaching, laying, and bundling involve a sense of behavior and applied forces that produce effects, and the urgency of such activity and affecting in Whitman seems not only to happen in and outside the writing, but to even characterize his sense of how writing might itself, as an ornament, relate to the world—by being laid across or placed in relation to it in such a way as to affect it.[8] In that sense, rather than seeking to erase the difference between writing and other objects in the world, that difference becomes a site of contact which is itself exciting. My point here is that the sexual quality in Whitman is focused on a structure of relation which is fully embodied in neither living flesh nor literary text, but in gestures of contact and response, which in a paradigmatic sense, for Whitman, concern touching-upon the world.[9]

A major preoccupation in Whitman criticism concerns his attempts to meld the realm of written representation to that of embodied presence. In *Disseminating Whitman*, Michael Moon argues that "Whitman set himself the problem of attempting to project actual physical presence into a literary text. At the heart of this problem was the impossibility of doing so literally."[10] To remedy that impossibility, Whitman would "produc[e] metonymic substitutes for the author's literal corporeal presence," but nevertheless, the "generative contradiction" in *Leaves of Grass* is "that which exists between Whitman's repeated assertions that he provides loving physical presence in the text and his awareness of the frustrating but ultimately incontrovertible conditions of writing and embodiment that actually render it impossible for him to produce in his writing more than metonymic substitutes for such contact."[11] The sense of a profound and problematic division between what a text can represent and the presence of a living human is, itself, related to a poetic tradition grounded in representation, and to its cognate philosophical metaphysics, in which the speech of the subject is by definition separated from the world it would speak of. This understanding is surely present in Whitman, but it is overshadowed by his sense of an ornamental aesthetics and poetics, much like that in Dickinson and Thoreau. Here the focus is on behaviors of engagement, influence, and approach that do not fix on the axis of representational poetics' divide between written language and the present world. These behavioral forms in Whitman resemble the gestures of care and attending which Heidegger characterizes as basic to *Dasein*, and I would venture that in Whitman these forms of attending and laying-on are similarly ontological conditions. As such they are, in turn, the conditions upon which particular experiences—be they physical encounters or written words—are founded. Both forms of activity would spring, for Whitman, from an underlying, felt relationship of the human being to the world. Moon has written that Whitman "discovered and made available to readers a way of re-experiencing their and our worlds as multiple, serial phenomena of a richness and intensity so strong that one's response would perforce be an erotic one."[12] I would extend this to say that it is not only the subject's response to phenomena that is erotic, but also Whitman's intuition of the underlying condition of human existence in the world—being placed upon it, moving across it, and reaching toward and handling things within it. In contrast, then, to materialist approaches that might emphasize Whitman's attempt to come closer to the primary world of the body,[13] I am stressing that Whitman's world begins in the pressing compartment that characterizes both his erotics and his ornamental aesthetics. This pressing-upon is something that can't really be addressed by moving between the registers of the written and thought or the embodied and material; it's a basic principle of force and affecting relation that undergirds them both.

Whitman's sense of poetics as touching behavior can be clarified through comparison to Susan Stewart's discussion of George Puttenham's *The Art of English Poesy*, an English Renaissance work on poetics that includes a major discussion of ornament.[14] She writes that Puttenham understood that "poetry is embedded in cultural systems of decorum and sensual regulation and at the same time has its own sphere of constraints, expectations, and permissions."[15] Rather than putting a profound divide between the poem and its world, this way of thinking stresses that culture entails liberties and constraints on behavior which operate within and without the poem; it also allows for permeability between the two realms. Stewart continues, discussing Puttenham:

> The regulation of the senses, of mouth and speech, is [for Puttenham] completely bound up with processes of social decorum: with who may do and say what in the presence or absence of whom on what occasions. The notion of poetic *kinds* is tied to the specificity of their use and occasion: the epithalamion, the elegy, and the aubade are at once works of art independent of their particular context of production and use and social acts tied to specific rules of decorum. Poems are in this sense acts of social intent and consequence not things in a world of things.[16]

Considered an act of social intent, Whitman's poetry often seeks to create an occasion for social behavior. His instigations to the reader serve as occasions for particular kinds of behavior, and engagement, which happen in relationship to the poem rather than being fully represented in it, or exist as a self-standing reality in relation to which the poem could be positioned.

The importance of ornamentation to Puttenham's work is clear in the text's division into three books: "Of Poets and Poesy," "Of Proportion Poetical," and "Of Ornament." As Frank Whigham and Wayne Rebhorn comment, "The *Art* is many things," "a poetics and a rhetoric, a theoretical treatise on prosody and a manual of courtly trifles, a work on education and a courtesy book," as well as "a work of self-fashioning."[17] It focuses on poetry as a politically engaged behavior, and as a mode of seduction and assertion. Puttenham's poetics is, according Whigham and Rebhorn, significant primarily for the overt nature of its combination of poetics with conduct. This is evident even in the English names he gives to classic figures of rhetorical ornament. He names them in terms that evoke person-to-person conduct or action, such that "Puttenham's Englishings invite the reader to imagine a person actually uttering the figure in some sort of localized social context":[18] "Anaphora, or the Figure of Report"; "Symploche, or the Figure of Reply"; "Insultatio, or the Disdainful"; and "Meiosis, or the Disabler."[19]

As does Cicero in *De Oratore*, Puttenham thinks ornament is a matter of providing pleasure to draw in and engage an audience. But whereas in Cicero that involved managing the limited time span of pleasure and interest, to Puttenham the whole issue is one of *approach*. This emerges within his discussion of decorum, that aspect of ornament which, in Puttenham's chapter title, "generally makes our speech well pleasing and commendable."[20] He explains:

> Our own Saxon English term is seemliness, that is to say, for his good shape and utter appearance well pleasing the eye. We call it also comeliness for the delight it bringeth coming towards us, and to that purpose may be called pleasant approach.[21]

Puttenham here says that poetic decorum, which is for him an aspect of ornamentation, concerns what makes a decent, graceful, "coming-towards us," or an "approach" that brings "delight" and pleasure.

Whigham and Rebhorn point out that one of the *Art*'s innovations is using "the Gorgeous" as the finale of its review of poetic ornaments. Somewhat mysteriously, the Gorgeous doesn't refer to any particular ornamental device or figure:

For the glorious luster it setteth upon our speech and language, the Greeks call it *exergasia*, the Latin *expolitio*, a term transferred from these polishers of marble or porphyrite, who, after it is rough hewn and reduced to that fashion they will, do set upon it a goodly glass, so smooth and clear as ye may see your face in it; or otherwise as it fareth by the bare and naked body, which, being attired in rich and gorgeous apparel, seemeth to the common usage of the eye much more comely and beautiful than the natural. So doth this figure (which therefore I call the Gorgeous) polish our speech and as it were attire it with copious and pleasant amplifications and much variety of sentences all running upon one point and to one intent, so as I doubt whether I may term it a figure, or rather a mass of many figurative speeches, applied to the beautifying of our tale or argument.[22]

The gorgeous is an ornamentation that becomes so identified with poetry in general that Puttenham finally "doubt[s]" whether there is any "term" for it or particular form to it, beyond sheer "mass" of "appli[cation]." In this regard, the Gorgeous retains the quality of application so central to all ornament—"the glorious luster it *setteth upon* our speech and language" (my emphasis)—while emphasizing an activity of polishing and attiring, which shares the quality of movement with his earlier examples of ornamentation.

Whitman also engages the "sett[ing] upon" and lavished attention that are the heart of Puttenham's "Gorgeous." For instance, Whitman's drawn-out lines and syntaxes recurring to similar phrasings have the quality of repeatedly "amplif[ying]" phrases and formulations. They are placed in a highly laden "running" along of language, which Puttenham identifies with ornamentation. Consider the lavished increase and attention in a catalogue in "Song of Myself":

> Walking the path worn in the grass and beat through the leaves of the brush,
> Where the quail is whistling betwixt the woods and the wheat-lot,
> Where the bat flies in the Seventh-month eve, where the great gold-bug drops through the dark,

> Where the brook puts out of the roots of the old tree and flows to the meadow,
> Where cattle stand and shake away flies with the tremulous shuddering of their hides,
> Where the cheese-cloth hangs in the kitchen, where andirons straddle the hearth-slab, where cobwebs fall in festoons from the rafters;
> Where the trip-hammers crash, where the press is whirling its cylinders,
> Wherever the human heart beats with terrible throes under its ribs,
> Where the pear-shaped balloon is floating aloft, (floating in it myself and looking composedly down,)
> Where the life-car is drawn on the slip-noose, where the heat hatches pale-green eggs in the dented sand,
> Where the she-whale swims with her calf and never forsakes it.
> ("S," 732–42)

The lines stretch the sentence out beyond its limit, carrying the grammar so beyond its bounds that even when traced back through about three pages of settings ("By the city's quadrangular houses . . . Along the ruts of the turnpike . . . Where the rattlesnake suns his flabby length on a rock . . . Under Niagara, the cataract falling like a veil over my countenance . . . Through patches of citrons and cucumbers with silver-wired leaves . . . I tread day and night such roads" ["S," 717–97]) the result is not exactly comprehension. This is because the text is about the numerous places in which the speaker "treads," and the number of clauses that could iteratively modify the frame grammar of "I tread." The passage doesn't contain a manageable image we need to work to decipher; it is, instead, a stringing out of attentive placements, line across line across line, to the effect of dazzling excess.

A focus on segmented activities is another aspect of ornamentation identified by Puttenham and evident in Whitman. This is visible in phrasings such as, "By the cot in the hospital reaching lemonade to a feverish patient" ("S," 784), "the brook puts out of the roots of the old tree and flows to the meadow," and even the "cheese-cloth hangs in the kitchen." There is enormous stress on isolated places at which an act is performed, or where a person and object are placed:

> The canal boy trots on the tow-path, the book-keeper counts at his desk, the shoemaker waxes his thread,
> The conductor beats time for the band and all the performers follow him,
> The child is baptized, the convert is making his first professions,
> The regatta is spread on the bay, the race is begun, (how the white sails sparkle!)
> The drover watching his drove sings out to them that would stray,
> The pedler sweats with his pack on his back, (the purchaser higgling about the odd cent;). ("S," 297–302)

Puttenham's sense of poetic ornamentation as a brief action is kindred to Whitman's focus on making a poem out of a string of isolated figures of activity, even if that activity is as simple as the hanging of the cheesecloth.[23] Each of these little acts or events is placed in its clause, line after end-stopped line, one after the other. The very lack of an account of the motion from one scene to another, and the lack of any narrative development within such scenes, creates a sense that the poem is a string of emblematic gestures, cut and set together in a way that constrains our ability to understand them as representation. (I think here of a point made by Grabar, that in ornamentation, "otherwise identified features—for instance, a rinceau of flowers and leaves or heart-shaped dots set in rows—are decoration rather than representations of something or significant of something else.")[24] Both the iteration and the animation of such lines—the sense of a little motion in a situation, one after another—are akin to the ornamentation in Puttenham, in which turns of phrase are effective, impressive actions. Such passages in Whitman also work an aesthetic of increase and piling-on, which serves as ornamentation by sheer amplification. In this light, the swelling of Whitman's sentences and lines is essentially ornamental, for they are so laden with clauses as to overflow with an abundance that piles over the content of the words.

The question of the appropriate has been central to a number of the accounts of ornament that I have considered, but for Puttenham the link of ornamentation to both appropriateness and decorous behavior is especially vivid. In his discussion of decorum, he observes of the appropriate use of ornamentation: "The Greeks call this good grace of everything in his kind το πρεπον, the Latins *decorum*; we in our vulgar call it by a scholastical term *decency*."[25] But what does decency have to do with Whitman, a poet known for abandoning ideas of social decorum and, for example, putting the President in the same sentence as a prostitute?

> The prostitute draggles her shawl, her bonnet bobs on her tipsy and pimpled neck,
> The crowd laugh at her blackguard oaths, the men jeer and wink to each other,
> (Miserable! I do not laugh at your oaths nor jeer you;)
> The President holding a cabinet council is surrounded by the great Secretaries. ("S," 305–308)

The objection that such a passage instances Whitman's rejection of decorum actually cuts to the heart of the ornamental quality of Whitman's poetry. Insofar as ornamentation (linked to an account of poetry as ceremonial behavior at appropriate occasions, and to an account of rhetoric in which art is applied when seemly or pleasant) is all about decorous behavior, it is the quality of poetry that most concerns Whitman. It is a misrecognition of Whitman to think of him as embracing all that might have seemed indecent (Puttenham is quite a bit more indecent than Whitman).[26] Whitman is obsessed with the question of appropriate behavior, and wishes not to abolish it but to expand its reach. In the passage on the prostitute, in addition to placing her in the vicinity of the President, he implicitly chastises those who "jeer and wink at each other" for their inappropriate response to her abjection. His rejection of a decorum that abhors the lowly is tied to a decorum that offers a different sense of the appropriate response to the world:

> This is the meal equally set, this the meat for natural hunger,
> It is for the wicked just the same as the righteous, I make appointments with all,

I will not have a single person slighted or left away,
The kept-woman, sponger, thief, are hereby invited,
The heavy-lipp'd slave is invited, the venerealee is invited;
There shall be no difference between them and the rest.
("S," 372–77)

Whitman's answer to what is decent and appropriate may be radically inclusive, but his idea that poetry is the place to explore and perform questions of the decent is absolutely in line with an ornamental poetics of appropriate bearing. The statement, "I wear my hat as I please indoors or out" ("S," 397) stresses that democracy, like aristocracy, will have its own mode of the graceful or the appropriate.[27]

Appropriateness in Whitman means writing as if both poet and poem were adorning the world, rather than fully holding that world within the ambit of words. For instance, in the twenty-ninth bather passage, Whitman's observation that the water in "[l]ittle streams pass'd all over their bodies" ("S," 211), is followed by the detail that "[a]n unseen hand also pass'd over their bodies" ("S," 212). Even when the fantasy becomes more involved, there is still a ritualistic application of touch that involves running all over a person, as the woman's motions (she "puffs and declines with pendant and bending arch") turn riding into a rising and falling arch, but also something hanging, "pendant" ("S," 215). Whitman has his moments of calling out "Undrape!" ("S," 145) and inveighing against ornamentation, but even his address in that same passage turns into an opportunity for the poetic voice to become a draped-on attendant to what it mentions: "I see through the broadcloth and gingham whether or no, / And am around, tenacious, acquisitive, tireless, and cannot be shaken away" ("S," 146–47). One is wrapped "around" by Whitman, or draped on Whitman—"O despairer, here is my neck ... hang your whole weight upon me" ("S," 1012–13). At one point, Whitman refers to his being through the poem as a decorated object "bestow[ed]" on others: "Adorning myself to bestow myself on the first that will take me" ("S," 261). This feeds the way that the work appears to sweep across items—to brush along them, even. This brushing-along often serves to pull groups together as well, as in the way that "[a] few ... a few ..." and then an embrace are placed together, but the grouping always has a quality of occasionality rather than necessity. In one sentence, these beings are grouped together; in another, a different cluster might be made. This clustering matters less for what might be said to motivate it (why these and not others) and more as an exploration of how long lines of the poem could be seen to move along and across objects in the world. In this respect, they temporarily rather than necessarily draw along and gather up objects of attention.

Thinking about Whitman's poetry as a behavior of attending or "withness" sheds light on his sense that literary form is part of lived experience. For literature as a mode of ornamental behaving is not concerned with the existence of the text as an autonomous object, inscribed in material and linguistic form. Puttenham, too, has no interest in complete written works, or the form of a text as a settled object separate from the world of its writer and its maker. He's only interested in the right time and the right way to apply or deploy an ornament. Additionally, the concept of ornamentation as attending positions language—be it thought, spoken, or written down—as an accoutrement to life. To think of poetry as ornamentation is to think of language as attending or approaching both us and our world.

Anne Carson prefaces *Economy of the Unlost* with a quotation that emphasizes language as accompaniment:

> Think of the Greek preposition πρός. When used with the accusative case, this preposition means "toward, upon, against, with, ready for, face to face, engaging, concerning, touching, in reply to, in respect of, compared with, according to, as accompaniment for." It is the preposition chosen by John the Evangelist to describe the relationship between God and The Word in the first verse of the first chapter of his Revelation:
>
> πρὸς Θεόν
>
> "And The Word was with God" is how the usual translation goes. What kind of withness is it?[28]

Carson writes that words are first present neither as what God speaks, nor as how he conveys his presence through language to persons. Words are, instead, what *attends* God, and what approaches and accompanies him. For Whitman, poetry is what attends the world, and is in this sense its ornament: "O days of the present, I adorn you."[29]

UNREPRESENTATIVE WHITMAN

A significant current of criticism on Whitman has been grounded in the relationship of his poetry's representative form to democratic politics. For example, Betsy Erkkila writes that in the opening poem of the "Calamus" section, "Whitman resolves to publish and give voice to the 'not yet published' standard of manly love."[30] She adds that his work was part of a "movement toward giving public and written voice to the masses of common men and women who made up the American people."[31] Michael Warner observes that "Whitman's poetry may in fact be the earliest instance of a theme that has come to be taken for granted in Euro-American culture: the idea of sexuality as an expressive capacity of the individual."[32] In a different vein, George Kateb sees Whitman's poetry turning on the making-known of persons, so as to participate in a democracy in which "[t]he deepest moral and existential meaning of equal rights is equal recognition granted by every individual to every individual."[33] There is something peculiar about organizing a sense of Whitman around representation and expression, given that, Kerry Larson writes, "[a]s has long been recognized, Whitman's poetic is largely organized around the suspension of sense,"[34] but the issue of Whitman's democratic representativeness has been so crucial to discussions of Whitman that it merits further investigation. I do so, in this section, first by way of Allen Grossman's essay "The Poetics of Union in Whitman and Lincoln," which directly links poetry's representative and honorific functions.

Grossman argues that Whitman's is a "language that intends as a function of its structure a just order of the human world,"[35] one which depends upon inclusive representation. In particular, Grossman identifies Whitman's "discovery of a regulative principle that permitted an art based in the representative function itself," in which what is to be represented is chosen simply on the "index" of "mere being-at-all."[36] He connects a sense of representation to poetry's potential to praise and honor, for in a democracy, "the perfect equality of all human beings requires, as Whitman understood, an infinite resource of fame."³⁷ If the ancient poetic tradition of praise saw representation as the privilege and boon of the special few, in Whitman's poetics representation was made available to one and all: "Whitman's 'greatest poet' inferred from the traditional fame-powers of his art a fundamental principle of undifferentiated representation, which constituted a massive trope of inclusion."³⁸ Notwithstanding his evident respect for Whitman, it is Grossman's devastating view that Whitman was unable to truly represent even one person, let alone all of them.

> It is opposition to the meaning-intending will by the resistance of abstract form that produces, in the English poetic line, the sentiment of the presence of the person as a singular individual; and this Whitman could not restore.³⁹

Grossman is sympathetic to Whitman's intention in "tend[ing] more and more to modify his regulative principles to release the world from the overdetermination of all systems of representation."⁴⁰ But, still, it is not praise to say that "the master of social love ... was unable ... to enter the world by any act, except the deathwatch of the wounded in Lincoln's war."⁴¹

At least two Whitman poems engage the tradition of poetry as a memorial of the person, but then turn it into a gestural project based on draping and holding, rather than on depictions of the human form or eidos in the sense that matters to Grossman. Each poem is from the "Calamus" group: "Recorders Ages Hence" and "What Think You I Take My Pen in Hand?"⁴² The first poem begins in dialogue with persons in the future, seeking to remember and know Whitman:

> Recorders ages hence,
> Come, I will take you down underneath this impassive exterior,
>   I will tell you what to say of me,
> Publish my name and hang up my picture as that of the tenderest lover,

> The friend the lover's portrait, of whom his friend his lover was fondest,
> Who was not proud of his songs, but of the measureless ocean of love within him, and freely pour'd it forth. ("R," 1–5)

Whitman casts the poem as a direct address to his readers, soliciting the recorders to "come" in the present moment and meet up with him.[43] This move is juxtaposed with another, more traditional work of poetry: speaking for the poet after his death. "[T]his impassive exterior" evokes the immobility of the corpse's face, not a living person's face, and the language of "tak[ing]" readers "down" to it heightens the impression that this is an invitation to speak with the dead.[44]

In both "Recorders" and "What Think You I Take My Pen in Hand?" Whitman writes poetry as a work of official memorial-making. In "Recorders," he directs the recorders to "[p]ublish my name and hang up my picture" once he has passed on. And in "What Think You I Take My Pen in Hand?" he considers that his poem is meant to record important public events, if not persons: "The battle-ship, perfect-model'd, majestic" ("W," 2), "Or the vaunted glory and growth of the great city spread around me" ("W," 4).

In contrast to the work of memorializing persons or public events, each of these poems memorializes the love of men for one another. The idea is to transfer the dignity of the great man or great scene onto the lovers and friends, but Whitman makes that transfer by abandoning the recorded name, form, and outline. Each poem ends with arms draped:

> Who oft as he saunter'd the streets curv'd with his arm the shoulder of his friend, while the arm of his friend rested upon him also.
> ("R," 10)

> But merely of two simple men I saw to-day on the pier in the midst of the crowd, parting the parting of dear friends,
> The one to remain hung on the other's neck and passionately kiss'd him,

> While the one to depart tightly prest the one to remain in his arms. ("W," 5–7)

Perhaps the most elegant moment in these two poems is when Whitman writes that he is the one who "curv'd with his arm the shoulder of his friend." The phrasing makes taking the abstract form of the curve into a mode of embracing. Each scene is about actions in relation, and yet not of mutual or mirrored activity. That is, while Whitman curves his friend's arm, the other "rested upon him also," and if "also" suggests similarity, the difference between curving and resting is nevertheless preserved. The second poem ends with a hug that is precisely distinguished: one man "hung on the other's neck," the other "tightly prest the one . . . in his arms." Through such gestural notation, these memorial images become emblems of attending to and draping upon, and exemplify formal relations that do not point toward the specificity of human beings but to the specificity of how they might relate to one another. While on one level each passage is a representation, just of two men hugging rather than of a human countenance or a historical event, what is represented becomes an emblem of arms and bodies that rest on, curve around, and contact each other.

I have already said that within "Song of Myself," Whitman's lines attend to, rather than represent, the persons and acts with which they are concerned. He himself says something comparable in avowing in the 1855 "Preface" that "the expression of the American poet . . . is to be indirect and not direct or descriptive or epic" ("P," 712). This eschewal of direct description produces more than indirect description (allusion, implication, fragmented views); it leads Whitman into a process that, in "Song of Myself," he calls "adorning" ("S," 261). In the 1855 "Preface," this is implied in claims such as "He bestows on every object or quality its fit proportions neither more nor less" ("P," 712). This bestowing is tied to the American poet's assertion that persons and things are appropriately placed: "Nothing out of its place is good and nothing in its place is bad" ("P," 712). Indeed, the poet's work in bestowing "fit proportions" is one of rendering appropriate and well-harmonized everything before him: "he supplies what wants supplying and checks what wants checking" ("P," 712).

Whitman also characterizes himself as attentively bestowing, with language that evokes reaching across and laying upon, back in the 1855 "Preface":

> When the long Atlantic coast stretches longer and the Pacific coast stretches longer he easily stretches with them north or south. He spans between them also from east to west and reflects what is between them. ("P," 711)

This action of "stretch[ing] with" and "span[ning] between" is interlaced with one of hanging, which we should think of in line with the interest in draping already considered in "Song of Myself"—where "cobwebs *fall in festoons* from the rafters" ("S," 737; my emphasis). In the "Preface," just after speaking about how the poet stretches and spans,

> On him rise solid growths that offset the growths of pine and cedar and hemlock and liveoak and locust and chestnut and cypress and hickory and limetree and cottonwood and tuliptree and cactus and wildvine and tamarind and persimmon. . . . and tangles as tangled as any canebrake or swamp. . . . and forests coated with transparent ice and icicles hanging from the boughs and crackling in the wind. ("P," 711)

The way that Whitman speaks about growths "[o]n him," of the "coat[ing]" of forests with ice "hanging from the boughs" (like Thoreau's icicle forest), pinpoints draping and resting as central to the poet's work of bestowing and stretching. He is along and across, but also weighing and pulling. In this sentence, these two motions are specifically "tangled" with Whitman's syntactic assertions, with its extended "ands" and of ellipses that grammatically perform both accretion and stretching alike.

Whitman states repeatedly in the 1855 "Preface" that American poets are to be "kosmoses." He writes of "the poets of the kosmos," who "[a]s they emit themselves facts are showered over with light" ("P," 721), as if simply in the act of being, this poet covers the world with light. He continues to speak about how the "poets of the kosmos advance through all interpositions and coverings and turmoils," how "priests" will be replaced with "gangs of kosmos and prophets en masse," iterating that the kind of poet he wishes to be, and to evoke, is a "kosmos" ("P," 721, 727). This is an inspired speaker whose very being *as* a cosmos is what marks him as a poet, not his poems as such. As Whitman observes of "the greatest poet," "[t]he touch of him tells in action": the poet is concerned with the touch that is an action, an ornamental contact like the brushing across and hanging from I have discussed earlier ("P," 725, 727).

The word *cosmos* also suggests a basic order, in which things are placed where they belong ("Each has his or her place in the procession"),[45] and ornamentation as a tribute to the appropriateness of that order.[46] And yet in Whitman's work, the beautiful cosmos is more fluctuating than that. When Whitman writes in the 1855 "Preface" that "[w]ho troubles himself about his ornaments or fluency is lost" ("P," 714), he treats "ornaments" and "fluency" as aligned words. That link of ornamentation to fluency is also evident in his phrase "richest fluency," which defines fluency as a form of lavishness. This "richest fluency" is a quality that the potential poet will have in himself, not in his stilted rhymes: "your very flesh shall be a great poem and have the richest fluency not only in its words but in the silent lines of its lips and face . . . and in every motion and joint of your body" ("P," 715). "[R]ichest fluency" is also at issue in the "candor" that Whitman repeatedly urges on his poet, for candor is a type of openly flowing speech: "The great poets are also to be known by the absence in them of tricks and by the justification of perfect personal candor. . . . How beautiful is candor! All faults may be forgiven of him who has perfect candor" ("P," 722). Open-handed candor also contains that aspect of bestowing approval of which Whitman spoke earlier, defining it as part of the adorning that the American poet performs. The word "candor" means openness in the sense of honesty or full disclosure, but it also has an obsolete meaning of "[b]rilliant whiteness; brilliancy," which explains how Whitman's indecorous abandonment of proprieties aligns with an ornamental aesthetic of the fluid bestowal of honoring light, setting the shine of approval on the world.[47] In his account linking Whitman to praise poetry, Grossman focuses upon the representation of the person as the work of praise: to be praised is to have one's eidos memorialized, lit, and presented to others. But praise is not inherently twinned to representation,[48] and in Whitman the dignity and value of praise poetry is conferred through the flux of ornamental applications, placings, and light.

Whitman's praise is shot through with qualities of fluidity and light that are, as I discussed in the Introduction, central to the ornamental qualities of *kleos* poets such as Simonides and Pindar. I want to briefly return to the topic of archaic poetry, both to remind us that poetic honor was not always linked to representation, and because Leslie Kurke's discussion of it illustrates a question about its political implications that pertains to Whitman. Kurke observes that Pindar's poetry functioned within a system of gifts exchanged to solidify social bonds. The games Pindar celebrates were played by aristocrats, since no one else had the money and time to train for contests without monetary reward. The rewards for victory were ornamental objects, such as laurel crowns or treasures made of gold or other precious metals. Such tokens were, in Kurke's account, used to exemplify a glory and fame that redounded not just upon the athlete, but upon his ancestors and his estate. She points out, for instance, that in Pindar's Isthmian I the victors "adorned their house with tripods and cauldrons and phials of gold."[49] The poem is filled with "light imagery," and this lightness "merges the golden prizes with their symbolic value" to denote the glory of "the house."[50] More broadly, the light-shedding quality of prize ornaments serves to link the house and the household to public glory. Hence the prizes, as well as the value they denote, "must be installed at home to be made available as community property."[51]

> [T]he house in Pindar organizes a moral landscape: out to achievement, success, the winning of prizes, and then back. Light imagery makes this circuit clear. Never to leave home or never to reach the end of achievement leaves the individual shrouded in obscurity.... In contrast, success and return generate a radiance that shines from afar.[52]

This bringing home of prizes and adorning of the home with them is a public display of value, a means of boasting about one's own victory and spreading one's esteem in the form of a radiance that "shines" out onto the larger world.

Kurke notes that the treasure-gift, or *keimelion*, has a specific bond to aristocrats, who mark their private and privileged bonds to one another, in contrast to the rest of their society. "As Louis Gernet observes, expenditure on such closed aristocratic occasions was rightly perceived by the polis as a challenge to its communal ideology."[53] Thus, Kurke argues, when Pindar presents his poetry as a type of *keimelion*, he presses for a world structured around aristocratic houses and not around the democratic polis. The whole language of poetic gracing and the shedding of light, including the identification of poetry with ornamental objects, accomplishes the work of "social glue."[54] And, Kurke observes, the identification of ornamentation with the natural order indicated in the dual meaning of the word *cosmos* bespeaks the use of ornamentation to naturalize social bonds so as to push back on the rise of the polis and democratic culture. However, she also argues that such ornamentation could be adapted to the emerging democratic order. In Pindar, bestowing praise and ornament, either in ritual or in the poetry, is at least potentially a way of *sharing* aristocratic grace with the community at large. For instance, Kurke quotes Pindar's Pythian 9: "I wish, heralding the bronze-shielded Pythian victor Telesikrates together with the deep-girdled Graces, to sing of this fortunate man, crown of Kyrene."[55] To be an ornament to one's town—here, a "crown of Kyrene"—is to share one's grace with it by dedicating one's extraordinary merit to society at large.

Dickinson clearly thought of ornamentation as a means of marking out for notice; that marking is, we are now in a position to see more clearly, about the marking out of what is extraordinary or outstanding. In her poem on the dew leaving drops like pearl necklaces on the grass, Dickinson observes that even "[a] Duchess, were too common / For such a noticing" (379 B), explicitly connecting ornamental notice to not only the uncommon but the noble. Thoreau also identifies traditions of ornament with aristocracy, as is evident in a quotation also cited earlier:

> Bring a spray from the wood, or a crystal from the brook, and place it on your mantel, and your household ornaments will seem plebeian beside its nobler fashion and bearing. It will wave superior there, as if used to a more refined and polished circle.[56]

In this light, ornamentation may now seem so fundamentally connected to admirable outshining and aristocracy that its democratic stature is deeply compromised. Still, Kurke's reading of Pindar raises the possibility that ornament's aristocratic elements may be transferred to a democracy. Thus Whitman's bestowing of praise may take the principle of the elite and the glorious and indiscriminately shed it across the nation at large. This would make Whitman's ornamental poetry one in which esteem and the brilliant candor of beauty, pride, and grace retain their element of discriminating achievement while also making it possible to think of that esteem as shareable with all.

To Grossman, Whitman's fundamental project is one of universal representation, and the problem with it is its difficulty preserving the particular image of the specific person. Similarly, Wai Chee Dimock argues that Whitman's poetry emphasizes democratic universality to the degree that it has no language of particularity. The specific experiences and individual preferences of persons were erased in Whitman as, in her account, they had been in the entire philosophy of liberalism.[57] I am suggesting that Whitman's work may universally shed ornamental glory, rather than offer universal representation. And given that ornament need in no way specifically pertain to who or what it ornaments, it does not bring up the classic problem of democratic universalism's potential erasure of particularity, which so concerns the readings focused on representation. This might make Whitman's ornament more democratically universal than representation: a form that sustains indiscriminate, free-flowing application to all, as in the ornamentation of the town in Pindar.

But is universally accorded ornament really democratic in any necessary or meaningful sense? According to the political theorist Nancy Fraser, honor, esteem, or outshining are not, in principle, anathema to democracy. In *Redistribution or Recognition?* she discusses a democratic politics grounded in the equal means to seek to attain acclaim, recognition, or status. Everyone should have the same abilities and resources to seek high standing, but this does not mean it is just or possible to demand that everyone have it. She observes that "the view that everyone has an equal right to social esteem . . . is patently untenable, of course, because it renders meaningless the notion of esteem."[58] Her footnote elaborates that she is "assuming the distinction, now fairly standard in moral philosophy, between respect and esteem. According to this distinction, respect is owed universally to every person in virtue of shared humanity; esteem, in contrast, is accorded differentially . . . the injunction to esteem everyone is . . . an oxymoron."[59] Insofar as Whitman's representation in the poem is implicitly equated with representation in either the state (universal suffrage) or the public sphere, the equation of universality with democracy is entirely logical. But, if we focus on honor apart from representation, the problem shifts. Does democracy require universal honor? Are the issues raised by a universal honor political in nature? For Fraser, to universalize honor or praise is not only unneccessary to democracy but is in itself meaningless (if we're all special, none of us is). And yet, in his invocations of the poetic praise of an ordered cosmos, Whitman *does* raise hopes of a universal praise. In taking up these questions in the next and final sections, I find that the universality at issue in Whitman's ornament goes beyond that of democratic universality, into a broader concern about what it could mean to laud the world, or to approve of reality. Here, the fluid, laid-upon qualities of Whitman's gorgeous decorations elaborate an ethically complex abandonment of the desire to govern the world on standards that would seem to us to merit approval.

WHITMAN'S DECORUM

In *Democratic Vistas*, Whitman lays out the importance of decorum and manners to democracy, particularly as a countermeasure to what he deems "the appalling dangers of universal suffrage in the United States" (*DV*, 363). "I say democracy is only of use there that it may pass on and come to its flower and fruits in manners, in the highest forms of interaction between men, and their beliefs" (*DV*, 389). Such ornamental behavior is posed as a counterpoint to representative democracy, which cannot "be vivified and held together merely by political means, superficial suffrage, legislation, &c" (*DV*, 368). Examples of democratic manners include a woman who "holds her own with unvarying coolness and decorum, and will compare, any day, with superior carpenters, farmers, and even boatmen and drivers" (*DV*, 400) and the "decorum" of wounded soldiers in Civil War hospitals (*DV*, 378). This might be bracketed as a symptom of Whitman's late pessimism about the United States, given that in *Democratic Vistas* he finds "the People" to be "ungrammatical, untidy, and their sins gaunt and ill-bred" (*DV*, 376) and laments, "In vain have we annex'd Texas, California, Alaska, and reach north for Canada and south for Cuba" (*DV*, 370). But the call in *Democratic Vistas* for beautiful "manners" (*DV*, 372) is very much in line with the earlier poetry's investment in the laying-on of ornamentation. And in the 1855 "Preface," Whitman was already focused on the deportment of the American "common people":

> Their manners speech dress friendships—the freshness and candor of their physiognomy—the picturesque looseness of their carriage . . . their deathless attachment to freedom—their aversion to anything indecorous or soft or mean— . . . their susceptibility to a slight—the air they have of persons who never knew how it felt to stand in the presence of superiors—the fluency of their speech— . . . . are unrhymed poetry. It awaits the gigantic and generous treatment worthy of it. ("P," 710)

So even in this early text, Whitman was already interested in a democracy of "manners" and the "[ ]decorous." For all its informality and its lack of apparent respect for the concept of "superiors," this "unrhymed poetry" is about carrying a "flu[id]" and "elegan[t]" "air" that signals innate superiority.

One of the most enduring frames for thinking about Whitman's poetry is that it takes upon itself the work of applying principles of universal equality. It takes seriously, that is to say, the ideals of the Declaration of Independence and seeks to write a poetry that fully embodies them. This can, as I considered in the previous section, be thought of as an ambition to write a poetry of universal representation, analogous to the universal suffrage. But it can also be thought of as a question of representation in a more philosophical sense: how can human life express a principle? Whitman's ongoing interest in decorous behavior might well fit with a view of Whitman carrying out democracy on beautifully equable lines, so that persons live and comport themselves in manners that portend their absolute equality to one another. But Whitman's commitment to manners and decorum actually supplants this metaphysics of representation, in which living democracy would carry out the ideal of equality.[60] His commitment to the decorous, and to appropriate behaving, make it hard to think of his poetry as a question of how an ideal can be brought fully into the life of experience. It suggests a quite contrary sense of a practice negotiated as a matter of in-process, proposed behavior.[61]

In "These I Singing in Spring," a poem from the "Calamus" section, the poet declares himself free to travel at will, even at random, from moment to moment:

> Now along the pond-side, now wading in a little, fearing not the wet,
> Now by the post-and-rail fences where the old stones thrown there, pick'd from the fields, have accumulated.[62]

Whitman moves in a place of detritus, where stones removed from cultivated fields have been randomly "thrown." This is a place of non-cultivation (not a field), but still shaped by human action (since it's filled with thrown-away stones). As he moves, he is "[c]ollecting" ("T," 4) tokens from nature "for lovers" ("T," 1). These tokens are thrown aside (like the stones) to a "troop" that "gathers around" ("T," 10).

> Collecting, dispensing, singing, there I wander with them,
> Plucking something for tokens, tossing toward whoever is near me,
> Here, lilac, with a branch of pine,
> Here, out of my pocket, some moss which I pull'd off a live-oak in Florida as it hung trailing down,
> Here, some pinks and laurel leaves, and a handful of sage.
> ("T," 13–17)

Each piece of this bevy of ornamental branches and flowers is gathered in some fashion, be it the "lilac, with" pine or the pink flowers bunched with "leaves" and "sage." The tokens are also all gathered in Whitman's syntax, and by the iterated word "[h]ere," which tells us repeatedly, in the same place (the start of the line: "Here") but also in the next line, hence in the *next* place, that these objects are offered. The way that the lines create an ongoing "[h]ere" out of different things and lines inflects how the poem seeks to bind together Whitman and his speaker, the reader with the "great crowd" around the speaker ("T," 12), and each or all of them to one another. For while Whitman's dispensing and sharing circles in on ornamental exchanges as a means to draw persons into cliques and clusters, the distribution of preferential and ornamental tokens is not an ideal or equal parceling out. In this poem, the bestowing of ornamental tokens is doubly restricted: first to his "troop" of lovers, then to those to whom he offers his "calamus-root" as the "token of comrades" ("T," 20): "only to them that love as I myself am capable of loving" ("T," 28). And yet these groups are thrown together, and their bonds merely proposed, rather than argued or fully inhabited. Like the space that is neither an open nor a tilled field through which Whitman moves, the parcels his tokens indicate are moved toward or tried on, so that the world is neither left as is nor fully settled into any one frame of reference.

The poem's sequential ordering of multiple "[h]ere[s]" indicates that it has a token blossom to offer to anyone, and in one of its final lines it suggests, for at least the second time, that its concern is with an open throwing-off of tokens that could go to any and all:

> And twigs of maple and a bunch of wild orange and chestnut,
> And stems of currants and plumb-blows, and the aromatic cedar,
> These I compass'd around by a thick cloud of spirits,
> Wandering, point to or touch as I pass, or throw them loosely from me,
> Indicating to each one what he shall have, giving something to each. ("T," 22–26)

Yet just around this elaboration of equal dispensation, "giving something to each," Whitman asserts the counter-principle that such tokens are used to make bonds that reduce the sphere of attention, first to the class of all lovers, and then to the class of "comrade"-lovers who receive the calamus. Although Whitman's openness in this poem may evoke a fair and equal distribution, at times it also sounds like a random throwing-away, as with the stones tossed out of the field. (Similarly, in "As I Ebb'd with the Ocean of Life," Whitman's "me and mine" are like "[a] limp blossom or two, torn, just as much over waves floating, drifted at random.")[63] And while Whitman speaks in terms that resemble those by which he might call to a special beloved, he specifically invokes a class of lovers which, in part by the vagueness of its naming, feels incompletely portioned-off from the class of all persons. Such unresolved conjuring of indifference and bonded particularity evinces Whitman's dedication to conferring ornamental notice in a fluctuating fashion.

If glory can be unevenly thrown off, it is also notoriously ladled upon Whitman himself. In "Song of Myself," by writing, "I know I shall not pass like a child's carlacue cut with a burnt stick at night" ("S," 408), Whitman bids for his right to outshine others and to burn brightly enough to win acclaim after his death. And in "These I Singing in Spring," he stands apart as the one making and rearranging collations of persons and ornamental tokens: "These I compass'd around," "point to or touch," "[i]ndicating ... giving." The adorning Whitman wields the capacious authority to bequeath tokens of esteem, which also form social bonds, and this means that in an additional respect, while in this poem ornamental tokens of esteem are strewn widely, the unevenness of such strewing and its relation to personal whim make the effect far from one of universal or equable apportionment.

The issue this raises is distinct from the more familiar concern with Whitman's democratic poetics, in which universal representation struggles to be adequate to the claims of particularity. Instead, the issue begins with a question regarding the aspiration to universal *praise* and esteem, rather than to universal *representation*: how can he adequately praise everyone and everything? The question comes up because his bestowals of esteem by forms of poetic notice, including the tossing of "twigs of maple and a bunch of wild orange and chestnut," seem neither incomplete nor inadequate but thrown off balance. But rather than think of the issue as a problem in Whitman—wondering why he can't better practice universal equality—we can take it as evidence that the application of equal praise is not what is at stake. The skewed and tossed disequilibrium in Whitman's ornamental notice evinces a lack of commitment to more perfectly embodying the ideal of human equality by means of distributing *either* representation or honor more evenly.

Considering Bonnie Honig's work on Sophocles' *Antigone* helps explain this side of Whitman. The character of Antigone has, Honig explains, long been read as a quintessential figure of democratic protest. Honig reads Antigone's clamorous and out of proportion lamentation of her brother in relation to a political and social conflict between democratic Athens and the aristocratic culture that it had unseated. Democratic Athens, she points out, had passed laws forbidding extended, showy burial practices in order to emphasize "a democratic economy of substitution" in which all persons mattered equally as citizens of the polis.[64] In contrast, aristocratic burial practices focused on the extraordinary, irreplaceable value of particular persons, evincing the values of "Homeric honor" and a "heroic ethics and politics of individuality and distinction."[65] Here, democracy's universal equality is opposed not simply to particularity, but to "honor" and "distinction." While Antigone's cries are indebted to the aristocrat's rejection of both the burial practices of the polis and its principle of equality, Honig argues that Antigone leverages an aristocratic ethos *within* a democratic sphere, thereby creating a fruitfully contentious resistance to democratic indifference to the person. While at some moments Honig seems concerned by the question that concerned Grossman and Dimock (how does democratic universality make room for the claim of particularity?), at others she asks a different question: How can universal human equality accommodate the claims of the extraordinary? Her answer to the latter question isn't in more perfectly realizing the ideal of universal equality, but in creating a clamorous political contentiousness.

In *Dis-agreement*, Jacques Rancière argues that in the story of classical political theory, democratic politics happens when people begin to consider "distributing *common* lots and evening out communal shares and entitlements to these shares."[66] This democratic appeal to "the common good, whose telos is contained in human nature" institutes "an ideal geometry," in which "shares and entitlements to these shares" are distributed across a community whose identity remains unquestioned. This "democracy" is at its base a project of arranging and ordering and thus is not truly political: he calls it "policing."[67] In contrast, the concept of the radical equality of persons means, to Rancière, treating persons as something other than individuals or groups with claims for the allotment of various goods and benefits. Political subjectivity, he argues, depends on a split between a person and his or her particular share, identity, or class role, because political subjectivity by its nature must link a part to the universal. This is the primary meaning of the *demos*: a part that claims a right to partake of the government of the polis but that has no particular share, claim, or identity for which to plead. It is, as "the people," a part that claims to speak for all. This produces a schismatic universalism anathema to modern liberal democracy's managerial ethos in which politics is seen as the allotment of shares to separate individual concerns. In this light, the entire approach to Whitman of wondering how he might fail to distribute either representation or ornamentation equally would be misguided, for the equal distribution concept is a misunderstanding of democracy's basic sense of a miscount, in which a part claims the voice of the whole people. In that miscount, Rancière isolates "the constitutive wrong or torsion of politics as such."[68]

Rancière's discussion of politics maintains the importance of rendering the visibility of the difference between equality as a principle of valuation and the way a community distributes goods and privileges.

> What is usually lumped together under the name of political history or political science in fact stems more often than not from other mechanisms concerned with holding on to the exercise of majesty, the curacy of divinity, the command of armies, and the management of interests. Politics only occurs when these mechanisms are stopped in their tracks by the effect of a presupposition that is totally foreign to them yet without which none of them could ultimately function: the presupposition of the equality of anyone and everyone, or the paradoxical effectiveness of the sheer contingency of any order.[69]

Politics in common usage means some process based on the belief that a social order can be justly founded in a guiding principle. In contrast, Rancière argues, there is no such foundation for the partitioning out of the goods in any society: true democracy is the eruption of a sense of wrong about the non-naturalness and the radical contingency at the root of all organizations of human communities—a force that cannot be philosophized, and which goes beyond historical logics or class interests. It is for this reason that his is a kind of anti-political theory: the political is not susceptible to theorization in the sense that it cannot be grounded in any principle or value outside human contentions, even if it must exist in relation to the overriding principle of equality. Much American thinking expects that equality can, properly processed, legitimate an appropriate distribution of economic goods and status recognition. This principle underlies the enormous faith of not only American culture but of its literary criticism in the power of universal representation.[70] But if Rancière is right, a democratic society must aim more at disruptions than at perfecting allotment among persons.

The Whitman who imposes on us, abrogating to himself the power to declare what is assumed and what is of value, tossing a limp blossom here or there, does not encourage us to imagine that democracy should aspire to the perfect embodiment of the ideal of equality.[71] Nor does he imply that there *is* a mode of apportioning honor that would ever be amenable to the demand of equality. However, in his recent book *Aisthesis*, Rancière himself reads *Leaves of Grass* as a straightforward application of the principle of equality, as if the poetry begins with a theory that can then simply be practiced: "The title" of *Leaves of Grass* "not only affirms the poetic thesis that governs it: all things are equal because the most infinitesimal contains the universe. . . . It incarnates this egalitarian procession in its very layout."[72] Rancière sees Whitman's poetry as a means of rejecting the ordering of the world in terms of economic exchange value or sheer utility; much like Grossman, he also sees Whitman abandoning an old poetic logic in which being seen and celebrated in poetry was an elite privilege. He writes that Whitman's work exemplifies a nascent modernist view that "there is a mode of presenting common things that subtracts them both from the logic of the economic and social order and the artificiality of poetic exception."[73] Thus Rancière's Whitman is the poet of achieved egalitarian distribution, in which—contrary to the elitism of traditional poetry and the demands of a market culture—each being is seen in full equality.[74] For him, Whitman's cosmos is "a microcosm of the community," engaged in a "universal intellectual capacity" to see the "sensible world" as the "exterior form of a divine thought."[75]

This isn't a perverse way to read Whitman, but I do think it is mistaken. It is true that at one point in "Song of Myself" Whitman claims as his goal the possibility of a society entirely ordered on the principle of equality: "I will accept nothing which all cannot have their counterpart of on the same terms" ("S," 507). But even in that moment the point is avowed as a personal fiat or eccentric demand: "I will have" is not the same as "it will be so in general," or in the world, or for all of us. So even in one of its prouder articulations, the idea of a human world fully ordered on universal equality is pressed off course. Behind Whitman's presence there is a looming sense that life is not about living out the principle of equality but about contingent behavior.

In this regard, the torn and thrown-off blossoms in Whitman indicate a disequilibrium more fundamental than the political one to which Honig and Rancière direct us. Whitman's thrown tokens of esteem bring a sense of discord into his work, one that can seem profoundly lacking in a poet who confidently announces, "I celebrate myself, and sing myself / And what I assume you shall assume, / For every atom belonging to me as good belongs to you" ("S," 1–3). But the very sense of overstepping in such a claim—its unjustified and off-kilter prerogative—*is* what fosters the sense of discord. This is the discord of uneasy disequilibrium, rather than of disagreement or differences susceptible to discussion. Concerning potential discrepancies and disagreements about exactly *who* or *what* will be taken as extraordinary, lauded with a blossom or a candid look, it is not discord in terms of rational argument, nor even about personal preference. It is discord about who and what is to be selected for acclaim, and in which fluid acclaim feels profoundly imbalanced and unpredictably showered.

Even with its lyrical, encompassing tone, "When Lilacs Last in the Dooryard Bloom'd" is a poetry of broken-off adornments curiously apportioned. The poem is set in motion by breaking off a piece of the blooming lilac, with an awkwardly phrased line that stresses the beginning of Whitman's poetic work in a selective breaking-off by the poet, which produces the ornamental blossom: "A sprig with its flower

I break."⁷⁶ The poem's mourning works, on one level, to identify the mourning of the extraordinary Lincoln with the mourning of all the Civil War dead. As it travels the country and the fame of Lincoln is spread "through lanes and streets" ("W," 33), the coffin becomes an honorific object spread throughout the world. Indeed Whitman emphasizes how his tribute to Lincon is also a tribute to all:

> (Nor for you, for one alone;
> Blossoms and branches green to coffins all I bring,
> ....
> All over bouquets of roses,
> O death, I cover you over with roses and early lilies.
> ("W," 46–47, 49–50)

But this universal blanket of ornament, with blossoms, branches, and flowers "[a]ll over" gives way to Whitman's insistence on the partiality and breaking of ornament:

> O death, I cover you over with roses and early lilies,
> But mostly and now the lilac that blooms the first,
> Copious I break, I break the sprigs from the bushes,
> With loaded arms I come, pouring for you,
> For you and the coffins all of you O death. ("W," 50–54)

Whitman emphasizes the mass quality of ornamentation that is "loaded" down and placed "[a]ll over," but such generality is countered by how he breaks specific "sprigs" of his preferred, "first"-blooming lilac. Even in the last line of this section, the motley sense of "you" and "the coffins of all of you" confounds the specific and general senses of the word "you." Whitman brings up both "you" and your "coffins" and then without punctuation turns to address "death" as if it were part of or included in the complexity of multiple "you[s]", coffins, and flowers. The resulting image of ornamental mourning presents the difficulty and unevenness with which one and all receive Whitman's ministering sprigs. By the poem's end, even as Whitman overall suggests that his memory of Lincoln will serve also as a memorial to others, the impression of "[c]omrades mine and I in the midst" ("W," 203) is of yet another oddly clustered bunch, as indeed the ornamental emblem of "[l]ilac and star and bird twined with the chant of my soul, / There in the fragrant pines and the cedars dusk and dim" ("W," 205–206) ends on the note of the artfully selected and placed bouquet. The prettiness of the image of the "twined" objects and the sense of pleasure in the conceit of their placement "[t]here in the fragrant pines and the cedars" emphasizes a sense of the poetic notice ornament contains, even in the form of elegy, as an intensely effected gesture of selection, which does not wrap Lincoln's exemplariness fully back into the ordinary, equal being of all other dead.

What tends to disturb people about Whitman is the powerful license of his "I" in the face of his claims of radical equality: Kateb writes, "a democratic individual, if he or she is to be true to the spirit of democracy, should not (on one hand) aspire to become a shaped presence, like a work of art, resplendent in its integrity and unmistakable in its attainment, or (on the other hand) try to disclose one's true 'genius.'"[77] But the eruption of a grand and candid "I" in Whitman, and his ongoing gestures of breaking and throwing off tokens of esteem, as in "These I Singing in Spring" or "When Lilacs Last in the Dooryard Bloom'd," makes us see that his bestowals are imposed and laid down, and that they are not expressions of any necessary principle underlying phenomenal reality. Whitman's brilliance is nothing if not uncomfortable, and much of the interest of Whitman's ornamentation is that it explicitly produces a felt sense of the uneasy quality of praise in general. Rather than seeking a perfect incarnation of equality and failing to deliver, the poet produces a sense of the ill-fitting and egregious, and at other times charmingly selected if unjustifiable, qualities of the adornments and brilliancy which together make his work so beautiful.

Whitman shifts the terms of the fame- and praise-bestowing qualities of poetry as adornment not in asking us to see everyone and everything as genuinely meritorious, but in rendering the category of the praiseworthy so startling. Consider the intentional ugliness of a number of the objects he calls out, from "[t]he scent of these arm-pits" ("S," 525) to "the alligator in his tough pimples" ("S," 724). There is an unpleasantness or strangeness in praising such things; I think in celebrating Whitman's democracy it's tempting to think that everything in his world is truly laudable and accepted. But this utopian sense of a world where we feel affection and pleasure at everything is different from Whitman's world, where we might praise even what we don't feel admiration or affection for. Consider how confusing the inclusion in "Song of Myself" of "the overseer" watching slaves work "from his saddle" is if you think that Whitman actually means us to understand that everything he "celebrate[s]" is good, beautiful, or likable ("S," 286, 1). So, too, the "mash'd fireman with breast-bone broken" ("S," 847). Rancière emphasizes precisely this point, observing that "no one had ever seen such an extravagant succession of prosaic activities and tools, this gallery of insignificant, vulgar or horrible genre scenes, offered up as a poetic work."[78] For him, the stress is on Whitman's ability to redeem and thus override the "horrible" quality of what is seen, as it is for Bennett in her discussion of Whitman's "solar judgment" as a nonjudging illumination of the world. His light is, she argues, evidence of "a mind that is open and quiet enough—that has slackened its reflex to categorize and rank" and is thus able to "accept all with equanimity."[79] She continues by granting that "[t]his magnanimity is dangerous—the sun falls on deadly viruses, on torture equipment, and not only on flowers, works of art, and the strong and lovely bodies of workers. But Whitman still seems to think that it is worth the risk, perhaps in part because such solar moments are necessarily fragile and fleeting."[80] In contrast, my suggestion here is that Whitman does not illuminate the world with a purified, nonpreferential, and recessive form of attention. If ornamentation, in some phases of my argument, featured as a potential version of such open, nonpossessive interest, the significance of Whitman is his insistence upon the *impressed* and inflected quality of ornamental attending. And the disarticulation of praise from justice, in Whitman, leads to something less perfectly open and balanced than both Rancière and Bennett find in him.

The praise in "Song of Myself" never feels truly right in the sense that an applied ideal of universal equality would. Nor is the poem so clearly about a democratic love in which what has been cast aside—from homosexuality to prostitution to slavery—is redeemed by Whitman's liberal heart. My point in linking those three is that for Whitman democracy cannot be about appreciative openness to everything, for he understands that everything includes what is not loved and acceptable. That some things (homosexuality) might be able to shift from one category to another is certainly a hope Whitman has; but the hope that democracy would mean the opening of arms wide enough to finally both like and love everything, including slavery, is one his ornamental poetic practices abjure. The ugliness in aspects of "Song of Myself," at least—even its grotesque form—render it intentionally resistant to the perfection of democratic representation and, more relevant to his own project, intentionally resistant to the comfortable sense of praise for the universe in either the archaic or Christian precedents of poetry that praises the world, the cosmos, as just and right.

Moreover, Whitman's free verse is less so in the sense of being open and capaciously liberated, and more in the sense of being somewhat random, applied, and even forced. There's no principle to govern why the canal-boy, the book-keeper, and the shoemaker must crowd into a single line—"The canal boy trots on the tow-path, the book-keeper counts at his desk, the shoe-maker waxes his thread"—while, a few lines down, a drover can stretch out with a whole line to himself ("The drover watching his drove sings out to them who would stray") ("S," 297–301). Nor is there a principle for the length of any of Whitman's numbered sections, which do not match one another. And yet Whitman keeps introducing what look like rules for his lines, as with the following passage's repeated "In vain[s]":

> In vain the speeding or shyness,
> In vain the plutonic rocks send their old heat against my approach,
> In vain the mastodon retreats beneath its own powder'd bones,
> In vain objects stand leagues off and assume manifold shapes,
> In vain the ocean settling in hollows and the great monsters lying low,
> In vain the buzzard houses herself with the sky,
> In vain the snake slides through the creepers and logs,
> In vain the elk takes to the inner passes of the woods,
> In vain the razor-bill'd auk sails far north to Labrador,
> I follow quickly, I ascend to the nest in the fissure of the cliff.
>
> ("S," 674–83)

The indefatigable force of Whitman's attention, which is surely at stake in this boasting and threatening of how fruitless all efforts to elude him will be, could be as adequately expressed by seven or twelve "In vain" lines as it is by the nine that are here. There's no necessary limit that makes Whitman stop at nine rather than twelve, and no principle, even of space to fill, that compels him to go as far as nine. The unnecessary, even artificial accretion of iterated phrasings, catalogues, and segmentations runs throughout "Song of Myself," a poem of willed exaggerations and roaming deviations.

When Whitman delightedly rejects meter, rhyme, and fancy images, he implies that poetry is a matter of one's relationship to a set of formal rules, which might simply be abandoned. In contrast, the egregiousness of Whitman's sudden calling-outs of himself by name (*"Walt you contain enough, why don't you let it out then?"* ["S," 568]), along with the violations of order in his extended catalogues (which flout not only poetic forms but norms of sentence formation), calls up a sense that poetry is instead a varying relationship to assembled situations. Poetic form is, like manners, a question all about what can be pulled off, or made to stick, rather than a rule one might follow or break. The life in this work is its ongoing curiosity about how a sense of the appropriate can be summoned up, resisted, varied, or extended without ever coming up against any actual rule.

Puttenham's sensitivity to whether and how a word or deed could be appropriately used is so delicate that, Jonathan Goldberg concludes, if Puttenham's text is always asking, "how is one to parse the proportions that govern the unspeakable and the admissible?" its only real answer is "that there is no determinate answer to such a question."[81] There is no rule by which a body or act can or cannot be granted or allowed; its decorousness or indecorousness is a matter of finesse, timing, and even chance. A comparably in-process negotiation of manners, this time in the face of a lack of relation between the principle of equality and social being, animates Whitman's poetry. It pursues a lived transformation in the sense of what is appropriate or proper. Far from being a term for the prissy or the polite, the *appropriate* is a term for that terrain in which the vision of incarnating an ideal has been abandoned. In this respect, Whitman's poetry reveals arrangement in its basic contingency and hence its basic force, by which I mean simply its having-been-effected. At issue here is the difference between formalism that sees form as something that is performed in the sense of having been caused or brought forth into being (like the arch of bent-over trees in Thoreau), and formalism that considers form to be a justified or necessary abstraction. The imposing quality of Whitman's bestowing, laying-upon presence is itself part of this poetry of effected form. This is a poetry about the effects of behavior, exertion, and placement—not a poetry of enforcing, then, but about force in the sense of intentions to impress, test, and affect.

In Heidegger, theories of knowing in which a subject represents a world to himself through concepts, and is basically outside of and not conditioned by the world, contain a foundational violence. This is the violence of, first, the transformation of the world into conceptual form, and also of the person's reduction to the abstraction of the thinking subject. Of course, this charge—that the subject's use of representation is basically violent—has a wide influence in the humanities.[82] In Whitman criticism, it emerges as a way of thinking about the ways his poetry declines to communicate or to represent clearly. Larson observes that "Song of Myself" contains the "radical idea that the poem is essentially indifferent to meaning, especially as a token held out to us to 'possess' or 'get at.'"[83] He attributes this to the belief that for the American writer to define meaning is to violate democratic openness: as a corollary, to refuse to define meaning is to refuse to be any higher than, or any more powerful than, one's readers. For Larson, the important point is the basic illogic of this idea that there *is* a violence or domination in the use of representation to convey meaning, or of one mind to specify meaning. Ornamental aesthetics has, as I have shown, a value in its sensitivity and responsiveness to the world, but it isn't inherently an ethically restrained alternative to whatever violence may, rightly or wrongly, be attributed to representation.[84] For it also contains other forms of violence, following from its impressed, impacted, and affected qualities. In Whitman (as in Thoreau and Dickinson), ornamental attending does not abjure all control or forcefulness. This is partly the point of his sense of ornamentation as a form of behavior, decorum, and manners: it is something done (twined, brought, given), whether gently or magnanimously.

Such doing is to be distinguished from the more current sense of performative action. Performativity contains a basic sense of liberty, in the subject's ability to shift and reconstruct reality due to its lack of natural foundation or ground. To the contrary, ornamental aesthetics, by its very dependent, related quality, doesn't have the same implication of separation from the given that performativity does.[85] Instead, its focus in Whitman, but also more broadly as a theory of ornamental behavior, is as an understanding of reality as neither materially given *nor* constructively created, but as fundamentally influenced. In my earlier discussion of Dickinson, I argued that ornamentation is in Dickinson and Heidegger a name for phenomenal form in light of the Open. Unlike readings of phenomenology that locate an essential home in things, I suggested an ornamental quality of transient, uncertain appearing of things in and as the world. Whitman has a comparable sense of phenomenal appearing, in which lived experience is neither an expression of ideals nor of performed liberty, but a field of impressed, contingent responses—some of them to Whitman's own bearing-down on the world. His ornament is attuned to the appearance of the world as an array of affected and caused phenomena, rather than the reflection of essential truth or an underlying logic. This is the source of the erotic quality of his sense of Being, and of the element of submission to the world in his work.

It is here that Whitman's poet as an ornament to the cosmos ceases to suggest a gracing of the appropriate order of the world and instead suggests what Heidegger called the "thrownness" of the world. This is the emergence of human experience in conditions already happening, and in an engagement with the world that precedes a subject's intentional response to it. Steiner calls it a matter of the "primordial banality" that conditions come before human knowing.[86] It appears in, for instance, Heidegger's sense that knowing always occurs through and in a mood, for "[a] state-of-mind not only discloses Dasein in its thrownness and its submission to that world which is already disclosed with its own Being."[87] If phenomenology locates the human being within the world, this is not so much to find one ensconced there, but "*delivered over*" to a world, constituted in response to relations that precede one and constitute the temporal, uncertain conditions of life.[88] Out of his own sense of reality's ongoing pressure upon the person, Whitman's praise of the cosmos by his poetic adornment shines on a world that is not rightly made and yet is here: influenced (in part by his own presence), underway, past argument.

The desire to reshape the world is a major source of critical consciousness; in Edward Said's words, "And what is critical consciousness at bottom if not an unstoppable predilection for alternatives?"[89] That comment expresses a sense of freedom more deliberately asserted in Alexandre Kojève's reading of Hegel:

> Freedom can *be* and *exist* only as *negation*. Now in order to negate, there must be something to negate: an existing given and hence an identical given-Being. And that is why man can exist freely—that is, humanly—only while living as an animal in a given natural World. But he lives *humanly* only to the extent that he *negates* this natural or animal given.[90]

If Kojève speaks here of the negation of animal reality, more broadly his reading of Hegel asserts a freedom found in the negation of whatever is present, given in experience, toward an idea of something absent. However beneficial a critical consciousness bound up in the negation of the present reality is, it does depend on a rejection of present experience.

I share with that critical tradition a sense that the obvious, apparent necessity of things as they appear to be given is to be questioned, not embraced as in recent critical work trained on the surfaces of literature engaged as a mass of facts. I have also argued, earlier, against the critical hope that repressing or exploding the human presence in the world would be the answer to the destructive qualities of human beings. What I want to propose now is that underlying a broad range of philosophical and political questions about the desirability and the politics of the subject's ability either to reject and transcend immediate conditions, or else to dissolve and disperse itself into conditions so as to cease controlling them, is an ongoing belief that there is a mismatch between the mind and the world. Since the human mind is a part of the world, such questions appear to pertain more to whether one *wants* the world, perhaps even *likes* or *approves* of it. These are the questions that ornamental aesthetics opens up, precisely because it works out of a tradition in which ornament announces approval of the world—the world seen as appropriate and worthy of praise.

Such questions do not pertain to justice or equality in the relations between persons. They fall outside the domain of the political, in that sense, and they may not even be philosophical in nature; they are perhaps religious, although to say this is to realize the need for a way of thinking of the intellectual interest of religious questions. At any rate, the question of whether the mind ought to be violent or kind, dominant or open, is either an easy or a foolhardy question. Setting it aside, what is one to do with a mind that thinks it has the ability to assess the laudability of reality? What is at issue in considering if the world is appropriately set forth? Perhaps to approve or disapprove of reality is to concede that it is not of our own creation. If in "Cædmon's Hymn" poetic praise marked the beauty of God's creation, that already marks praise of the world as a recognition of its status as something other than a human creation. For Thoreau, Dickinson, and Whitman, praise accompanies a world we may affect, but do not direct and perhaps do not even understand. The sense of beauty and even honor are, in this context, forms of concession to a reality that is beyond one's choice. Such an aesthetic judgment, far from being a moral or rational judgment of the world, and far from being an attempt control and objectify it, is a concession to the inapplicability or irrelevance of views of how the world ought to be. In this sense, praising the world is a way to come into relationship with it, rather than seek to negate it or search for an alternative to it.

IN CONCLUSION: SHEEN AND MOSS

"And now in four weeks more – you are mine, *all* mine," Dickinson wrote to Sue Gilbert in May 1852.[91] One month earlier, she sent her these words:

> I gathered something for you, because you were not there, an acorn, and some moss blossoms, and a little shell of a snail, so

whitened by the snow you would think 'twas a cunning artist had carved it from alabaster – then I tied them all up in a leaf with some last summer's grass I found by a brookside, and I'm keeping them all for you.[92]

Charmingly, the snail shell seems made by "a cunning artist" but is only carved by nature and "whitened by the snow." But in this sweet, seductive ornamentation, actions of binding and holding are at stake. Dickinson would keep that moss and shell "tied ... all up," as if this ornament were a charm to tie and keep Sue herself.

This identification of ornament with binding can be seen in Ovid's tale of Apollo and Daphne, in which, as Barbara Johnson has argued, Daphne escapes sexual violence by turning into a tree, only to have Apollo take her branches as the ornaments of poetry. It is not even quite true to say that Daphne's transformation into a tree saves her from violence, for the assault continues as Apollo "pressed his lips to the wood; but the wood still shrank from his kisses."[93] And the transformed Daphne still hears this:

> [Y]ou must at least be Apollo's tree. It is you who will always be
>   twined in my hair, on my tuneful lyre and my quiver of arrows.
> The generals of Rome shall be wreathed with you, when the
>   jubilant paean
> of triumph is raised and the long procession ascends the Capitol.[94]

An attempt at sexual violence is transformed into the cutting and bestowing of the laurel tree's branches, which become Apollo's ornaments and, by extension, those of poetry itself.[95] Apollo, unable to possess Daphne in person, dictates fresh terms: "you must at least be Apollo's tree." Daphne, according to Ovid, takes this sentence as if it were an offer: "With a wave of her new-formed branches, / the laurel agreed, and seemed to be nodding her head in the treetop."[96] Yet there is an unsettling motion in that last line—what "seem[s]" to be happening? The tree looks like a head, nodding assent, but what choice did Daphne have? "[Y]ou must ... be Apollo's tree." The violent possession in these laurels, like the bound up snail shell with moss, indicates an ornamental poetry of taking possession, in which the fluttering of the leaf is just the agitated motion of being forced.⁹⁷

"When Winds take Forests in their Paws – The Universe – is still – " (477 A): Dickinson's treetops, like Daphne's, toss in the air even while bound by force. The universe's stillness is a waiting and watching what may happen under the pressure of wind—will the tree break or simply wave? And some of that stillness may be shock at the mere "hold[ing]" (477 B) and taking of the forest, or at how the tree, like any being, is under the impress of forces outside itself. It's as if ornamentation to the world is suddenly reversed: the "Universe," in a fearsome repose, attends to the way the wind tosses and threatens to destroy the branches of trees.

Grossman's dedication to the poetics of representation was centered in his belief that it made it possible for persons to see one another, and hence to value one another, so as to protect against human violence. Comparably, Stewart writes that "poetry is a force against effacement," and that its work "is to make visible, tangible, and audible the figures of persons."⁹⁸ This "cultural, or form-giving work of poetry is to counter the oblivion of darkness," in which one cannot maintain "the outline, the figure, of the person" and lives instead in a terror "that the darkness will not end."⁹⁹ But, in his book *Being Numerous*, Oren Izenberg argues that modern and postmodern poets, in response to the failures of poetry to protect persons against mass atrocity, reconceived of poetry in order to make it a more durable index of human commonality. Izenberg distrusts representative poetics for an original reason: its reliance on the human valuation of specific objects is not strong enough to preserve the world. In its place, he discusses a poetics grounded in universal laws.

A key example of this is Paul Celan's image of an *"Atemkristal,"* or "breathcrystal." This is "[a] crystallization of vapor into ice" which

> may in a sense be *expressed*, or precipitated out of the human breath; but it does not *express* anything internal to the person. . . . Expressing nothing, it stands as the "expression" of the general laws that structure the world in which particular crystals reside.¹⁰⁰

For Celan to class a poem with an *Atemkristall* is to make, Izenberg writes, "a kind of argument that there exist forces of attraction that draw all things together and that are (under ideal circumstances) irresistible and perfecting."[101] The poetry that makes such an argument is not concerned with representing a subject's thought or experience. Nor is it a thing for someone to interpret or really read, let alone enjoy. Instead, it is a "rational" poetry that testifies to "a priori" laws.[102] Such poetry might be said to abandon much of what would draw readers to poetry in order to shore up its ability to maintain human community.

That is, however unlike Grossman's poetics Izenberg's is, it absolutely shares the view that poetry is central to securing human communities from violence through a commitment to shared value. He writes that Frank O'Hara offers "a reconceptualization of poetic history, less as a sequence of valuable objects, and more as a *medium* in which we can privilege our disposition to value altogether."[103] Here valuing can be separated from a commitment to one set of "valuable objects" but not from the principle or even law of value as about picking some objects over others. (Although if we are "privileg[ing] our disposition to value," we are still valuing a specific object, this time valuing itself.) Izenberg continues by arguing that O'Hara's work seeks "to elevate valuing as such in order to demonstrate that *that* is an activity that is not bound by particular histories or restricted to particular communities."[104] The law of human universality that such poetry reveals is that we may value different things for different reasons, but we all value things.

In light of the violence with which Apollo values Daphne, and with which Dickinson values Sue, one can question the belief that valuing persons or objects is, in itself, a nonviolent activity. At the least, what passes for value might be rather different in its true nature. That said, Johnson herself reminds us that the articulation of force, as distinct from violence, may be ethically fruitful: "Respect and distance are certainly better than violence and appropriation," she asks, but "is ethics only a matter of restraint?"[105] Discussing the work of D. W. Winnicott, she notes that there is "a danger arising not just from infantile destructiveness but from the infantile *terror* of destructiveness—its exaggerated and paralyzing repression. Winnicott describes the process of learning to overcome *that* terror, which allows one to trust to play, and to experience the reality of both the other *and* the self."[106] And if we could see no effects arising from our behavior, far from having attained a virtuous state of noninterference, we would be unable to understand how our being relates to that of anyone, or anything, else. Could Apollo take seriously Daphne's recoil, it would reveal to him the difference between his experience and hers.

But there is a different discomfort with the concept of valuing, other than its possibly coercive relationship to its objects or the differences between the objects that persons value. Is valuing, at its heart, a relationship to objects? Or is the ability to value, love, and even honor diminished or at least put to secondary use when it is attached to an object? Dickinson, for one, questions the necessity of attaching value to objects. One poem at first seems to insist that *sheen*—a word meaning value, love, and beauty—must be attached to a particular object:

> The pattern of the sun
> Can fit but him alone
> For sheen must have a Disk
> To be a sun – (1580)

The poem has the tone of an edict, as if in the business of poetry as law-evincing object. But then, the declarative form betrays the non-necessity of the very thing it would make law: if it is not law until it is pronounced, it is neither an a priori nor a natural law. There is further question about this truth that "sheen must have a Disk," for the claim that the two cannot be parted is made by a phrasing that digs up a capacity to part them, which one would have been unlikely to imagine otherwise (it asks, in essence, does this light need some disk?). And there is the qualification of the last line: it's not that sheen must always have a disk, to be sheen at all. It is only "[t]o be a sun" that sheen must take an object. Before the world composed of sun, even sky and grass and tree, there is a sheen that has nothing.

We think of sheen now most often as "[s]hining, brightness," or "radiance as of a body reflecting light," but the *Oxford English Dictionary* notes that as an adjective it can mean "beautiful."[107] This adjectival form of sheen (and of course Dickinson frequently uses adjectives as nouns, and vice versa) references the beauty "[o]f persons," and their "appearance, features, etc."[108] Indeed, the Gothic origins of the word indicate that sheen "may originally have meant 'having (a certain) appearance,'" so that this shining beauty is also associated with form.[109] In regard to the meaning "[b]right, shining, resplendent," "[i]n early use this sense may have been merely contextual, the adj. being applied in the sense 'beautiful' to objects (e.g. heavenly bodies, jewels, metals) the beauty of which is dependent on their brightness. In later use . . . the sense 'shining' is felt as primary."[110] This sense of beauty as shining is specifically used "[o]f a day, the sky, etc."[111] as it is in Dickinson's usage—in fact, one meaning of sheen just *is* "the bright sun."[112] If these meanings already indicate a sense of beautiful light that is both apart from things (it shines on and off of them) but also is identified with them, as in the meaning of the bright sun or the beautiful form of a person, it is entirely appropriate that it should also denote ornamentation: "[g]orgeous or bright attire."[113]

Recalling Coomaraswamy's sense of ornamentation as an addition that completes or is necessary to its object, sheen as ornamenation evokes a resplendent brightness which is both part of and different from what it adorns. All of this is to suggest that the question Dickinson raises about sheen—if it must take a "Disk"—is a quintessential question about ornamentation's relationship to the appearance of specific objects. When Dickinson writes, "sheen must have a Disk," she asserts that the light of beauty must shine in and upon an object. It cannot just glow, but must tend to, be bestowed upon, an object. And yet such light beauty is indifferent to form, even indifferent to the object it glorifies. Thus even in insisting that light takes an object, the poem allows that this taking might be an indifferent bestowing, one that lights a form without seeing it. Underlying much of the restlessness or agitation of ornamentation which I have discussed throughout is this sense of a light that is both of and not of things, and is thus in a critical sense neither transcendent nor grounded.

Whitman's "I Saw in Louisiana a Live-Oak Growing," which recalls seeing a tree that is magnificently solitary and self-sufficient, conducts its own inquiry into the attachment of value to objects. The live-oak beckons to Whitman that he, too, might partake of its "growing" and "joyous" being—"its look, rude, unbending, lusty, made me think of myself."[114] The poem insists on the solitude of the tree, "standing alone there without its friend near" ("I," 5), "without a friend a lover near" ("I,"

12) and suggests that, unlike this lonely tree, Whitman could not exist "uttering joyous leaves" ("I," 3, and again at 12) in self-sufficient solitude. The tree offers something to Whitman: unbound being, "solitary in a wide flat space" ("I," 11), which is a pure open clarity of growing without audience, direction, or even preference. But Whitman chooses to reject it: his double "I could not" ("I," 5, 13) has the tone of steeling himself against it, and calling resistance by the name of incapacity. Resistance to the tree is identified with cutting off a piece of it for an ornament: "And I broke off a twig with a certain number of leaves upon it, and twined around it a little moss, / And brought it away, and I have placed it in sight in my room" ("I," 6–7). Unlike the open increase of the tree's "growing," with its unspecifiable bounty of "joyous leaves," Whitman's "curious token" ("I," 10) has a specific number of leaves, and concerns limitation, from the broken-off twig (just a piece) to the moss "twined around" in an act of binding off.

In light of the overall scenario of the poem—Whitman's turning away from this tree to a life in which he "think[s] of little else than" his "own dear friends" ("I," 9, 8)—I am tempted to read Whitman's ornament as of a piece with his choice to remain at the level of particular attachments rather than that of the "wide flat space" in which the oak "glistens," under a light of unlimited beauty. Whitman does say that the "curious token . . . makes me think of manly love," which would seem to strengthen such a reading. And yet, to "think of manly love" is not really the same as holding onto a token that is a bond to a specific person. Whitman's "curious token" is open-ended, for it enables looking toward specific connection and the "wide flat space" of Being. Even that love of Being is laced up with a turning toward the tree, as the ornament is a sign of having been there and felt the "look" of the tree. It's here that Whitman's token is truly "curious," in the sense of being uncommitted to what it connects to and able to extend in two separate directions, both to open, plentiful totality and to the specific love of one for another.

To even say that these are two directions, as if this twig with moss were a binary switch, is to oversimplify. For the human love of a valued object is expressly vacant in this poem: first of all, the missing conjunction in "a friend a lover" has a loose diffidence over whether those roles are distinct or additive, or are revisions of one another. And the relation of the speaker to friend or lover remains only possible here: these are categories of relation without the directed focus of another poem in the "Calamus" section, "To a Stranger" which addresses a "[p]assing stranger!" who may still be unnamed, but is addressed as a "you" whom the poet would speak to and adore—a level of one-to-one connection the "live-oak" poem lacks.[115] The token only suggests "manly love" as a phenomenon and category of love; it is not directed toward a particular beloved, even an anonymous lover or one among many.

As the love of men is less specific than one first thinks, so the tree is less clearly a vision of undifferentiated completeness. The live-oak is laden with leaves, which Whitman thinks of as different from the tree, making the tree into an assemblage of tree *and* leaves. The tree is also laden as "the moss hung down from the branches" ("I," 2), so it's already ornamented by nature even before Whitman breaks it off and twines it with moss. In the 1859 manuscript the entire "Calamus" section had been entitled "Live Oak, with Moss," suggesting that the oak's key quality is not autonomy but being attended: being "with Moss."[116] That Whitman would have titled the section that way also links the oak to the homosexuality the whole cluster of poems considers, so that it's not quite fair to say—as I tried to above, and as Whitman tries to more than once—that the poem is about rejecting totality for the specificity of love. Even the way the oak tree is so clearly present *in* a space counters a reading of it as a vision of autonomy: "*in* Louisiana" is said twice in the poem, and once in its title, and the tree is also placed "*in* a wide flat space."

I argued earlier that in Dickinson ornamentation is form that attends to the Open, to a sense of that which is beyond the limits of the world of separation. Following that line, I would say that the tree is here a form of such ornamentation, as its leaves and moss and being glisten "in" a place, and the tree is set out upon this space to call attention to that flat open litness and to make it bearable and attractive (it has a seductive but also barely tolerable "look, rude, unbending, lusty"). In this sense, the live-oak is from the outset partaking in a scene that is about ornamental attending to the Open's indivisible litness. Thus it isn't, finally, the case that the poem performs a turn away from the Open to specific human love; as the intertwining of oak and friend and lover evinces, what is known in this poem is that a love that is felt for one object is not fully separable from a love for Being itself, or from a love unconnected to objects. And this isn't a lovelorn poem either, because it understands that the love it can offer—to Being or to a lover—is incommensurable with any particular object on which it may be trained. There may be sadness that *no* object—from light to tree to person—can fully absorb or contain its eros, or even that, since that lit live-oak is in a place, adorned with moss, there seems to be no doing without objects altogether, however unmotivated their selection might be. Such dissatisfactions explain the subtle violence around the broken and twined token, as if there were no acceptable or right mediation between love, its specific objects, and the openness of a lit world without distinction. And they explain the lingering sense that the world should be furnished so as to make sense to us, even if that meant seeing it furnished with nothing at all.

Some confusion regarding the world's status as an object of attention is at issue in the sentence from Thoreau's *Journal*, "Why should just these sounds & sights accompany our life?" (*J*, 4:468). In *Writing Nature*, Cameron comments that Thoreau revised that sentence into a more traditional one for *Walden*, where he asks, "Why do precisely these objects which we behold make a world?" (*W*, 225). She observes that in the *Journal*'s version "impressions have not yet been abstracted into objects" or into a world; instead, it "intimates companionship, suggesting that man, not fronting nature, has it alongside of him."[117] The revision replaces a sense of Thoreau "accompany[ing]" impressions with a sense of him as a subject beholding an object world, thereby making a transition from attending into conceptual framing. What I want to add is that even in his *Journal* phrasing, which has him accompanied by "sounds and sights," there is a sense of disorientation and possibly fear at the thrown, unmotivated quality of appearance. Why are these things and not others our life? Why are phenomena not under our control? While a strong line of criticism suggests that knowing is problematic because of the control it evinces over objects, such concern with conceptual domination might obscure a terror and confusion easily provoked by contact with the essential inability of the mind to control phenomena.[118] This is the fear I hear in Thoreau's disoriented wondering at why certain "sounds & sights accompany our life," and even in Whitman's praise of a world so clearly not right.

I have just now been writing as if it were obvious that there is an opposition between value for specific persons and things, and a value that attends to everything, whether this is thought of as Being or the world. In principle, that is, I have maintained that there is a conflict between value considered as a process of selection and as a non-selecting, openhanded approach to the world. In the work of Thoreau, Dickinson, and Whitman alike, the complexity of the shifts between the shine of distinct forms and of the Open, together with their range of restless, sometimes violent adjustments to such shifts, may be taken instead as an experienced alteration between ways of thinking about shine at all. On the one hand, Fraser lays out for us that it is nonsensical to think of esteem without linking it to some objects and persons rather than to others, and this is a point clearly present in Izenberg's account of value as a relation to things. On the other hand, in the traditions which identify ornamentation with the cosmos it is indeed possible to conceive of a praise that encompasses everything. These are simply two distinct modes of thinking about what valuing is, and they entail different understandings of what persons are capable of. Rather than praise Thoreau, Dickinson, and Whitman for choosing one side, I would say that the fluctuations of their ornamental formulations evince the mental fluctuation that personal experience entails, in which it is possible, if not logical, to move between not only different beliefs, but different registers of belief. The uncertainty about why such choices and ideas occur—why such thoughts happen—is a form of vulnerability, akin to that which Thoreau voices regarding the uncertainty about why particular phenomena appear to us. In my own estimation, there is often a peculiar quality of accompaniment between my own thoughts and the texts that I read throughout this project, as there is a circumstantiality with which thoughts occur in relation to objects. To read as I have in this project brings out the contingent, ornamental quality of the relation between a critical mind and what interests it.[119] These thoughts have occurred upon the occasion of reading these texts; seen in detail, reading, itself a form of thinking, *happens that way*.

In addition, an ornament to the world stands as a particular item that both lauds and attends a totality toward which it bears a peculiar relationship. Think of the wind-tossed forest against which, in Dickinson, the universe stands. As a particular item made to stand out from the universe (as from, in other cases, the object which it may serve to make stand out), the ornament is a unique form of particular. It is a particular (a rosette, a pearl necklace, a twig with moss on it) which belongs to no whole and exemplifies nothing larger than itself, but which leads toward a whole, and in this sense introduces and acclimates the mind to wholeness. The work of such particularity is not to resist, oppose, or be folded into the universe, but to serve as a means by which the person, more familiar with a life of particularities, might approach and relate to the Open. In so doing, it raises the possibility of seeing other particularities, such as particular attachments and concerns, as something quite different from a problematic opposite to intuitions of the Open. They too might, like Whitman's lovers and friends, become a way toward the Open, which, even being somewhat apart from it, does it a service.

The distinctive particularity of ornamentation has another power of acclimating the mind to the Open, which is found precisely in its askew and imposed qualities. The concept of praising the Open, and in some way approving of the totality of reality, is an affront to one's tendency to locate and object to that which is wrong in the world and with our life in it. But it is possible to separate ethical and moral judgments of what is beneficial or just from a judgment that reality is in some way different than it ought to be. It is possible to accept that on one level, it is right that things have occurred as they have, and that phenomena are as they are, without claiming that this is the rightness of moral or political judgment. To see that, though, one has to be able to tolerate the possibility that one's ideas of what would make sense or be best are distinct from reality and in a basic way set against it. The fugitive, intrusive qualities of ornamentation refuse to offer one the satisfaction of finding the world made as one thinks it ought to have been, and are a challenge to consider that it might be made right when, to one's own mind, it looks wholly otherwise. Ornamentation is both an irritant and a tonic to a mind that wants the world to follow its own logic, or to fit in some final way, and it thus invites us to a freedom that doesn't begin by negating what is present.

NOTES

Introduction

1. Walt Whitman, 1855 "Preface," in *Leaves of Grass: Comprehensive Reader's Edition*, ed. Harold W. Blodgett and Sculley Bradley (New York: New York University Press, 1965), 722. Hereafter cited parenthetically by page number and abbreviated as "P."
2. Henry D. Thoreau, *Walden* (1854), ed. J. Lyndon Shanley, *The Writings of Henry D. Thoreau*, gen. ed. Robert Sattelmeyer (Princeton, NJ: Princeton University Press, 1971), 193, 37. *Walden* is hereafter cited parenthetically by page number and abbreviated as *W*.
3. Susan Howe, *My Emily Dickinson*, with a preface by Eliot Weinberger (New York: New Directions, 1985; preface © E. Weinberger, 2007), 17.
4. Henry D. Thoreau, *Journal* vol. 5: 1852–1853, ed. Patrick F. O'Connell, *The Writings of Henry D. Thoreau* (Princeton, NJ: Princeton University Press, 1997), 176, 371. The *Journal* is hereafter abbreviated as *J* and cited parenthetically by volume and page number. Volumes of the *Journal* not yet published by Princeton are cited from *The Journal of Henry David Thoreau*, ed. Bradford Torrey and Francis H. Allen, with a foreword by Walter Harding (Boston: Houghton Mifflin, 1906), in fourteen volumes bound as two (New York: Dover reprint edition, 1962); this edition hereafter cited parenthetically by volume and page number and abbreviated as *Jo*.
5. Emily Dickinson, *The Poems of Emily Dickinson: Variorum Edition*, ed. R. W. Franklin (Cambridge, MA: The Belknap Press of Harvard University Press, 1998), poems 523, 510. Hereafter cited parenthetically by Franklin's poem number.

6. Walt Whitman, *Democratic Vistas*, in *Prose Works 1892*, Vol. II, *Collect and Other Prose*, ed. Floyd Stovall, in *The Collected Writings of Walt Whitman*, series eds. Gay Wilson Allen and Sculley Bradley (New York: New York University Press, 1964), 412, 404. Hereafter abbreviated as *DV* and cited parenthetically by page number.
7. Ralph Waldo Emerson, "The Poet" (1844), in *Essays and Lectures*, selected with notes by Joel Porte (New York: Library of America, 1983), 450.
8. In this respect, the ornamental aesthetics that this book argues for is comparable to the relational aesthetics which Nicolas Bourriaud describes in contemporary art, with its focus on "ways of living and models of action within the existing real" (*Relational Aesthetics*, transl. Simon Pleasance and Fronza Woods, with Mathieu Copeland [Dijon, France: Les Presses du réel, 1998, 2002, 2008], 13). The aspect of Bourriaud that is most relevant here is his focus on transitive artworks, which do not exist outside their engagement by persons. He writes that such "[t]ransitivity is as old as the hills. It is a tangible property of the artwork.... Any artwork might thus be defined as a relational object" (Bourriaud, 26). Claire Bishop argues that Bourriaud fails to see that "a democratic society is one in which relations of conflict are *sustained*, not erased," as she finds they are in the works Bourriaud tends to champion (Bishop, "Antagonism and Relational Aesthetics," *October* 110 [Fall 2004]: 51–79; 66). Thus, Bishop argues, relational aesthetics ought to be concerned with relationships of "antagonism," a focus on political dissensus that has much in common with the work of Jacques Rancière (Bishop, 66). In my accounts of the relational aspect of Thoreau, Dickinson, and Whitman, the possible modes of being-in-relation are still more wide-ranging than either harmonious collectivity or principled antagonism.
9. Art historian Oleg Grabar offers a theory of ornamentation grounded in the visual arts of "classical Islamic times" that is, in his view, "applicable to other times and other places" (Oleg Grabar, *The Mediation of Ornament*, The A. W. Mellon Lectures in the Fine Arts [1989], The National Gallery of Art, Bollingen Series XXXV.38 [Princeton, NJ: Princeton University Press, 1992], 5). In this theory, ornamentation becomes a mediating element between subjects and objects: "Like Plato's demons they are what some literary critics have called the prisms mediating between the world and the text or the text and its readers" (Grabar, 44). Overall, his account of ornamentation as a relational rather than a material category has importantly informed my own understanding of ornamentation, although his emphasis on the "sensory pleasure" of ornamentation and its strict role as a mediator between subject and object contains a distinct sense of the world from that which is, I argue, at issue in the writing of Thoreau, Dickinson, and Whitman (Grabar, 244).
10. My reading of Heidegger has primarily been informed by the way his work is engaged in literary criticism, but for philosophical background

NOTES

to Heidegger I've also found helpful: Hubert L. Dreyfus, *Being-in-the-World: A Commentary on Heidgger's* Being and Time, Division I (Cambridge, MA: MIT Press, 1991); George Steiner, *Martin Heidegger* (Chicago: University of Chicago Press, 1978); Robert Sokolowski, *Introduction to Phenomenology* (Cambridge: Cambridge University Press, 2000); Mark A. Wrathall, *Heidegger and Unconcealment: Truth, Language, and History* (Cambridge: Cambridge University Press, 2011); Charles B. Guignon, "Introduction," and Dorothea Frede, "The Question of Being: Heidegger's Project," each in *The Cambridge Companion to Heidegger*, 2nd edition, ed. Charles B. Guignon (Cambridge: Cambridge University Press, 2006).

11. Martin Heidegger, *Parmenides*, transl. André Schuwer and Richard Rojcewicz (1982; Bloomington: Indiana University Press, 1992), 48.
12. Heidegger, *Parmenides*, 49–50.
13. In *Being and Time*, Heidegger outlines the understanding of truth, which he argues against as follows: "There are three theses which characterize the way in which the essence of truth has been traditionally taken and the way it is supposed to have been first defined: (1) that the 'locus' of truth is assertion (judgment); (2) that the essence of truth lies in the 'agreement' of the judgment with its object; (3) that Aristotle, the father of logic, not only has assigned truth to the judgment as its primordial locus but has set going the definition of 'truth' as 'agreement' " (257). The topic of agreement is itself a representational one, insofar as it depends on seeking to match reality to a concept of the subject's formulating. Martin Heidegger, *Being and Time*, transl. Jon Macquarrie and Edward Robinson, foreword by Taylor Carman (New York: Harper Perennial, 1962, 2008).
14. In the earlier and more traditionally structured *Being and Time*, Heidegger also objects that this mode of understanding is insufficient because it has not looked into the underlying question of how the human being is present in relation to objects at all. Beneath the questions of subject and object, that is, are questions about the Being of the world at all. How does it arise as a reality in which we find ourselves and which we seek to understand?
15. Heidegger, *Parmenides*, 11.
16. Heidegger, *Parmenides*, 62. For a discussion of the enigmatic quality of Heidegger's sense of truth as what is brought to light and also held back from it, see Daniel Tiffany, *Infidel Poetics: Riddles, Nightlife, Substance* (Chicago: University of Chicago Press, 2009), 64–65 and *passim*.
17. Kaja Silverman, *World Spectators* (Stanford, CA: Stanford University Press, 2000), 2.
18. Silverman, 2.
19. Silverman, 2.
20. I discuss Silverman's phenomenology in more detail in Chapter Two.

21. Steiner, 83.
22. Heidegger, *Being and Time*, 127, 130.
23. Steiner, 83. Her work is more focused on Husserl and Merleau-Ponty, but Sara Ahmed's focus on orientation and the conscious experiences of bodies in space is an example of interest in phenemonology that focuses on its return to the sensory world, rather than on the dislocation from immediacy that Heidegger's investigation of Being produces. Sara Ahmed, *Queer Phenomenology: Orientations, Objects, Others* (Durham, NC: Duke University Press, 2006).
24. Heidegger, *Being and Time*, 59.
25. Heidegger, *Being and Time*, 99.
26. Heidegger, *Being and Time*, 61.
27. Heidegger, *Being and Time*, 89.
28. Heidegger, *Being and Time*, 89.
29. Heidegger, *Being and Time*, 120. In *On the Way to Language*, Heidegger describes language as a bud putting out petals: "Language, heard through this word, is: the petals that stem from *Koto*" (Heidegger, *On the Way to Language* [1959], transl. Peter D. Hertz [New York: Harper & Row, 1971], 47).
30. Heidegger, *Being and Time*, 176.
31. See Lucien Goldmann, *Lukács and Heidegger: Towards a New Philosophy*, transl. William Q. Boelhower (London: Routledge & Kegan Paul, 1977). Lukács himself points out that the topic of alienation at the heart of *History and Class Consciousness*, "following the publication of Heidegger's *Being and Time* (1927), . . . moved into the centre of philosophical debate" ("Preface to the New Edition," *History and Class Consciousness: Studies in Marxist Dialectics*, transl. Rodney Livingstone [Cambridge, MA: MIT Press, 1971], xxii). Of course, Lukács also considers Heidegger an instance of the "philosophical, cultural criticism of the bourgeoisie" (Lukács, xxiv).
32. Stephen Best and Sharon Marcus write that they "take surface to mean what is evident, perceptible, apprehensible in texts; what is neither hidden nor hiding; what, in the geometrical sense, has length and breadth but no thickness, and therefore covers no depth. A surface is what insists on being looked *at* rather than what we must train ourselves to see *through*" (Stephen Best and Sharon Marcus, "Surface Reading: An Introduction," *Representations* 108.1 [Fall 2009]: 1–21; 9). My work clearly does not perform the kind of critique which Best and Marcus were arguing against, but the relationship of ornament to Being and even the uncertain, changing quality of ornamental relations is antithetical to the surface readers' image that "what is evident, perceptible, apprehensible" is a simple matter of being there to "be[ ] looked *at*." While this book has a resemblance to work done in the name of rejecting a hermeneutics of suspicion or "symptomatic reading"

николай
(Best and Marcus, 1), at heart it is closer to both phenomenological and historicist work than to recent work that abjures interpretation in favor of a more literal way of taking things as they are.

33. "Rohitassa Sutta: To Rohitassa," *Anguttara Nikaya* 4.45, transl. Thanissaro Bhikku (1997), http://www.accesstoinsight.org/tipitaka/an/an04/an04.045.than.html (accessed July 22, 2015).

34. Friedrich Schiller, *On the Aesthetic Education of Man: In a Series of Letters*, transl. and ed. Elizabeth M. Wilkinson and L. A. Willoughby (Oxford: Clarendon Press, 1982), 9.

35. Schiller, 205.

36. Another example: William Hogarth, in Ronald Paulson's estimation, created a "practical aesthetics," which differed from "the theoretically pure aesthetics of Shaftesbury, where the human body can only be beautiful if divorced from function, fitness, and utility. Hogarth says that in the real world . . . the beautiful object cannot be separated from any of these—only that the moral judgment is replaced by a subtler, more 'disinterested' . . . 'pleasure,' the 'pleasure of pursuit.'" Ronald Paulson, "Introduction," William Hogarth, *The Analysis of Beauty*, ed. with intro and notes by Ronald Paulson (New Haven, CT: Yale University Press for the Paul Mellon Centre for British Art, 1997), xxxiii.

37. Sir Joshua Reynolds, *Discourses on Art*, ed. Robert R. Wark (New Haven, CT, and London: Yale University Press, 1975), 19.

38. Schiller, 125.

39. Immanuel Kant, *Critique of Judgment* (1790), transl. and intro. Werner S. Pluhar, foreword by Mary J. Gregor (Indianapolis and Cambridge: Hackett, 1987), 72.

40. Kant, 77.

41. Jacques Derrida, *The Truth in Painting*, transl. Geoff Bennington and Ian McLeod (Chicago: University of Chicago Press, 1987), 64.

42. Naomi Schor, *Reading in Detail: Aesthetics and the Feminine* (New York: Methuen, 1987), 16.

43. Schor, 22.

44. See Isobel Armstrong's critique of Derrida's view of the aesthetic, which she sees as "[r]emorseless" in its "emptying out" of the aesthetic, and violent in its reduction of the aesthetic to "rejected matter" or "vomit" (*The Radical Aesthetic* [Oxford: Blackwell, 2000], 47, 48). The project of running aesthetics in reverse—so that rather than uplifting us from materiality and desire it takes us back down to them—also animates Terry Eagleton's *Ideology of the Aesthetic* (Malden, MA, and Oxford: Blackwell, 1990).

45. Paul De Man, "Excuses (Confessions)," in *Allegories of Reading: Figural Language in Rousseau, Nietzsche, Rilke, and Proust* (New Haven, CT: Yale University Press, 1979), 279 (quoting Rousseau), 283.

46. De Man, 288.

NOTES

47. Steven Knapp and Walter Benn Michaels, "Against Theory," *Critical Inquiry* 8 (Summer 1982): 723–42; 734.
48. Susan Bernstein, *Housing Problems: Writing and Architecture in Goethe, Walpole, Freud, and Heidegger*, with photographs by Suzanne Doppelt (Stanford, CA: Stanford University Press, 2008), 58, 59–60, 60.
49. Gülru Neçipoglu, *The Topkapi Scroll: Geometry and Ornament in Islamic Architecture*, contrib. Mohammad al-Asad (Los Angeles: Getty, 1996), 221–222.
50. For example, see David Brett, *Rethinking Decoration: Pleasure and Ideology in the Visual Arts* (Cambridge: Cambridge University Press, 2005), 20.
51. At stake here is also the emergence of professional design studies, as distinct from the study of how to practice design. See Victor Margolin, "Design History and Design Studies," in *The Politics of the Artificial: Essays on Design and Design Studies* (Chicago: University of Chicago Press, 2002).
52. Henry Glassie, "Eighteenth-Century Cultural Process in Delaware Valley Folk Building," *Winterthur Portfolio* 7 (1972): 29–57; 30. Also see Henry Glassie, *Material Culture* (Bloomington: Indiana University Press, 1999).
53. Jules David Prown, "Mind in Matter: An Introduction to Material Culture Theory and Method," *Winterthur Portfolio* 17.1 (Spring 1982): 1–19; 6.
54. Kenneth L. Ames, *Death in the Dining Room; and Other Tales of Victorian Culture* (Philadelphia: Temple University Press, 1992), 72–73.
55. Katherine C. Grier, "Culture Made Material," *American Literary History* 8.3 (Autumn 1996): 552–65; 563.
56. Neçipoglu, 222.
57. This characterization also applies to Dorri Beam's compelling investigation of nineteenth-century women's "'highly wrought' writing" (Dorri Beam, *Style, Gender, and Fantasy in Nineteenth-Century American Women's Writing* [Cambridge: Cambridge University Press, 2010], 1). She offers a complex account of the claims made by female writers' ornate style, and of the ways that soul and materiality are conjoined in their work. Nevertheless, overall, Beam emphasizes that ornate and ornamental writing is especially attuned to its materiality, and her larger claim is that emphasizing the worked nature of such material style enabled the articulation of different accounts of female desire and agency. In her discussion, then, ornamental language is still concerned with the way that expression is found in and through the materiality of linguistic form, making ornamentation a form of linguistic representation, rather than a distinct practice. See, for instance, her comments on "the materiality and decorative nature that is assigned to women's labor through the label 'highly wrought'" (Beam, 4), her discussion of how a flower Margaret Fuller writes about is "symbolic and material at once" (Beam, 53), how Mary Clemmer's "language urges us to ... 'delight in the simple sensuous existence' of the words themselves, experiencing them as newly palpable" (Beam, 109), and on "the substance of expression" (Beam, 192).

58. Raymond Williams, *Culture and Society: 1780–1950* (New York: Columbia University Press, 1958, 1983), 130.
59. Williams, 130.
60. Anne Carson, *Economy of the Unlost: Reading Simonides of Keos with Paul Celan* (Princeton, NJ: Princeton University Press, 1999), 78. Andrew Ford describes the same watershed period in ancient Greece by pointing out that "the major difference between archaic and classical criticism . . . [is the new] approach to song as verbal craftsmanship. I call this change the invention of poetry because it was signaled by the popularization of a new vocabulary to describe singers as 'makers' or 'poets' (*poiētai*) and songs as 'made things' or 'poems' (*poiēmata*)" (Ford, *The Origins of Criticism: Literary Culture and Poetic Theory in Classical Greece* [Princeton, NJ: Princeton University Press, 2002], 93).
61. Carson, 78.
62. Ford, 94.
63. Ford, 95.
64. Ford, 95.
65. Considering Carson's and Ford's work puts a different light on Daniel Tiffany's view that "[i]n the humanities, the material substance of ordinary things is judged to be either an intuitive certainty or an arcane possession of physics" (Tiffany, 36). He maintains that the humanities need to reopen the question of what materiality is, which in his case means asking "what lyric poetry may be able to tell us about the material substance of things" (Tiffany, 37). But part of the reason for this humanistic habit of assuming that the material is beyond question may be that the concept of the literary object is related to the recording of poetry on stones, paper, and objects, as this containment in visible and touchable physical form made it possible for a text to have a stable identity. That which can be touched and seen is identified for a real reason with what seems not to change, for it is opposed to sung and spoken occasional verse.
66. Marcel Detienne, *The Masters of Truth in Ancient Greece*, transl. Janet Lloyd, foreword by Pierre Vidal-Naquet (New York: Zone Books, 1999).
67. Ford, 12.
68. Ford, 13.
69. Ford, 26.
70. Carson, 42.
71. This view is not unique to archaic Greece. In his study grounded in Islamic art, Grabar concluded that ornament often "seems to complete an object, a wall, or a person, by providing it with a quality," transferring that quality from itself to that which it adorns (Grabar, 25). He raises several examples of this principle in order to indicate "the agreement, in several highly literate and articulate societies, on the existence of an action that completes something,

that makes it perfect. That action is to decorate and the medium of its effectiveness is ornament" (Grabar, 26). Ananda K. Coomaraswamy similarly suggests that ornamentation, particularly in Vedic texts, is about an activity in relation to an object: "most of these words which imply for us the notion of something adventitious and luxurious, added to utilities but not essential to their efficacy, originally implied a completion or fulfillment of the artifact or other object in question; to 'decorate' an object or person meant to endow the object or person with its or his 'necessary accidents,' with a view to 'proper' operation" (Coomaraswamy, quoted in Naomi Schor, *Breaking the Chain: Women, Theory, and French Realist Fiction* [New York: Columbia University Press, 1985], 117). See Coomaraswamy, "A Figure of Speech or a Figure of Thought?" in *The Essential Ananda K. Coomaraswamy,* ed. Rama P. Coomaraswamy, foreword by Arvind Sharma, prologue by Marco Pallis (Bloomington, IN: World Wisdom, 2004), 21–51.

72. Ford, 36.
73. Ford, 43.
74. Carson, 34.
75. Carson, 73.
76. Carson, 60.
77. Carson, 61–62.
78. Ford, 99.
79. Ford, 99.
80. Ford, 101. Plato, *Phaedrus,* transl. Robin Waterfield (Oxford: Oxford University Press, 2002), 54.
81. Ford, 102.
82. Ford, 105, quoting Simonides.
83. Ford, 106.
84. Ford, 107, 105, 108. It's a little confusing, insofar as Simonides is a poet of the oral tradition whose poems were also inscribed. But the issue is, in Ford's view, how inscription is understood: "A statue, a burial mound, or any uninscribed artifact had been the silent partner rather than the rival of oral tradition; but once such objects make much of their engraved messages, Simonides attacks their hubristic guarantees of fame" (Ford, 108).
85. Ford, 112.
86. Ford, 111.
87. Leslie Kurke, *The Traffic in Praise: Pindar and the Poetics of Social Economy* (Ithaca, NY: Cornell University Press, 1991), 3.
88. Also see M. I. Finley, *The World of Odysseus* (1954), intro. Bernard Knox (New York: New York Review Books, 1978, 2002), on guest-friendship and gift exchange.
89. Pindar, Nemean V. 1, transl. Thoreau, "Pindar," *The Dial* 4 (January 1844): 379–90, in *Translations,* ed. K. P. van Anglen, *The Writings of Henry D. Thoreau* (Princeton, NJ: Princeton University Press, 1986), 123.

NOTES

90. Pindar, Nemean VIII, in *Pindar's Victory Songs*, transl. Frank J. Nisetich, foreword by Hugh Lloyd-Jones (Baltimore, MD: The Johns Hopkins University Press, 1980), Stand 1, ll. 11–17 in original.
91. Ford, 118.
92. Ford, 121. He quotes Deborah Tarn Steiner, "Pindar's 'Oggetti Parlanti,'" *Harvard Studies in Classical Philology* 95 (1993): 159–80; 176. Also see Deborah Tarn Steiner, *The Tyrant's Wit: Myths and Images of Writing in Ancient Greece* (Princeton, NJ: Princeton University Press, 1994). Ford observes that another critic, Segal, "has brought out 'a continuous dialogue within Pindar's work between song (poetry) on the one hand and monumentalization in statuary'" on the other (Ford, 122). Ford's reference is to C. P. Segal, *Pindar's Mythmaking: The Fourth Pythian Ode* (Princeton, NJ: Princeton University Press, 1986).
93. Ford, 122.
94. Tiffany, 11.
95. Tiffany, 156.
96. On the state of the university, see Chris Lorenz, "If You're So Smart, Why Are You under Surveillance? Universities, Neoliberalism, and New Public Management," *Critical Inquiry* 38.3 (Spring 2012): 599–629.
97. Jacques Rancière, *Dis-agreement: Politics and Philosophy*, transl. Julie Rose (Minneapolis: University of Minnesota Press, 1999), 104–105.
98. Jonathan Crary, *24/7: Late Capitalism and the Ends of Sleep* (London: Verso, 2013), 5.
99. Crary, 21.
100. Fredric Jameson, *The Political Unconscious: Narrative as a Socially Symbolic Act* (Ithaca, NY: Cornell University Press, 1981), 9. The critical departure from the person was as important to new historicism as to Marxist historicism such as Jameson's. For instance, in *The Gold Standard and the Logic of Naturalism*, Walter Benn Michaels argued against inquires into how a particular author might be said to relate to his or her culture, maintaining that "the only relation literature as such has to culture as such is that it is part of it" (Walter Benn Michaels, *The Gold Standard and the Logic of Naturalism* [Berkeley: University of California Press, 1987], 27).
101. I believe this emphasis on persons' fluctuating practices is amenable to an argument Imani Perry has made that racism should be considered a practice, rather than as either a structure or the identity of the individual. She argues that "[t]he theory of structural racism," "rooted in the profound influence of Marxist modes of analysis," is unable to account for the way that the actions and behaviors of individuals are what shape a culture (Imani Perry, *More Beautiful and More Terrible: The Embrace and Transcendence of Racial Inequality in the United States* [New York: New York University Press, 2011], 34).

102. Allen Grossman, "Summa Lyrica," in *The Sighted Singer: Two Works on Poetry for Readers and Writers* (Baltimore, MD: The Johns Hopkins University Press, 1992), 230.
103. Reginald A. Ray, *Touching Enlightenment: Finding Realization in the Body* (Boulder, CO: Sounds True, 2014), 337.
104. Ray, 339.
105. He cites it only as "[a] wise medieval Jewish saying" from Iraq (Grabar, 25).

Chapter 1

1. Sharon Cameron, *Writing Nature: Henry Thoreau's Journal* (Chicago: University of Chicago Press, 1985), 4.
2. Cameron, *Writing Nature*, 12.
3. Anne-Lise François, *Open Secrets: The Literature of Uncounted Experience* (Stanford, CA: Stanford University Press, 2008), 17.
4. François, xvi, xvii, 34.
5. Lawrence Buell, *The Environmental Imagination: Thoreau, Nature Writing, and the Formation of American Culture* (Cambridge, MA: The Belknap Press of Harvard University Press, 1995).
6. Buell, *Environmental Imagination*, 154–55.
7. Buell, *Environmental Imagination*, 11, 10. Although his later work on environmental criticism includes the humanly constructed world in its account of the environment, it does not contradict the reading of Thoreau in *The Environmental Imagination*, nor does it radically reverse that book's orientation around the opposition between anthropocentric and ecocentric values. See *Writing for an Endangered World: Literature, Culture, and Environment in the U.S. and Beyond* (Cambridge, MA: The Belknap Press of Harvard University Press, 2001), and *The Futures of Environmental Criticism: Environmental Crisis and the Literary Imagination* (Malden, MA, and Oxford: Blackwell, 2005).
8. Henry David Thoreau, *A Week on the Concord and Merrimack Rivers* (1849), ed. Carl Hovde, William L. Howarth, Elizabeth Hall Witherell, with an introduction by John McPhee (Princeton, NJ: Princeton University Press, 1980), 226–227.
9. Emerson, "The Poet," 459.
10. Emerson, "The Poet," 459–60.
11. Emerson, "The Poet," 460.
12. Thoreau's English translation is probably his own, as it differs from that in two available to him, Thomas Taylor's 1817 edition and the 1835 translation by William Gowan, and includes more of the phrase than Emerson does in "The Poet." I thank Edan Dekel for providing this information. For a discussion of the abandon with which Thoreau uses quotations, often heedless

of context, see Meredith McGill's "Common Places: Poetry, Illocality, and Temporal Dislocation in Thoreau's *A Week on the Concord and Merrimack Rivers*," American Literary History 19.2 (Summer 2007): 357–74.

13. Martin Heidegger, *What Is Called Thinking?*, transl. J. Glenn Gray (New York: Harper & Row, 1968), 203.
14. Henry George Liddell and Robert Scott, *A Greek-English Lexicon*, rev. and augmented throughout by Sir Henry Stuart Jones, with the assistance of Roderick McKenzie (Oxford: The Clarendon Press, 1940), accessed via Perseus Digital Library at Tufts University, www.perseus.tufts.edu/hopper/, *sub verbo* νόος.
15. Henry David Thoreau, "Walking," in *Excursions*, ed. Joseph J. Moldenhauer (Princeton, NJ: Princeton University Press, 2007), 216, 215.
16. Kant, 84.
17. "What is formal in the presentation of a thing, the harmony of its manifold to [form] a unity (where it is indeterminate what this unity is [meant] to be) does not by itself reveal any objective purposiveness whatsoever. For here we abstract from what this unity is *as a purpose* (what the thing is [meant] to be), so that nothing remains but the subjective purposiveness of the presentations in the mind of the beholder. Subjective purposiveness [is] merely a certain purposiveness of the subject's presentational state and, within that state, [an] appealingness [involved] in apprehending a given form by the imagination" (Kant, 74).
18. Sherman Paul, *The Shores of America: Thoreau's Inward Exploration* (New York: Russell & Lowell, 1958), 295, 351.
19. Frederick Garber, *Thoreau's Redemptive Imagination* (New York: New York University Press, 1977), 11. Another important critical work on how Thoreau plumbed experience to transform it into literary art is James McIntosh, *Thoreau as Romantic Naturalist: His Shifting Stance toward Nature* (Ithaca, NY: Cornell University Press, 1974).
20. Paul, 395.
21. Paul, 396.
22. Thus Stanley Cavell's view that *Walden* is an "epic" and that Thoreau is its "hero"—"knowledge is a heroic enterprise. The hero departs from his hut and goes into an unknown wood from whose mysteries he wins a boon that he brings back to his neighbors"—seems to mistake Thoreau's way of relating to his environment (Cavell, *The Senses of Walden: An Expanded Edition* [Chicago: University of Chicago Press, 1992], 6, 5, 119). For Cavell, Thoreau's world is a world made through language, and through the a priori conditions of human knowing; my suggestion is that, to the contrary, language and knowing accompany and respond to the world for Thoreau, but are not its grounding condition.
23. Louisa May Alcott, *Moods* (1864), ed. Sarah Elbert, *American Women Writers* (New Brunswick, NJ: Rutgers University Press, 1999), 1.

24. The quotation is from "Experience" (1844), where the punctuation and wording are slightly different: "Life is a train of moods like a string of beads, and, as we pass through them, they prove to be many-colored lenses which paint the world their own hue, and each shows only what lies in its focus" (Emerson, "Experience," in *Essays and Lectures*, 473).
25. Emerson, "Circles" (1844), in *Essays and Lectures*, 406.
26. Cameron, *Writing Nature*, 5.
27. Cameron, *Writing Nature*, 61.
28. Cameron, *Writing Nature*, 24.
29. Cameron, *Writing Nature*, 153.
30. Laura Dassow Walls, *Seeing New Worlds: Henry David Thoreau and Nineteenth-Century Science, Science and Literature*, ed. George Levine (Madison: University of Wisconsin Press, 1995), 140.
31. Walls, 164.
32. Walls, 52.
33. Elisa New, *The Line's Eye: Poetic Experience, American Sight* (Cambridge, MA: Harvard University Press, 1998), 2, 54.
34. New, 302.
35. Cameron, *Writing Nature*, 133.
36. Ananda K. Coomaraswamy, "Ornament," in Coomaraswamy, *Figures of Speech or Figures of Thought? The Traditional View of Art*, rev. edition with previously unpublished author's notes, ed. William Wroth, intro. Roger Lipsey (Bloomington, IN: World Wisdom, 2007), 72.
37. Coomaraswamy, "Ornament," 74.
38. Coomaraswamy, "Ornament," 74.
39. Coomaraswamy, "Ornament," 74.
40. Alan D. Hodder's "The Artist of Kouroo," in *Thoreau's Ecstatic Witness* (New Haven, CT: Yale University Press, 2001), gives a useful account of what Indian and other Asian texts Thoreau read. "Thoreau's engagement with South Asian literature began quite suddenly with his reading of Emerson's copy of William Jones's translation of *The Laws of Manu* in 1840," which "marked the beginning of a devotion to Asian, especially Hindu, classics that continued for the next fifteen years" (Hodder, 178, 179). This included "Charles Wilson's translation of the Bhagavad Gita, which did not arrive in Concord until 1845" (Hodder, 181). Thoreau was also "familiar with several other classic Hindu texts, including Wilson's translation of the *Viṣṇu Pūraṇa*, William Ward's translation of excerpts from the six systems of Indian philosophy, Rommohan Roy's translations of selected Upanishads, and Colebrooke's translation of the *Sāmkhya-kārikā*." Hodder argues that from his reading, Thoreau developed an association of Vedic texts with music, which helped him to develop his own understanding of "literary organicism" (Hodder, 186). (Even though "Thoreau did not have access

NOTES

to translations of any Vedic hymns themselves," Hodder notes, "*Manu* does provide a definitive statement of how Indian tradition conceived and understood 'the Veda'" [Hodder, 185]). I am not arguing for as strict a link between Hindu texts and Thoreau's aesthetics as Hodder sees; while I think it possible that Thoreau's understanding of ornament was subtly affected by his readings in these texts, the important point is that Coomaraswamy's terms help us to see what is happening in Thoreau.

41. Thoreau, *A Week*, 149.
42. Coomaraswamy, "Ornament," 79.
43. Coomaraswamy, "Ornament," 79.
44. Coomaraswamy, "Ornament," 76.
45. And, from 1852: "The barren flowers of gnaphalium ... are like a diamond set in pearly very dry & pure & pearly like a breast pin" (*J*, 5:58); an iris is "a little too showy & gaudy like some women's bonnets. Yet it belongs to the meadow & ornaments it much" (*J*, 5:90).
46. The late essay "Autumnal Tints" encompasses this argument explicitly. It contains familiar anxiety about the difficulty of finding the meaning of a natural object: "Each humblest plant, or weed, as we call it, stands there to express some thought or mood of ours; and yet how long it stands in vain!" (Thoreau, "Autumnal Tints" [1862], in *Excursions*, 230). But this worry is overwhelmed by the essay's confidence in Thoreau's ability to locate the beauty of nature in its last, dying phase. His confident commitment to seeing natural beauty even when it has no symbolic meaning leads him to reflect on nature as an ideal source of ornamental beauty. He asks, "What School of Design can vie with this?" referencing the Kensington School of Design, where modern industrial design was first being taught in Britain, and approvingly recommends that "manufacturers of cloth and paper, and paper-stainers" might be "educated by these autumnal colors" (Thoreau, "Autumnal," 244). Later in the essay Thoreau exclaims, "How differently the poet and the naturalist look at objects!" (Thoreau, "Autumnal," 257), but in its fascination with colors and design over the meaning of nature, the essay evinces how fully his sense of poetic seeing had become enfolded into ornamentation.
47. Ralph Waldo Emerson, "Thoreau" (1862), in *Emerson's Prose and Poetry*, sel. and ed. Joel Porte and Saundra Morris (New York: Norton, 2002), 410–11.
48. Emerson, "Thoreau," 409.
49. Hannah Arendt has written about "the relentlessness inherent in sheer thinking, whose need can never be assuaged," and of how thought "harbors within itself a highly self-destructive tendency" (Arendt, *The Life of the Mind*, one-volume edition [New York: Harvest, Harcourt, 1977, 1978], 55, 56). Although Arendt is concerned with speculative thinking, not with the kind of observations Thoreau is engaged in, her words help us account for the virtue of Thoreau's commitment to a project of attending that he

is finding not to yield even a "small fruit." Arendt continues, "To expect truth to come from thinking signifies that we mistake the need to think with the urge to know" (Arendt, 61). Thoreau's willingness to continue looking, to continue noting, even though he often feels that he is failing in his response is, however painfully and even embarrassingly, a willingness to pursue the mind's demand for knowing. This demand is both out of sync with, and determined to far outpace, the demand to have an answer, to have a shape to give what is apprehended. We could also appeal here to Cameron's contentions about the way that the *Journal* is pressing thought to its limits, as "[w]e suppose 'thinking' is the exploration of a delineated subject, and we presume, in addition, that successful thinking has a point, whether it be the solution of a problem or the completion of an idea. What would count as completion apparently involves finding the end of an idea" (Cameron, *Writing Nature*, 132). Such propositions about thinking are ones that, Cameron argues, Thoreau's *Journal* confronts, with the result that "the problem in the *Journal* is that thinking is endless" (Cameron, *Writing Nature*, 134). This quality of thinking in the *Journal* brings Thoreau close to Emerson, for whom, as Branka Arsić has argued, "thinking should be wandering and excursional," "a process, unconcerned with final results" (Arsić, *On Leaving: A Reading in Emerson* [Cambridge, MA: Harvard University Press, 2010], 63).

50. Heidegger, *What Is Called Thinking?* 38.
51. Heidegger, *What Is Called Thinking?* 38, 39.
52. Heidegger, *What Is Called Thinking?* 39.
53. Heidegger, *What Is Called Thinking?* 41–42.
54. Heidegger, *What Is Called Thinking?* 42.
55. Heidegger, *What Is Called Thinking?* 44.
56. Heidegger, *What Is Called Thinking?* 139.
57. Heidegger, *What Is Called Thinking?* 141.
58. Heidegger, *What Is Called Thinking?* 144.
59. Heidegger, *What Is Called Thinking?* 145.
60. Heidegger, *Being and Time*, 83.
61. Heidegger, *Being and Time*, 84.
62. Heidegger, *What Is Called Thinking?* 199.
63. Heidegger, *What Is Called Thinking?* 203.
64. Heidegger, *What Is Called Thinking?* 211.
65. Heidegger, *What Is Called Thinking?* 236.
66. Heidegger, *What Is Called Thinking?* 237.
67. Heidegger, *What is Called Thinking?* 237.
68. Steiner, 100.
69. New, 3. Also see her *The Regenerate Lyric: Theology and Innovation in American Poetry* (Cambridge, MA: Cambridge University Press, 1993).

70. New, 3.
71. William Bartram, *The Travels of William Bartram* (1791), ed. Thomas P. Slaughter (New York: Library of America, 1996), 303, 435.
72. Kant, 59.
73. Kant, 76–77.
74. Jonathan Loesberg, *A Return to Aesthetics: Autonomy, Indifference, and Postmodernism* (Stanford, CA: Stanford University Press, 2005), 6.
75. Art is always a secondary example of the aesthetic for Kant, according to Loesberg, because we know that art, unlike nature, was intended. Thus art does not provide the problem of apparent but unverifiable design that motivates the third *Critique*. Perhaps the less clearly intentional aspects of decorative art, in Kant's eyes, made it appear closer to nature than to other arts.
76. Naturally, to Emerson the distinction I am making would seem rather forced, since to him the meaning that God puts into the world is the same meaning that we find in it. But I do not think it is quite that way for Thoreau (since he does not seem to identify his soul with God), and in critical terms it is useful to make a distinction between these two meaning sources, even if Emerson understood them to be one and the same.
77. Frances Ferguson, *Pornography, the Theory: What Utilitarianism Did to Action* (Chicago: University of Chicago Press, 2004), 73.
78. Ferguson, 74. The passage I am quoting from explains how these qualities are shared by both Kant's aesthetics and de Sade's pornography.
79. In addition to Buell's work, discussed earlier, see *Thoreau's Sense of Place: Essays in American Environmental Writing*, ed. Richard J. Schneider, foreword by Lawrence Buell (Iowa City: University of Iowa Press, 2000); John Hildebidle, *A Naturalist's Liberty* (Cambridge, MA: Harvard University Press, 1983).
80. Thoreau, *A Week*, 21.
81. Laura Saltz discusses Thoreau's interest in actinism, the process by which light produces chemical changes in physical substances (Saltz, "'Corn Grows in the Night': Thoreau, Actinism, and the Natural Laws of Rhyme," in *Imponderables: Photography and the Science of Light in American Romantic Literature* [Unpub. MS]). Actinism is critical to photographic processes, and is responsible for the ability of a flower to open in response to light falling on it.
82. Thoreau, "Natural History of Massachusetts" (1842), in *Excursions*, 22.
83. Susan Stewart, *Poetry and the Fate of the Senses* (Chicago: University of Chicago Press, 2002), 149.
84. Stewart, 149. One translation of "Cædmon's Hymn" reads: "Now sing the glory of God, the King / of Heaven, our Father's power and His perfect / Labor, the world's conception, worked / In miracles as eternity's Lord

made / The beginning. First the heavens were formed a roof / For men, and then the holy Creator, / Eternal Lord and protector of our souls, / Shaped our earth, prepared our home, / The almighty Master, our Prince, our God." *Poems and Prose from the Old English*, transl. Burton Raffel, ed. Alexandra H. Olsen and Burton Raffel, intro. Alexandra H. Olsen (New Haven, CT: Yale University Press, 1998), 55.

85. Stewart, 150. Stewart goes on to connect this aspect of poetry—a praising that is also a reaching-toward—with a history of thinking of poetry as the offering of a bouquet. She includes two cases pertinent to this study, Dickinson's fascicles and Whitman's *Leaves of Grass*, but also the wonderful example of the English poet John Clare, who titled a collection of poems *The Midsummer Cushion*, after a custom of bringing a piece of turf with flowers blooming on it into the house for a decoration.

86. Stewart, 164–65.

87. Louis Althusser, "The Underground Current of the Materialism of the Encounter," in *Philosophy of the Encounter: Later Writings, 1978–87*, ed. François Matheron and Oliver Corpet, transl. and intro. G. M. Goshgarian (London: Verso, 2006), 167–68.

88. Althusser, 168.

89. Althusser, 169.

90. Althusser, 191.

91. Althusser, 191–92.

92. Althusser, 167.

93. Jane Bennett, *Vibrant Matter: A Political Economy of Things* (Durham, NC: Duke University Press, 2010), viii.

94. Bennett, xii.

95. Bennett, 32.

96. Bennett, 33.

97. Bennett, 112.

98. On the tension between randomness and order in Thoreau, see William Rossi, "Poetry and Progress: Thoreau, Lyell, and the Geological Principles of *A Week*," *American Literature* 66.2 (June 1994): 275–300. Rossi locates that tension in relation to the principles of contemporary geology, in which over long spans of time the world appears to be moving progressively forward, albeit in a jaggedly and seemingly haphazard fashion. Also see John C. Broderick's "The Movement of Thoreau's Prose," *American Literature* 33.2 (May 1961): 133–42, which describes Thoreau's form as one of circles that recur erratically and contingently, rather than in perfect wholeness.

99. See Jeffrey A. Auerbach, *The Great Exhibition of 1851: A Nation on Display* (New Haven, CT: Yale University Press, 1999); Alf Bøe, *From Gothic Revival to Functional Form: A Study in Victorian Theories of Design* (New York: The Humanities Press, Da Capo Press, 1979; Oslo: Oslo University Press, 1957; Oslo: Scandinavian University Press, 1997);

Joseph Bizup, *Manufacturing Culture: Vindications of Early Victorian Industry* (Charlottesville: University of Virginia Press, 2003).

100. See F. O. Matthiessen on Horatio Greenough and Thoreau in *The American Renaissance: Art and Expression in the Age of Emerson and Whitman* (New York: Oxford University Press, 1941); Theodore M. Brown, "Thoreau's Prophetic Architectural Program," *NEQ* 38.1 (March 1965): 3–20; William J. Griffin, "Thoreau's Reactions to Horatio Greenough," *New England Quarterly* 30.4 (December 1957): 508–12; Richard N. and Jean Carwile Masteller, "Rural Architecture in Andrew Jackson Downing and Henry David Thoreau," *NEQ* 54.4 (December 1984): 483–510. Bill Brown locates an anti-decorative impetus in America in the late nineteenth century, countering the narrative of Victorian excess to be trumped by the revolution of modernism, but still sees Thoreau as an iconoclast against the untrammeled ornament of the earlier nineteenth century (Brown, *A Sense of Things: The Object Matter of American Literature* [Chicago: University of Chicago Press, 2003], 223).

101. Katherine C. Grier, *Culture and Comfort: Parlor Making and Middle-Class Identity, 1850–1930* (Washington, DC: Smithsonian, 1997).

102. Gillian Brown argues that Stowe, "in her insistence on use value [in *House and Home Papers*,] differentiates household possessions, the stuff of sentimental associations, from the ephemeral objects in the marketplace" (*Domestic Individualism: Imagining Self in Nineteenth-Century America* [Berkeley: University of California Press, 1990], 45). But economics and the market are never far from Stowe's mind: she would be more likely to brag about how little she paid for an object than to pretend it was purchased with love. *House and Home Papers* is a quite direct attempt to think about how beauty could be attained, as Stowe puts it, on the "cheap" (Christopher Crowfield [Harriet Beecher Stowe], *House and Home Papers* [Boston: Ticknor and Fields, 1865], 102). Lora Romero has also investigated domestic ideology in relation to Stowe; see her *Home Fronts: Domesticity and Its Critics in the Antebellum United States* (Durham, NC: Duke University Press, 1997). Lori Merish's argument that *House and Home Papers* is "a *reductio ad absurdum* of liberalism's ideal of consensual authority, articulating a fantasy of noncoercive ownership in which relations of power and force are imaginatively reconstituted, and masked" seems itself reductive (Merish, *Sentimental Materialism* [Durham, NC: Duke University Press, 2000], 152).

103. Stowe, *House and Home Papers*, 111.

104. Stowe, *House and Home Papers*, 13, 301.

105. In *The Environmental Imagination*, Buell comments on Thoreau's connections to nature writers Elizabeth Wright, Susan Cooper, and Mary Austin and suggests that Thoreau is misread if placed too heavily in line with "the

NOTES

antisocial, individualistic flight from the settlements featured in masculine wilderness romance" (Buell, *Environmental Imagination*, 49).

106. In fact, the mid- to late nineteenth century in Britain and the United States was a time of both widespread and intense critique of ornamentation. As Alf Bøe points out, "It is a singular fact concerning the design typical of the period that it was disliked not only by the generations following immediately after, but by a great many among the Victorians themselves" (Bøe, 5). On the intensity of discussions about ornamentation in the period, also see Isabelle Frank, "Introduction: The History of the Theory of the Decorative Arts," in *The Theory of Decorative Art: An Anthology of European & American Writings, 1750–1940*, ed. Frank, with transl. by David Brett (New Haven, CT: Yale University Press, 2000).

107. Ursula K. Heise, *Sense of Place and Sense of Planet: The Environmental Imagination of the Global* (Oxford: Oxford University Press, 2008), 34–35. For her dismissal of environmentalist accounts of Thoreau's relation to place, see 41–43.

108. Such readings of Thoreau may be misreadings, but they are long-standing ones. See the account of early publicity for, and reviews of, *Walden* in Robert Sattelmeyer, "Walden: Climbing the Canon," in *More Day to Dawn: Thoreau's* Walden *for the Twenty-first Century*, ed. Sandra Harbert Petrulionis and Laura Dassow Walls (Amherst: University of Massachusetts Press, 2007).

109. In addition to Bennett, see Jonathan Kramnick, *Actions and Objects: from Hobbes to Richardson* (Stanford, CA: Stanford University Press, 2010), which questions the distinction between person and mind on the one hand, and the world of materiality on the other, or Owen Flanagan, *The Bodhisattva's Brain: Buddhism Naturalized* (Cambridge, MA: MIT Press, 2011), which makes much of the fact that the current state of the field of brain science indicates that "there are no such things" as "immaterial mental properties" (Flanagan, 6). It is unclear to me that brain science has in fact proved the nonexistence of immaterial mental properties, but, more to the point, it is unclear why pointing out that the mind might only be a form of material activity should serve to invalidate the concept of the mind or the person, since there are plenty of material entitities that we nonetheless conceive as distinct from one another (my neighbor's car does not become mine, or undifferentiated from me, simply because we are both material entities).

Chapter 2

1. On Dickinson's use of "syntactic doubling" and other grammatical strategies, see Cristanne Miller, *Emily Dickinson: A Poet's Grammar* (Cambridge, MA: Harvard University Press, 1987), 37.

NOTES

2. Robert Weisbuch, *Emily Dickinson's Poetry* (Chicago: University of Chicago Press, 1975), 16.
3. Suzanne Juhasz, *The Undiscovered Continent: Emily Dickinson and the Space of the Mind* (Bloomington: Indiana University Press, 1983), 10.
4. See Sharon Cameron's *Choosing Not Choosing: Dickinson's Fascicles* (Chicago: University of Chicago Press, 1992); Susan Howe's reading of Dickinson in *The Birth-Mark: Unsettling the Wilderness in American Literary History* (Hanover, NH: Wesleyan University Press at University Press of New England, 1993); and Barton Levi St. Armand's *Emily Dickinson and Her Culture: The Soul's Society* (Cambridge: Cambridge University Press, 1984).
5. Diana Fuss, "Dickinson's Eye: The Dickinson Homestead, Amherst Massachusetts," in *The Sense of an Interior: Four Writers and the Rooms That Shaped Them* (New York: Routledge, 2004), 24.
6. Fuss, 4. She writes: "To attribute substance and materiality to architecture, and imagination and metaphor to literature, misreads both artistic forms. It is by no means clear that literature is less embodied than architecture, or that architecture is less visionary than literature. Neither the materiality of writing nor the metaphysics of building can be quite so readily elided. My own view on the relation between literature and architecture is one part Martin Heidegger, one part Gaston Bachelard" (Fuss, 4), but, as I see it, this view is not fully followed through in the reading of Dickinson.
7. Fuss, 54.
8. Paula Bernat Bennett, "Emily Dickinson and Her American Women Poet Peers," in *The Cambridge Companion to Emily Dickinson*, ed. Wendy Martin (Cambridge: Cambridge University Press, 2002), 215–35; 233.
9. Bennett, 229.
10. Dickinson's poetry "was not exclusively literary in nature but originated in Dickinson's situation as a nineteenth-century woman who was part of a community where many nonliterary or nonacademic arts were practiced. Whereas the art of the portfolio is manifestly an elite pursuit, the art of quilting offers an alternative model for coherence and design. May not Dickinson's art also be an art of assemblage, a 'quilting' of elite and popular ideas onto a sturdy underlying folk form, frame, or fabric?" (St. Armand, 9).
11. Daneen Wardrop, *Emily Dickinson and the Labor of Clothing* (Durham, NH: University of New Hampshire Press, 2009), 39, 40.
12. Jerome McGann, *Black Riders: The Visible Language of Modernism* (Princeton, NJ: Princeton University Press, 1993), 20, xiii.
13. McGann, 5.
14. McGann, 112.
15. Betsy Erkkila, "Emily Dickinson and Class," in *Mixed Bloods and Other Crosses: Rethinking American Literature from the Revolution to the Culture Wars* (Philadelphia: University of Pennsylvania Press, 2005), 172.
16. Erkkila, 174.

17. Karl Marx, *Capital: A Critique of Political Economy*, vol. 1, intro. Ernest Mandel, transl. Ben Fowkes (London: Penguin, in association with New Left Review, 1976; 1990), 126.
18. Marx, 126.
19. Marx, 131.
20. Marx, 163.
21. Alexandre Kojève, *Introduction to the Reading of Hegel: Lectures on the Phenomenology of Spirit*, assembled by Raymond Queneau, ed. Allan Bloom, transl. James H. Nichols Jr. (Ithaca, NY: Cornell University Press, 1969), 27.
22. Lukács, 19.
23. Lukács, 88.
24. Marx, 163–64.
25. Roland Barthes, *Mythologies*, transl. Annette Lavers (New York: Farrar, Straus and Giroux, 1972), 78.
26. Barthes, 79.
27. Barthes, 79.
28. Barthes, 54–55.
29. Calling our attention to the seriousness of "placing" in Dickinson's work, Cameron argues in *Choosing Not Choosing* that "the fascicles . . . were essential to her placing of" the poems, "with the idea of placing as identification and the idea of placing as materially establishing *what* they are in relation to *where* they are" (Cameron, *Choosing*, 12). But in the cases I have been considering, placing is less a matter of defining and more of being susceptible to being "borne away."
30. Arendt, 106.
31. Oren Izenberg has suggested that in Dickinson it is revealed that "ordinary sense experience is more mysterious than revelation," and I agree that Dickinson can upend one's faith in the accessibility of external objects ("Poems Out of Our Heads," *PMLA* 123.1 [2008]: 216–22; 219). Still, I do not quite agree that Dickinson is concerned with "what in the philosophy of mind go by the name *qualia*," "the subjective or phenomenal aspects of conscious experience—what it is like to see a color or hear a sound" (Izenberg, "Poems," 219). In Izenberg's work, the concern remains focused upon the relationship of an observing subject to an object, albeit with a distinct twisting toward what it is like, for the subject, to perceive the object (how, say, redness manifests itself in consciousness). In my reading, Dickinson finds that qualities of external phenomena can also appear within herself. This may resemble concerns about how one knows, or experiences, external objects, but the topics are distinct.
32. Dickinson's manuscripts include three drafts of letters addressed to "Master." Scholars have debated the possible identity of that addressee, whether final versions were ever sent, and whether these are drafts of

actual letters or literary exercises. See Richard Sewall, *The Life of Emily Dickinson* (New York: Farrar, Straus and Giroux, 1974); Martha Nell Smith, *Rowing in Eden: Rereading Emily Dickinson* (Austin: University of Texas Press, 1992); Ellen Louise Hart and Martha Nell Smith, eds., *Open Me Carefully: Emily Dickinson's Intimate Letters to Susan Huntington Dickinson* (Ashfield, MA: Paris Press, 1998); Marietta Messmer, *A Vice for Voices: Reading Emily Dickinson's Correspondence* (Amherst: University of Massachusetts Press, 2001); Alfred E. Habegger, *My Wars Are Laid Away in Books: The Life of Emily Dickinson* (New York: Random House, 2001).

33. *The Master Letters of Emily Dickinson*, ed. Ralph W. Franklin (Amherst, MA: Amherst College Press, 1986), 35.
34. Sharon Cameron, *Lyric Time: Dickinson and the Limits of Genre* (Baltimore, MD: The Johns Hopkins University Press, 1979), 145.
35. Cameron, *Lyric Time*, 145.
36. Cameron, *Lyric Time*, 157.
37. *The Letters of Emily Dickinson*, 3 vols., ed. Thomas H. Johnson, assoc. ed. Theodora Ward (Cambridge, MA: The Belknap Press of Harvard University Press, 1958), L 233.
38. The claim that Dickinson wrote neither letters nor poems but a new genre, the "letter-poem," is central to Smith and Hart's *Open Me Carefully*.
39. Many of Dickinson's manuscripts include extensive markings of additions to, and variants of, the phrasings in the main document. Scholarly opinion is divided over whether these are addenda and markings that Dickinson would eventually have incorporated into a finished text, or whether she understands her finished work to include variations in wording and other formal aspects of the text. See Cameron, *Choosing Not Choosing*; Smith, *Rowing in Eden*; Domhnall Mitchell, *Measures of Possibility: Emily Dickinson's Manuscripts* (Amherst: University of Massachusetts Press, 2005). It is Mitchell's view that Dickinson's writings are not experimental but unfinished.
40. Here I touch on Virginia Jackson's claim that "the framing of Dickinson's writing as a set of lyrics is not only an ongoing, collective historical process, but also a mistake." Although confident that it is a "mistake" to call the poems lyrics, she is on principle unwilling to say what they should be rightly called, since she argues for "the messiness that [she] would like to attach to what are often purified terms" (Jackson, *Dickinson's Misery: A Theory of Lyric Reading* [Princeton, NJ: Princeton University Press, 2005], 235).
41. See Cameron's argument in *Choosing* that the fascicles are to be read not as individual lyrics or lyric sequences in the traditional sense, but as an interrelated series of poems.
42. See, for instance, Ellen Louise Hart with Sandra Chung, "Hearing the Visual Lines: How Manuscript Study Can Contribute to an Understanding

of Dickinson's Prosody," in *A Companion to Emily Dickinson*, ed. Martha Nell Smith and Mary Loeffelholz (Malden, MA: Blackwell, 2008), 348–67; Howe, *The Birth-Mark*; Jerome McGann, *Black Riders*.

43. Mitchell's contention that manuscript study "is a means, not an end: the end is the reading of Emily Dickinson's letters and poems" indicates how fully the question of interpreting Dickinson has been replaced by, or united with, the question of "what constitute[s] a book of Dickinson's poetry or even a Dickinson poem" (Mitchell, 324, 29).

44. Walter Benn Michaels, *The Shape of the Signifier: 1967 to the End of History* (Princeton, NJ: Princeton University Press, 2004), 7.

45. Michaels, *The Shape of the Signifier*, 3.

46. To claim that Dickinson criticism is preoccupied with the material object is no surprise; as Suzanne Juhasz observed, "In the 1990s, we have been struck by certain material facts about Dickinson as a writer.... As a consequence, the way she wrote, the materiality of her writing, has everything to do with what and how we read when we are 'reading Dickinson'" (Juhasz, "Materiality and the Poet," in *The Emily Dickinson Handbook*, ed. Gudrun Grabher, Roland Hagenbüchle, and Cristanne Miller, intro. Richard Sewall [Amherst: University of Massachusetts Press, 1998], 427).

47. Jackson, 116.
48. Jackson, 1.
49. Jackson, 219.
50. Jackson, 231, 232.
51. Jackson, 17.
52. Mitchell, quoted in Bennett, *Vibrant Matter*, 2.
53. Bennett, *Vibrant Matter*, 3.
54. Bill Brown, "Thing Theory," *Critical Inquiry* 28.1 (Autumn 2001): 1–22; 16.
55. Jackson, 123.
56. Jackson, 125.
57. Brown, "Thing Theory," 15.
58. Martin Heidegger, "Letter on Humanism," in *Basic Writings*, ed. David Farrell Kell, with a new foreword by Taylor Carman (New York: Harper-Collins, 1977, 1993), 251.
59. Bill Brown, "Objects, Others, and Us (The Refabrication of Things)," *Critical Inquiry* 36.2 (Winter 2010): 183–217; 207.
60. Brown, "Objects, Others, and Us," 207 n. 69.
61. Silverman, 145.
62. Arendt, 19.
63. Arendt, 29.
64. Silverman, 144.
65. This is also the view of the Buddhist tradition; in the words of the monk and teacher Ajahn Sucitto, "*our perceptions and state of consciousness are aspects of*

the raw material of the experiential whole. This is what is meant by 'world' in the Buddhist sense: *it is the holistic entirety of psychophysical experience, not trees, rocks, planets, and stars*" (Ajahn Sucitto, *Turning The Wheel of Truth: Commentary on the Buddha's First Teaching* [Boston: Shambhala, 2010], 42).
66. See New, *The Regenerate Lyric*.
67. Elizabeth Petrino, *Emily Dickinson and Her Contemporaries: Women's Verse in America, 1820–1885* (Hanover, NH: University Press of New England, 1998), 135.
68. Petrino, 136.
69. Petrino, 136.
70. Petrino, 136.
71. Petrino, 136.
72. Petrino, 125.
73. Cicero, *De Oratore*, in *De Oratore III; De Fato, Paradoxa Stoicorum; De Partitione Oratoria*, ed. T. E. Page, E. Capps, W. H. D. Rouse, L. A. Post, E. H. Warmington, transl. H. Rackham, *Loeb Classical Library* 26.2 (Cambridge, MA: Harvard University Press, 1960), III. xxv. 96.
74. Cicero, *De Oratore*, III. xxv. 96–97.
75. Cicero, *De Oratore*, III. xxv. 98, 97.
76. Cicero, *De Oratore*, III. xxv. 98–101.
77. Naomi Schor's discussion of this passage from Cicero, and of ornament's status in Quintilian, leads to the statement that "the rhetorical imaginary" is "a sexist imaginary where ornament is inevitably bound up with the feminine, when it is not the pathological—two notions Western culture has throughout its history had a great deal of trouble distinguishing. This imaginary femininity weighs heavily on the fate of the detail as well as of ornament in aesthetics, burdening them with the negative connotations of the feminine: the decorative, the natural, the impure, the monstrous" (Schor, *Reading*, 45). She quotes Quintilian on the need for ornament to be "bold, manly, and chaste, free from all effeminate smoothness and the false hues derived from artificial dyes" (Schor, *Reading*, 44).
78. Detienne, 114, 111.
79. I am countering a view of Dickinson's flowers in which they are understood as carriers of symbolic meaning. Both Petrino and Judith Farr argue that Dickinson uses flowers as symbols like those of the language of flowers. Petrino contends that flowers became a means "through which women communicated to each other without reserve feelings that were unacceptable to a reading public and staked out new emotional territory for themselves" (Petrino, 130). Similarly, Farr suggests that by consulting floral dictionaries, we can decode the meaning of some of Dickinson's poetry and her gifts (Farr, *The Gardens of Emily Dickinson* [Cambridge, MA: Harvard University Press, 2004]). However, as Petrino notes and according to Beverly Seaton, "There

is almost no evidence that people actually used these symbolic lists to communicate" (Seaton, *The Language of Flowers: A History* [Charlottesville: University Press of Virginia, 1995], 2). Jack Goody also found that the language of flowers "had only a minimal relation with contemporary practice" (Goody, *The Culture of Flowers* [Cambridge: Cambridge University Press, 1993], 282). For a critique of the view that the language of flowers was a form of code, see Beam, "Chapter One: Florid Fantasies: Fuller, Stephens, and the 'Other' Language of Flowers."

80. Emerson, "Experience," 473.
81. Francisco J. Varela, Evan Thompson, and Eleanor Rosch, *The Embodied Mind: Cognitive Science and Human Experience* (Cambridge, MA: MIT Press, 1991), 60–61. Also see Varela, *Ethical Know-How: Action, Wisdom, and Cognition* (Stanford, CA: Stanford University Press, 1992).
82. Martin Heidegger, "The Thinker as Poet," in *Poetry, Language, Thought*, transl. and intro. Albert Hofstadter (New York: HarperCollins, 1971), 9.
83. Heidegger, "The Thinker as Poet," 9.
84. Bernstein, 125.
85. Bernstein, 131.
86. Grossman, "Summa Lyrica," 225.
87. Heidegger, "The Origin of the Work of Art," quoted in Grossman, "Summa Lyrica," 86.
88. Grossman, "Summa Lyrica," 226.
89. Cameron comments that Grossman "sees [Dickinson's] poems as preserving the very distinction between the interior and the exterior that ... her poems contest" (*Choosing*, 184 n. 5). More like Grossman, New writes that Dickinson's "poems reveal, even exhibit, the perceptual process that localizes an experience that was not before and will not be after" (New, *Line's Eye*, 148). New aligns the choice to depict a bounded experience—"poetry finds its subject where something has happened"—with the closure and limitation in the lyric form (New, *Line's Eye*, 3).
90. Cameron, *Choosing*, 185.
91. Cameron, *Choosing*, 183.
92. Cameron, *Choosing*, 188.
93. Cameron, *Choosing*, 191.
94. Cameron, *Choosing*, 191–92. Consequently, when Jackson wonders why Cameron continues "hold[ing] tenaciously to the lyric as the genre governing Dickinson's composition" (Jackson, 43), this shows not that Cameron didn't go far enough, but that Jackson failed to grasp the full extent of Cameron's argument. In Cameron's reading, as Dickinson drops into the Open, abandoning all questions of "objects and subjects," she has gone far past the concern with identifying a poem as a poem, or as part of a genre.
95. Cameron, *Choosing*, 182.

NOTES

96. Heidegger, "The Origin of the Work of Art," in *Poetry, Language, Thought*, 66.
97. Heidegger, "Letter on Humanism," in *Basic Writings*, 230, quoted in Bernstein, 128.
98. Bernstein, 129.
99. Heidegger, "Letter on Humanism," 260, quoted in Bernstein, 130.
100. Bernstein, 130.
101. Heidegger, "Letter on Humanism," 260.
102. Howe, *My Emily Dickinson*, 112.
103. Heidegger, *Being and Time*, 171.
104. Wrathall, 242.
105. Howe, *My Emily Dickinson*, 105.
106. Howe, *My Emily Dickinson*, 17.
107. Richard Chase, *Emily Dickinson's Poetry* (Chicago: University of Chicago Press, 1975), 134.
108. Chase, 229.
109. Chase, 215 ("uninteresting"), 221.
110. Chase, 225.
111. Chase, 109, 236.
112. Franklin, editorial comment, *Poems* 1:161.
113. Coomaraswamy, "Ornament," 80.
114. Helen Vendler, *On Dickinson: Selected Poems and Commentaries* (Cambridge, MA: Belknap Press of Harvard University Press, 2010), 277.
115. Cameron, *Choosing Not Choosing*, 191; quoting *The Letters of Rainer Maria Rilke, 1910–1926*, transl. Jane Bannard Greene and M. D. Herter Norton (New York: Norton, 1969), 373.
116. Stewart, 3.
117. Grossman, "Summa Lyrica," 233.
118. Grossman, "Summa Lyrica," 270, 284.
119. Grossman, "Summa Lyrica," 232.
120. Grossman, "Summa Lyrica," 286.
121. Detienne, 15.
122. Detienne, 16.
123. Pindar, quoted in Detienne, 46.
124. Bernstein, 124.
125. Heidegger, "The Origin of the Work of Art," 19.
126. Heidegger, "The Origin," 20.
127. Heidegger, "The Origin," 40.
128. Heidegger, "The Origin," 44.
129. Heidegger, "The Origin," 44.
130. Heidegger, "The Origin," 43, 44.
131. Heidegger, "The Origin," 44–45.
132. Heidegger, "The Thing," in *Poetry, Language, Thought*, 164–65.

133. Heidegger, "The Thing," 165, 166, 164.
134. Heidegger, "The Thing," 179.
135. Heidegger, "What Are Poets For?" in *Poetry, Language, Thought*, 124.
136. Heidegger, "What Are Poets For?" 125.
137. Heidegger, "What Are Poets For?" 129–30.
138. Heidegger, "What Are Poets For?" 129.
139. Heidegger, "The Origin," 47.
140. New, *Line's Eye*, 123, 135.
141. New, *Line's Eye*, 21.
142. New, *Line's Eye*, 60.

Chapter 3

1. Walt Whitman to Ralph Waldo Emerson, 1856, in *Leaves of Grass, Comprehensive Reader's Edition*, 734.
2. Stephen Cushman, *Fictions of Form in American Poetry* (Princeton, NJ: Princeton University Press, 1993), 35, 37.
3. Cushman, 25.
4. In a significant twentieth-century account of American poetry, Edwin Fusell follows the line that "[o]ur poetic history begins with the necessary emancipation from English tradition" (Edwin Fusell, *Lucifer in Harness: American Meter, Metaphor, and Diction* [Princeton, NJ: Princeton University Press, 1973], 11). And yet, to Fusell this freedom did not mean that Whitman abandoned metaphor: rather, his poems turn on "constituting metaphor[s]," which give many poems "an unobtrusively figurative flavor" (Fusell, 79, 54.) Kenneth Price is much less persuaded of Whitman's ability to free himself from tradition. True, "Whitman objected to the romantic poets' polished poetic surface and heavy reliance on simile and metaphor" and "established the severest of his goals for his own verse: 'No ornamental similes at all—not one'" (Kenneth Price, *Whitman and Tradition: The Poet in His Century* [New Haven, CT: Yale University Press, 1990], 21). But Price concludes that Whitman's work reveals "that he absorbed much from his poetic contemporaries and romantic predecessors," and hardly performed the break with the poetic tradition he claimed (Price, 53). Angus Fletcher's *A New Theory for American Poetry: Democracy, the Environment, and the Future of Imagination* (Cambridge, MA: Harvard University Press, 2004) places Whitman within a newly theorized poetic tradition that includes both British and American poets.
5. Walt Whitman, "Song of Myself" (1881 version), in *Leaves of Grass: A Textual Variorum of the Printed Poems*, 3 vols., ed. Sculley Bradley,

NOTES

Harold W. Blodgett, Arthur Golden, William White (New York: New York University Press, 1980), I: 1026. "Song of Myself" hereafter abbreviated "S" and cited parenthetically by line number from Volume I of this edition.

6. Not that the location of sexuality in formal qualities is unprecedented; consider Leo Bersani's readings in *The Freudian Body: Psychoanalysis in Art* (New York: Columbia University Press, 1986).

7. Examples of this would be Derrida's work on ornament in "The Parergon" section of *The Truth in Painting*, and Schor's discussion of ornament's association with femininity and desire in *Reading in Detail*.

8. This is due in part to Whitman's understanding of rhetoric, in which language is always linked to the production of an effect (See C. Carol Hollis, *Language and Style in Leaves of Grass* [Baton Rouge: Louisiana State University Press, 1983]).

9. Critics in the 1980s and 1990s maintained that focusing on aesthetics or form in Whitman was a means to impose normative sexual values upon him. This may be true about earlier Whitman criticism, but it is not true that thinking about Whitman's aesthetics or his form is of necessity to erase his sexuality. I am questioning here the idea that Whitman's sexuality is clearly of the body, and clearly distinct from or prior to his interest in how poetry adorns the world. Michael Moon's influential argument is that Whitman's literary innovations are "subordinate to other, primary, essentially nonliterary considerations" (Moon, *Disseminating Whitman: Revision and Corporeality in* Leaves of Grass [Cambridge, MA: Harvard University Press, 1991], 8). In practice, the rejection of early critical formalism's anti-homosexual cast did not lead Moon or other critics to discount Whitman's language, but only to argue that it is secondary to his political and social ambitions. M. Jimmie Killingsworth argued that "Whitman's tropes involve excesses, deformations, and deviations that, in blending politics and sexuality, explicitly demonstrate the Kristevan notion that in revolutionary language, 'the rhythms of the body and the unconscious have managed to break through the rational defenses of conventional social meaning'" (M. Jimmie Killingsworth, *Walt Whitman's Poetry of the Body* [Chapel Hill: University of North Carolina Press, 1989], xiv). The value of the troping is, for Killingsworth, in its ability to rupture social norms, as is evident in his rejection of the later Whitman's "depoliticized aestheticism in which art is seen not as a motivator of political and moral action but as an artifact embodying the soul of the genius" (Killingsworth, xix).

10. Moon, *Disseminating Whitman,* 5. Also see Kerry Larson's discussion of Whitman's complicated attempts to supersede the vagaries of the mediated communication between author and reader which representation entails, in *Whitman's Drama of Consensus* (Chicago: University of Chicago Press, 1988).

NOTES

11. Moon, *Disseminating Whitman*, 5–6. Max Cavitch's *American Elegy: The Poetry of Mourning from the Puritans to Whitman* (Minneapolis: University of Minnesota Press, 2007) is an interesting example of this. Although he operates on the "extravagant idea" that elegy "is not consolation for the deaths of others, but fulfillment, rather, of a specifically political, shared happiness that 'loss' misnames" (Cavitch, 24), this does not entirely displace the premise that poetry begins in loss and in compensation delivers a new creation. Hence he speaks of Whitman's poetry as containing "opportunit[ies] to audition substitutes for what Joseph Roach calls 'the doomed search for originals.'" Out of this "longing for a referentiality" that would also be a reconnection to original objects, Whitman generates "creativity" and the chance to not only grieve but attain the hitherto "unfulfilled aspirations of erotic life" (Cavitch, 251).

    It might also be said that the discourse of new materialism, in its continuing focus on the separation of materiality from subjectivity, continues this long strain of intellectual concern with how human consciousness pertains to what it takes as the object-matter that forms its world but is not of it. For a discussion of this materialism and its relation to theories of subjectivity, see Mark Noble's *American Poetic Materialism from Whitman to Stevens* (Cambridge: Cambridge University Press, 2015).

12. Moon, "Solitude, Singularity, Seriality: Whitman vis-à-vis Fourier," *ELH* 73.22 (Summer 2006): 303–23; 308.
13. Jane Bennett's "The Solar Judgment of Walt Whitman," in John Seery, ed., *A Political Companion to Walt Whitman* (Lexington: University Press of Kentucky, 2011) emphasizes Whitman's receptivity to the immanent life of things in themselves.
14. Puttenham's text has been a strong influence on Western poetics, and was in print in the nineteenth century: see *The Arte of English Poesie* (London: printed by Harding and Wright, for R. Triphook, 1811).
15. Stewart, 26.
16. Stewart, 26–27.
17. Frank Whigham and Wayne A. Rebhorn, "Introduction," George Puttenham, *The Art of English Poesy* (1589), *A Critical Edition*, ed. Whigham and Rebhorn (Ithaca, NY: Cornell University Press, 2007), 24.
18. Whigham and Rebhorn, "Introduction," 59.
19. Puttenham, 282, 283, 294, 304.
20. Puttenham, 347.
21. Puttenham, 348.
22. Puttenham, 333.
23. See Ezra Greenspan, "The Poetics of 'Participle-Loving Whitman,'" in *The Cambridge Companion to Walt Whitman*, ed. Ezra Greenspan (Cambridge: Cambridge University Press, 1995), on Whitman's frequent use of strings of present participles. Although Greenspan reassures us

that Whitman was not "attracted to them simply for the sake of decoration or elaboration" (Greenspan, 95), his account of the present participles in Whitman as evidence of "'sprawl'—of life as ceaseless, unauthorized (except as self-authorized) motion; of experience as an ongoing process of self-propelled thrust out into the world" (Greenspan, 96) reveals Whitman's work with series of activities, and the sense of a world in the process of being made and pressed forward, which I consider ornamental.

24. Grabar, 9.
25. Puttenham, 347–48.
26. See Jonathan Goldberg's *Sodometries: Renaissance Texts, Modern Sexualities* (Stanford, CA: Stanford University Press, 1992). Goldberg argues that the *Art* entails a play of power and desire that rejects the division between desires for bodies and for political power, and between desires for male or female bodies. Goldberg refutes a prominent argument by Louis Montrose, in which the language of sexual desire in Puttenham was a cover for its essential political desire (Montrose, "Of Gentlemen and Shepherds: The Politics of Elizabethan Pastoral Form," *ELH* 50.3 [Autumn 1983]: 415–59). For a discussion of the prominence of Puttenham in new historicist criticism, see Robert Matz, *Defending Literature in Early Modern England: Renaissance Literary Theory in Social Context* (Cambridge: Cambridge University Press, 2000).
27. Emerson also imagined replaying aristocratic bearing in a democratic key. In "Self-Reliance," he admires "[t]he nonchalance of boys who are sure of their dinner, and would disdain as much as a lord to do or say aught to conciliate one." Such confident, artful ease is one of the attributes of courtly bearing, and Emerson's parlor boy is said to be acting like "a lord," unwilling to deign to another: "You must court him; he does not court you" ("Self-Reliance," in *Essays and Lectures*, 261). This boy's "nonchalance" is seen in much imagery of young white men in the period (see Edward L. Widmer, *Young America: The Flowering of Democracy in New York City* [New York: Oxford University Press, 1999]). On the translation of aristocratic concepts of manners into democratic terms in nineteenth-century American culture more broadly, see Grier, *Culture and Comfort*.
28. Carson, viii.
29. "By Blue Ontario's Shore," I:120, in Variorum *Leaves of Grass*.
30. Betsy Erkkila, "Whitman and Political Theory," in *Whitman East and West: New Contexts for Reading Walt Whitman*, ed. Ed Folsom (Iowa City: University of Iowa Press, 2002), 26.
31. Erkkila, 118.
32. Michael Warner, "Whitman Drunk," in *Publics and Counterpublics* (New York: Zone Books, 2005), 287. While he emphasizes that Whitman complicates the principle of sexuality as self-expression, he still contends

that a crucial part of what Whitman accomplishes is to link sexual experience to public discourse.
33. George Kateb, "Whitman and the Culture of Democracy," in *A Political Companion to Walt Whitman*, ed. John E. Seery (Lexington: University Press of Kentucky, 2011), 26.
34. Larson, *Whitman's Drama of Consensus*, 99.
35. Allen Grossman, "The Poetics of Union in Whitman and Lincoln: An Inquiry Toward the Relationship of Art and Policy," in *The American Renaissance Reconsidered*, ed. Walter Benn Michaels and Donald Pease (Baltimore, MD: Johns Hopkins University Press, 1985), 183–208; 186.
36. Grossman, "Poetics," 188.
37. Grossman, "Poetics," 192.
38. Grossman, "Poetics," 187.
39. Grossman, "Poetics," 188–89.
40. Grossman, "Poetics," 199.
41. Grossman, "Poetics," 203.
42. Both poems are in Volume II of the Variorum edition of *Leaves of Grass*. Hereafter abbreviated as "R" and "W" and cited parenthetically by line number.
43. Whitman is, I mean, preempting the work of remembering himself after his death. This is perhaps a case of what Larson has called the "proleptic drive" in much of Whitman's work (Larson, *Drama of Consensus*, 18).
44. That work is, as Barbara Johnson writes, a central task of much poetry: "What an epitaph accomplishes, then, is what all literature has to accomplish: to make poetry that convinces the reader that the poet speaks, that the poem gives access to his living voice—even though the individual author may have been buried for more than two hundred years" (Barbara Johnson, *Persons and Things* [Cambridge, MA: Harvard University Press, 2008], 14).
45. Whitman, "I Sing the Body Electric," in Variorum *Leaves of Grass* I: 87–88: "Each belongs here or anywhere just as much as the well-off, just as much as you, / Each has his or her place in the procession."
46. Both David Reynolds and Laura Dassow Walls note that Alexander von Humboldt's *Kosmos* is the source of Whitman's choice of this term (Laura Dassow Walls, *The Passage to Cosmos: Alexander von Humboldt and the Shaping of America* [Chicago: University of Chicago Press, 2009]; David Reynolds, *Walt Whitman's America: A Cultural Biography* [New York: Alfred A. Knopf, 1995]). In both of their accounts, the beauty of Humboldt's cosmos is in its harmonic order, whereas here I am arguing that Whitman's ornamental world is precisely not ordered in that sense. The human presence in the universe which both Reynolds and Walls locate in Humboldt's cosmos is, for Whitman, more dislocating and troubling than their accounts allow. There is real kinship between this book's humanism and Walls's argument against versions of ecocriticism that valorize the

negation of human subjectivity, and her observation that the term *cosmos* insists on the relationship of the world to mind is one I agree with. Yet her understanding of beauty and aesthetics—and even of the mind itself—is limited by her focus on harmonic order (which is a feature of her earlier work on Thoreau). For instance, she writes: "In *Cosmos*, the imagination of the viewer—whether poet, artist, or scientist—fused information into a new and beautiful whole" (Walls, *Passage to Cosmos*, 223). Although she observes in passing that *cosmos* means beauty as adornment, this in her treatment only means beauty as the perception of ordered unity in the world.

47. "Candor, n.," *OED Online* (Oxford: Oxford University Press, December 2014), http://www.oed.com/view/Entry/27009?redirectedFrom=candor (accessed January 3, 2015).

48. Anne Anlin Cheng has argued that ornamental shine can signal the value of a person in a way that resists objectification. Discussing a film starring Anna May Wong as the dancer Shosho, Cheng writes that Shosho's golden, ornamented costume "overwhelm[s] its wearer's skin with its metallic brilliance" (Cheng, "Shine: On Race, Glamour, and the Modern" *PMLA* 126.4 [October 2011]: 1022–1040; 1031). In Cheng's reading, this shiny, ornamental coat and the general association of shine with filmic celebrity shows us that "[g]lamour's imperviousness"—its inorganic, industrial gleam—"draws on a crisis of personhood that is inherently political and may be even strangely liberating for a woman and a minority—liberating . . . in the sense of temporary relief from the burdens of personhood and visibility" (Cheng, 1032).

49. Kurke, *The Traffic in Praise*, 29. Kurke's citations of Pindar are to her own translations.

50. Kurke, 29.
51. Kurke, 35.
52. Kurke, 31.
53. Kurke, 89.
54. Kurke, 154–55.
55. Kurke, 207.
56. Thoreau, "Natural History of Massachusetts," 22.
57. In "Song of Myself," writes Dimock, "the 'Me Myself' is increasingly stripped bare, put through an increasingly rigorous set of refinements, until it is purified into no more than an idea, an empty form, but, for that very reason, a form of transcendent dignity. Like [John] Rawls, Whitman is quite willing to give up what is 'mine,' to write it over to the world as part of its bounty as well as part of its caprice, in order to rescue 'me' as an absolute concept, free from all circumstantial encumbrances, free from the vagaries of the accidental" (Wai Chee Dimock, *Residues of Justice: Literature, Law, Philosophy* [Berkeley: University of California Press, 1996], 114–15). In

NOTES

some of her discussions of the importance of the "affective" that is left out of Whitman, there is room to suggest that the concept of the exceptional is at issue for her (Dimock, 120). But the value of what is loved, for Dimock, is clearly in its particularity to the individual, as opposed to the emptiness of the universal. This leaves out the concept of a particularity that is exceptional, or of any one person being not just preferred by another particular person, but being recognized as greater than others. This latter concept, I am arguing, matters to Whitman.

58. Nancy Fraser, "Social Justice in the Age of Identity Politics: Redistribution, Recognition, and Participation," in Nancy Fraser and Axel Honneth, *Redistribution or Recognition? A Political-Philosophical Exchange*, transl. Joel Golb, James Ingram, and Christiane Wilke (London: Verso, 2003), 7–109; 32.
59. Fraser, "Social Justice," n. 32, 99.
60. Whitman is certainly aware of the concept that the phenomenal world might be at base an image of truth or "real" reality. Indeed this belief is quite powerful and troubling to him, as poems such as "Of the Terrible Doubt of Appearances" or "Eidòlons" explicitly consider.
61. In a chapter on "Manners" in Philadelphia literature and culture, Samuel Otter raises the question, "What happens to abstract rights as they become the focus of struggle on the pages and streets of the city?" (Otter, *Philadelphia Stories: American Literature of Race and Freedom* [New York: Oxford University Press, 2010], 81). One of the things that happens is that rights cease to seem like abstractions to be put into practice at all: even if "Manners became" in some cases "a form of expression and experiment" (Otter, 87), the flexibility of manners suggests a transformative performance.
62. Whitman, "These I Singing in Spring," in Variorum *Leaves of Grass*, II: 5-6. Hereafter abbreviated "T" and cited parenthetically by line number.
63. Whitman, "As I Ebb'd with the Ocean of Life," in Variorum *Leaves of Grass* II: 66.
64. Bonnie Honig, *Antigone, Interrupted* (Cambridge: Cambridge University Press, 2013), 106. This is a view that is, she observes, identified with Pericles' Funeral Oration (see Honig, 129–30 and *passim*).
65. Honig, 96, 103.
66. Rancière, *Dis-agreement*, 5.
67. Rancière, *Dis-agreement*, 5–6.
68. Rancière, *Dis-agreement*, 14.
69. Rancière, *Dis-agreement*, 17.
70. As John Guillory argues in *Cultural Capital*, in the liberal logic of the canon wars of the 1980s, more equal representation of social groups on literary syllabi was intended to lead to more equal economic and social relations. In Guillory's view, such a politics lacks an adequate consideration of how economic, institutional, and social power function (Guillory, *Cultural Capital:*

The Problem of Literary Canon Formation [Chicago: University of Chicago Press, 1993]).

71. Discussing nineteenth-century American culture, Larson writes, "Ever present as a social ideal, equality shrinks at the touch of the social. Perhaps *Democracy in America*'s most basic insight is that these two features do not cancel one another out but coexist and contend against one another.... The current practice, especially pronounced in scholarship on the antebellum era, of pitting an abstract equality against the real thing thus looks past the most crucial feature of modern democratic power" (Larson, *Imagining Equality in Nineteenth-Century American Literature* [Cambridge: Cambridge University Press, 2008], 4). Larson's point is that the misfit between belief in human equality and in a society premised on the maintenance of inequity wasn't an ideological mystification or even a failure to live up to principles; nineteenth-century American culture took universal human equality as a given, but never thought that the basic ambition of a democratic society was to utterly embody it.
72. Jacques Rancière, *Aisthesis: Scenes from the Aesthetic Regime of Art* (2011), transl. Zakir Paul (London and New York: Verso, 2013), 71.
73. Rancière, *Aisthesis*, 72.
74. In a reading of Whitman that also uses Rancière's work, Jason Frank contends that Whitman's poetry adopts a heteroglossic mode of representation, in which the multitudinous and agonistic reality of the people is brought into play as the voice of the poetry. This bringing of the people's voice into representation becomes a means for the people to be inspired to become a fuller expression of their own democratic being. In this there is a fundamental play in the poetry between articulating the phenomenal reality of the people and the ideal of their democratic being, as the work of the poetry and its reception becomes a means to bring this reality and ideal into ever closer alignment (Frank, *Constituent Moments: Enacting the People in Postrevolutionary America* [Durham, NC: Duke University Press, 2010]).
75. Rancière, *Aisthesis*, 69. His contention is that Whitman's catalogues are "related to the vast redemption of the empirical world proclaimed by German idealism: the redemption of a sensible world where spirit recognizes the exterior form of a divine thought that it knows from now on as its own thought" (Rancière, *Aisthesis*, 69).
76. "When Lilacs Last in the Dooryard Bloom'd," in Variorum *Leaves of Grass*, II:17. Hereafter abbreviated "W" and cited parenthetically by line number.
77. Kateb, 36.
78. Rancière, *Aisthesis*, 66.
79. Bennett, "Solar Judgment," 134, 138.
80. Bennett, "Solar Judgment," 138.
81. Goldberg, 53.

82. One instance of this argument is Hans Ulrich Gumbrecht's *The Production of Presence: What Meaning Cannot Convey* (Stanford, CA: Stanford University Press, 2004).
83. Larson, *Imagining Equality,* 104–105. He continues that Whitman's work, "so far from offering an alternative to the notion that authorship is inherently autocratic and hierarchical, is nothing if not the purest possible tribute to the ongoing power" in American culture of the idea that since "the authorial will is prone to cognitive imperialism," suppressing that will "should help set the reader free" (Larson, *Imagining Equality,* 105–106; 106).
84. Indeed, ornamentation in Western culture has often been charged with forms of violence. See E. H. Gombrich, *The Sense of Order: A Study in the Psychology of Decorative Art,* The Wrightsman Lectures (Ithaca, NY: Cornell University Press, 1979).
85. Also see Noble's argument that Whitman's abandonment of "cultural authorities" for "embodied experience" moves in a direction so radical that its use for specific political agendas is exploded (Noble, 58). He argues that "the political utility at stake in access to a material primordium of subjectivity" is dubious insofar as it estranges the subject into impersonal atoms (Noble, 60).
86. In Steiner's account: "We are 'thrown' (*geworfen*) into the world, proclaims Heidegger. Our being-in-the-world is a 'thrownness,' a *Geworfenheit.* There is nothing mystical or metaphysical about this proposition. It is a primordial banality which metaphysical speculation has long overlooked. ... Our *Dasein* is inseparable from it and ... there is a sense in which the world derives meaning from its *Dasein.* But the relationship is not causal; it is not, as in certain rigorously idealist models, our awareness that constructs the world" (Steiner, 87).
87. Heidegger, *Being and Time,* 178.
88. Heidegger, *Being and Time,* 174.
89. Edward Said, *The World, The Text, and the Critic* (Cambridge, MA: Harvard University Press, 1983), 247.
90. Kojève, 222.
91. Dickinson, *The Letters of Emily Dickinson,* L 93.
92. Dickinson, *The Letters of Emily Dickinson,* L 88.
93. Ovid, *Metamorphoses,* ed. David Raeburn, intro. Denis Feener (New York: Penguin Classics, 2004), 1:556.
94. Ovid, 1:558–60.
95. To underscore ornament's link to violence and submission: the architectural historian George Hersey argues that ancient Greeks believed that temple architecture evoked both the grove at which sacrifices were performed and the victims of such sacrifice. For example, the term "Aprophysis," denoting "the hollow curve between a column's base and shaft, is taken

from the word for part of a bone or blood vessel" (Hersey, *The Lost Meaning of Classical Architecture: Speculations on Ornament from Vitruvius to Venturi* [Cambridge, MA: MIT Press, 1988], 22). Having taught us to see the striations of classic columns as the lines of "three upright bones wrapped top and bottom with strands of dripping fat," Hersey adds that the capitals of columns evoke the leaves and flowers crowning victims of sacrifice (Hersey, 31). These crowns do not honor the victims but signify their bondage: prisoners are "said to be *sub corona*" (Hersey, 38). Considering Vitruvius's discussion of the caryatid figures (prisoner figures standing as architectural columns, as at the Erechtheum in Athens), he concludes that they "give to architecture a distinctly punitive aspect. They reinforce its role as the exhibitor of justice accomplished" (Hersey, 75).

96. Ovid, 1:566–67.
97. Johnson comments, "the seriousness of lyric in comparison with epic was won by making the sexual roles similar to those of conqueror and conquered" (Johnson, 78).
98. Stewart, 2.
99. Stewart, 1.
100. Oren Izenberg, *Being Numerous: Poetry and the Ground of Social Life* (Princeton, NJ: Princeton University Press, 2011), 28.
101. Izenberg, *Being Numerous*, 28.
102. Izenberg, *Being Numerous*, 23.
103. Izenberg, *Being Numerous*, 112.
104. Izenberg, *Being Numerous*, 128.
105. Johnson, 94.
106. Johnson, 105.
107. "Sheen, n. 1," *OED Online*, http://www.oed.com/view/Entry/177761?rskey =fBo9i2&result=1 (accessed January 3, 2015).
108. "Sheen, adj.," *OED Online*, http://www.oed.com/view/Entry/177764?rskey= LtVNJD&result=4 (accessed January 3, 2015).
109. "Sheen, adj.," *OED Online*.
110. "Sheen, adj.," *OED Online*.
111. "Sheen, adj.," *OED Online*.
112. "Sheen, adj.," *OED Online*.
113. "Sheen, n. 1," *OED Online*.
114. Whitman, "I Saw in Louisiana a Live-Oak Growing," in Variorum *Leaves of Grass*, II: 1, 3, 4. Hereafter abbreviated "I" and cited parenthetically by line number.
115. Whitman, "To a Stranger," in Variorum *Leaves of Grass*, II: 1.
116. Betsy Erkkila, "Manly Love in All Its Moods: A Preface," in *Walt Whitman's Songs of Male Intimacy and Love: 'Live Oak, with Moss' and 'Calamus'"* (Iowa City: University of Iowa Press, 2011), xi.

NOTES

117. Cameron, *Writing Nature*, 53.
118. Raymond Williams, for one, had a keen sense of the depth of the commitment to controlling life: "We live in almost overwhelming danger, at a peak of our apparent control. We react to the danger by attempting to take control, yet still we have to unlearn, as the price of survival, the inherent dominative mode. . . . It is as if, in fear or vision, we are now all determined to lay our hands on life and force it into our own image. . . . This is a real barrier in the mind, which at times it seems almost impossible to break down" (Williams, 336).
119. My investment in the relationship of the mind to what concerns it is, clearly, antithetical to Franco Moretti's vision of literary scholarship as "sharing raw materials, evidence—*facts*—with one another" (*Distant Reading* [London: Verso, 2013], 240). Moretti recalls conceding that two other critics were "right—and [Moretti] should have known better," and observes that it was "difficult" but "liberating" to discover the critical discussion was about facts rather than "about you," or himself. Moretti's idea that we have two choices—"narcissistic" discussions about ourselves, and "a world of facts that everybody agrees to share (and respect)"—disregards the specific claims of humanistic thinking to sustain a connection to both the objective and rational, and the personal, creative, and otherwise undeterminable and resistant aspects of existence (Moretti, 108). But, of course, his formalism is one based in the truth value of patterns and structures which are supposed to underlie individual experiences, a formalism utterly at odds with the ornamental aesthetics this book explores.

BIBLIOGRAPHY

Ahmed, Sara. *Queer Phenomenology: Orientations, Objects, Others*. Durham, NC: Duke University Press, 2006.

Alcott, Louisa May. *Moods*. 1864. Ed. Sarah Elbert. American Women Writers. New Brunswick, NJ: Rutgers University Press, 1999.

Althusser, Louis. "The Underground Current of the Materialism of the Encounter." In *Philosophy of the Encounter: Later Writings, 1978–87*. Ed. François Matheron and Oliver Corpet. Transl. and intro. G. M. Goshgarian. London: Verso, 2006.

Ames, Kenneth L. *Death in the Dining Room; and Other Tales of Victorian Culture*. Philadelphia: Temple University Press, 1992.

Arendt, Hannah. *The Life of the Mind*. One-volume edition. New York: Harvest, Harcourt, 1977, 1978.

Armstrong, Isobel. *The Radical Aesthetic*. Oxford: Blackwell, 2000.

Arsić, Branka. *On Leaving: A Reading in Emerson*. Cambridge, MA: Harvard University Press, 2010.

Auerbach, Jeffrey A. *The Great Exhibition of 1851: A Nation on Display*. New Haven, CT: Yale University Press, 1999.

Barthes, Roland. *Mythologies*. Transl. Annette Lavers. New York: Farrar, Straus and Giroux, 1972.

Bartram, William. *The Travels of William Bartram*. 1791. Ed. Thomas P. Slaughter. New York: Library of America, 1996.

Beam, Dorri. *Style, Gender, and Fantasy in Nineteenth-Century American Women's Writing*. Cambridge: Cambridge University Press, 2010.

Bennett, Jane. *Vibrant Matter: A Political Economy of Things*. Durham, NC: Duke University Press, 2010.

Bennett, Jane. "The Solar Judgment of Walt Whitman." In *A Political Companion to Walt Whitman*. Ed. John Seery. Lexington: University Press of Kentucky, 2011. 131–146.

Bennett, Paula Bernat. "Emily Dickinson and Her American Women Poet Peers." In *The Cambridge Companion to Emily Dickinson*. Ed. Wendy Martin. Cambridge: Cambridge University Press, 2002. 215–35.

Bernstein, Susan. *Housing Problems: Writing and Architecture in Goethe, Walpole, Freud, and Heidegger*. With photographs by Suzanne Doppelt. Stanford, CA: Stanford University Press, 2008.

Bersani, Leo. *The Freudian Body: Psychoanalysis and Art*. New York: Columbia University Press, 1986.

Best, Stephen M., and Sharon Marcus. "Surface Reading: An Introduction." *Representations* 108.1 (Fall 2009): 1–21.

Bishop, Claire. "Antagonism and Relational Aesthetics." *October* 110 (Fall 2004): 51–79.

Bizup, Joseph. *Manufacturing Culture: Vindications of Early Victorian Industry*. Charlottesville: University of Virginia Press, 2003.

Bourriaud, Nicolas. *Relational Aesthetics*. Transl. Simon Pleasance and Fronza Woods, with the participation of Mathieu Copeland. Dijon, France: Les Presses du réel, 1998, 2002, 2008.

Bøe, Alf. *From Gothic Revival to Functional Form: A Study in Victorian Theories of Design*. New York: The Humanities Press, Da Capo Press, 1979; Oslo: Oslo University Press, 1957; Oslo: Scandinavian University Press, 1997.

Brett, David. *Rethinking Decoration: Pleasure and Ideology in the Visual Arts*. Cambridge: Cambridge University Press, 2005.

Broderick, John C. "The Movement of Thoreau's Prose." *American Literature* 33.2 (May 1961): 133–42.

Brown, Bill. "Objects, Others, and Us (The Refabrication of Things)." *Critical Inquiry* 36.2 (Winter 2010): 183–217.

Brown, Bill. *A Sense of Things: The Object Matter of American Literature*. Chicago: University of Chicago Press, 2003.

Brown, Bill. "Thing Theory." *Critical Inquiry* 28.1 (Autumn 2001): 1–22.

Brown, Gillian. *Domestic Individualism: Imagining Self in Nineteenth-Century America*. Berkeley: University of California Press, 1990.

Brown, Theodore M. "Thoreau's Prophetic Architectural Program." *NEQ* 38.1 (March 1965): 3–20.

Buell, Lawrence. *The Environmental Imagination: Thoreau, Nature Writing, and the Formation of American Culture*. Cambridge, MA: The Belknap Press of Harvard University Press, 1995.

Buell, Lawrence. *The Futures of Environmental Criticism: Environmental Crisis and the Literary Imagination*. Malden, MA, and Oxford: Blackwell, 2005.

BIBLIOGRAPHY

Buell, Lawrence. *Writing for an Endangered World: Literature, Culture, and Environment in the U.S. and Beyond*. Cambridge, MA: The Belknap Press of Harvard University Press, 2001.

Cameron, Sharon. *Choosing Not Choosing: Dickinson's Fascicles*. Chicago: University of Chicago Press, 1992.

Cameron, Sharon. *Lyric Time: Dickinson and the Limits of Genre*. Baltimore, MD: Johns Hopkins University Press, 1979.

Cameron, Sharon. *Writing Nature: Henry Thoreau's Journal*. Chicago: University of Chicago Press, 1985.

Carson, Anne. *Economy of the Unlost: Reading Simonides of Keos with Paul Celan*. Princeton, NJ: Princeton University Press, 1999.

Cavell, Stanley. *The Senses of Walden: An Expanded Edition*. Chicago: University of Chicago Press, 1992.

Cavitch, Max. *American Elegy: The Poetry of Mourning from the Puritans to Whitman*. Minneapolis: University of Minnesota Press, 2007.

Chase, Richard. *Emily Dickinson's Poetry*. Chicago: University of Chicago Press, 1975.

Cheng, Anne Anlin. "Shine: On Race, Glamour, and the Modern." *PMLA* 126.4 (October 2011): 1022–40.

Cicero. *De Oratore III; De Fato, Paradoxa Stoicorum; De Partitione Oratoria*. Ed. T. E. Page, E. Capps, W. H. D. Rouse, L. A. Post, E. H. Warmington. Transl. H. Rackham. Loeb Classical Library 26.2. Cambridge, MA: Harvard University Press, 1960.

Coomaraswamy, Ananda K. "A Figure of Speech or a Figure of Thought?" In *The Essential Ananda K. Coomaraswamy*. Ed. Rama P. Coomaraswamy. Foreword by Arvind Sharma. Prologue by Marco Pallis. Bloomington, IN: World Wisdom, 2004. 21–51.

Coomaraswamy, Ananda K. "Ornament." In *Figures of Speech or Figures of Thought? The Traditional View of Art*. Rev. edition with previously unpublished author's notes. Ed. William Wroth. Intro. Roger Lipsey. Bloomington, IN: World Wisdom, 2007. 71–83.

Crary, Jonathan. *24/7: Late Capitalism and the Ends of Sleep*. London: Verso, 2013.

Cushman, Stephen. *Fictions of Form in American Poetry*. Princeton, NJ: Princeton University Press, 1993.

De Man, Paul. "Excuses (Confessions)." In *Allegories of Reading: Figural Language in Rousseau, Nietzsche, Rilke, and Proust*. New Haven, CT: Yale University Press, 1979. 278–301.

Derrida, Jacques. *The Truth in Painting*. Transl. Geoff Bennington and Ian McLeod. Chicago: University of Chicago Press, 1987.

Detienne, Marcel. *The Masters of Truth in Ancient Greece*. Transl. Janet Lloyd. Foreword by Pierre Vidal-Naquet. New York: Zone Books, 1999.

Dickinson, Emily. *The Letters of Emily Dickinson*. 3 vols. Ed. Thomas H. Johnson. Assoc. ed. Theodora Ward. Cambridge, MA: The Belknap Press of Harvard University Press, 1958.

Dickinson, Emily. *The Master Letters of Emily Dickinson*. Ed. Ralph W. Franklin. Amherst, MA: Amherst College Press, 1986.

Dickinson, Emily. *The Poems of Emily Dickinson: Variorum Edition*. Ed. R. W. Franklin. Cambridge, MA: The Belknap Press of Harvard University Press, 1998.

Dimock, Wai Chee. *Residues of Justice: Literature, Law, Philosophy*. Berkeley: University of California Press, 1996.

Dreyfus, Hubert L. *Being-in-the-World: A Commentary on Heidegger's* Being and Time, *Division I*. Cambridge, MA: MIT Press, 1991.

Eagleton, Terry. *Ideology of the Aesthetic*. Malden, MA, and Oxford: Blackwell, 1990.

Emerson, Ralph Waldo. *Emerson's Prose and Poetry*. Sel. and ed. Joel Porte and Saundra Morris. New York: Norton, 2002.

Emerson, Ralph Waldo. *Essays and Lectures*. Selected with notes by Joel Porte. New York: Library of America, 1983.

Erkkila, Betsy. "Emily Dickinson and Class." In *Mixed Bloods and Other Crosses: Rethinking American Literature from the Revolution to the Culture Wars*. Philadelphia: University of Pennsylvania Press, 2005. 37–61.

Erkkila, Betsy. *Walt Whitman's Songs of Male Intimacy and Love: "Live Oak, with Moss" and "Calamus."* Iowa City: University of Iowa Press, 2011.

Erkkila, Betsy. "Whitman and Political Theory." In *Whitman East and West: New Contexts for Reading Walt Whitman*. Ed. Ed Folsom. Iowa City: University of Iowa Press, 2002. 115–144.

Farr, Judith. *The Gardens of Emily Dickinson*. Cambridge, MA: Harvard University Press, 2004.

Ferguson, Frances. *Pornography, the Theory: What Utilitarianism Did to Action*. Chicago: University of Chicago Press, 2004.

Finley, M. I. *The World of Odysseus*. 1954. Intro. Bernard Knox. New York: New York Review Books, 2002.

Flanagan, Owen. *The Bodhisattva's Brain: Buddhism Naturalized*. Cambridge, MA: MIT Press, 2011.

Fletcher, Angus. *A New Theory for American Poetry: Democracy, the Environment, and the Future of Imagination*. Cambridge, MA: Harvard University Press, 2004.

Ford, Andrew. *The Origins of Criticism: Literary Culture and Poetic Theory in Classical Greece*. Princeton, NJ: Princeton University Press, 2002.

François, Anne-Lise. *Open Secrets: The Literature of Uncounted Experience*. Stanford, CA: Stanford University Press, 2008.

Frank, Isabelle. "Introduction: The History of the Theory of the Decorative Arts." In *The Theory of Decorative Art: An Anthology of European and American*

Writings, 1750–1940. Ed. Isabelle Frank. With transl. by David Brett. New Haven, CT: Yale University Press, 2000. 21–26.

Frank, Jason. *Constituent Moments: Enacting the People in Postrevolutionary America*. Durham, NC: Duke University Press, 2010.

Fraser, Nancy. "Social Justice in the Age of Identity Politics: Redistribution, Recognition, and Participation." In Nancy Fraser and Axel Honneth, *Redistribution or Recognition? A Political-Philosophical Exchange*. Transl. Joel Golb, James Ingram, and Christiane Wilke. London: Verso, 2003. 7–109.

Frede, Dorothea. "The Question of Being: Heidegger's Project." In *The Cambridge Companion to Heidegger*. 2nd edition. Ed. Charles B. Guignon. Cambridge: Cambridge University Press, 2006. 42–69.

Fusell, Edwin. *Lucifer in Harness: American Meter, Metaphor, and Diction*. Princeton, NJ: Princeton University Press, 1973.

Fuss, Diana. "Dickinson's Eye: The Dickinson Homestead, Amherst Massachusetts." In *The Sense of an Interior: Four Writers and the Rooms That Shaped Them*. New York: Routledge, 2004. 9–30.

Garber, Frederick. *Thoreau's Redemptive Imagination*. New York: New York University Press, 1977.

Glassie, Henry. "Eighteenth-Century Cultural Process in Delaware Valley Folk Building." *Winterthur Portfolio* 7 (1972): 29–57.

Glassie, Henry. *Material Culture*. Bloomington: Indiana University Press, 1999.

Goldberg, Jonathan. *Sodometries: Renaissance Texts, Modern Sexualities*. Stanford, CA: Stanford University Press, 1992.

Goldmann, Lucien. *Lukaçs and Heidegger: Towards a New Philosophy*. Transl. William Q. Boelhower. London: Routledge & Kegan Paul, 1977.

Gombrich, E. H. *The Sense of Order: A Study in the Psychology of Decorative Art*. The Wrightsman Lectures. Ithaca, NY: Cornell University Press, 1979.

Goody, Jack. *The Culture of Flowers*. Cambridge: Cambridge University Press, 1993.

Grabar, Oleg. *The Mediation of Ornament*. The A. W. Mellon Lectures in the Fine Arts, 1989. The National Gallery of Art, Bollingen Series XXXV.38. Princeton, NJ: Princeton University Press, 1992.

Greenspan, Ezra. "The Poetics of 'Participle-Loving Whitman.'" In *The Cambridge Companion to Walt Whitman*. Ed. Ezra Greenspan. Cambridge: Cambridge University Press, 1995. 92–109.

Grier, Katherine C. *Culture and Comfort: Parlor Making and Middle-Class Identity, 1850–1930*. Washington: Smithsonian Institution Press, 1997.

Grier, Katherine C. "Culture Made Material." *American Literary History* 8.3 (Autumn 1996): 552–65.

Griffin, William J. "Thoreau's Reactions to Horatio Greenough." *New England Quarterly* 30.4 (December 1957): 508–12.

Grossman, Allen. "The Poetics of Union in Whitman and Lincoln: An Inquiry toward the Relationship of Art and Policy." In *The American Renaissance Reconsidered*. Ed. Walter Benn Michaels and Donald E. Pease. Baltimore, MD: The Johns Hopkins University Press, 1985. 183–204.

Grossman, Allen. "Summa Lyrica." In *The Sighted Singer: Two Works on Poetry for Readers and Writers*. Baltimore, MD: The Johns Hopkins University Press, 1992.

Guignon, Charles B. "Introduction." In *The Cambridge Companion to Heidegger*. 2nd edition. Ed. Charles B. Guignon. Cambridge: Cambridge University Press, 2006. 1–41.

Guillory, John. *Cultural Capital: The Problem of Literary Canon Formation*. Chicago: University of Chicago Press, 1993.

Gumbrecht, Hans Ulrich. *The Production of Presence: What Meaning Cannot Convey*. Stanford, CA: Stanford University Press, 2004.

Habegger, Alfred E. *My Wars Are Laid Away in Books: The Life of Emily Dickinson*. New York: Random House, 2001.

Hart, Ellen Louise, with Sandra Chung. "Hearing the Visual Lines: How Manuscript Study Can Contribute to an Understanding of Dickinson's Prosody." In *A Companion to Emily Dickinson*. Ed. Martha Nell Smith and Mary Loeffelholz. Malden: Blackwell, 2008. 348–67.

Hart, Ellen Louise, and Martha Nell Smith, eds. *Open Me Carefully: Emily Dickinson's Intimate Letters to Susan Huntington Dickinson*. Ashfield, MA: Paris Press, 1998.

Heidegger, Martin. *Basic Writings*. Ed. David Farrell Kell. Foreword by Taylor Carman. New York: HarperCollins, 1977, 1993.

Heidegger, Martin. *Being and Time*. Transl. Jon Macquarrie and Edward Robinson. Foreword by Taylor Carman. New York: Harper Perennial, 1962, 2008.

Heidegger, Martin. *On the Way to Language*. 1959. Transl. Peter D. Hertz. New York: Harper & Row, 1971.

Heidegger, Martin. *Parmenides*. 1982. Transl. André Schuwer and Richard Rojcewicz. Bloomington: Indiana University Press, 1992.

Heidegger, Martin. *Poetry, Language, Thought*. Transl. with introduction by Albert Hofstadter. New York: HarperCollins, 1971.

Heidegger, Martin. *What Is Called Thinking?* Transl. J. Glenn Gray. New York: Harper & Row, 1968.

Heise, Ursula K. *Sense of Place and Sense of Planet: The Environmental Imagination of the Global*. Oxford: Oxford University Press, 2008.

Hersey, George. *The Lost Meaning of Classical Architecture: Speculations on Ornament from Vitruvius to Venturi*. Cambridge, MA: MIT Press, 1988.

Hildebidle, John. *A Naturalist's Liberty*. Cambridge, MA: Harvard University Press, 1983.

Hodder, Alan D. "The Artist of Kouroo." In Hodder, *Thoreau's Ecstatic Witness*. New Haven, CT: Yale University Press, 2001.
Hollis, C. Carroll. *Language and Style in Leaves of Grass*. Baton Rouge: Louisiana State University Press, 1983.
Honig, Bonnie. *Antigone, Interrupted*. Cambridge: Cambridge University Press, 2013.
Howe, Susan. *The Birth-Mark: Unsettling the Wilderness in American Literary History*. Hanover, NH: Wesleyan University Press at University Press of New England, 1993.
Howe, Susan. *My Emily Dickinson*. Preface by Eliot Weinberger. New York: New Directions, 1985. Pref. copyright Eliot Weinberger. 2007.
Izenberg, Oren. *Being Numerous: Poetry and the Ground of Social Life*. Princeton, NJ: Princeton University Press, 2011.
Izenberg, Oren. "Poems Out of Our Heads." *PMLA* 123.1 (2008): 216–22.
Jackson, Virginia. *Dickinson's Misery: A Theory of Lyric Reading*. Princeton, NJ: Princeton University Press, 2005.
Jameson, Fredric. *The Political Unconscious: Narrative as a Socially Symbolic Act*. Ithaca, NY: Cornell University Press, 1981.
Johnson, Barbara. *Persons and Things*. Cambridge, MA: Harvard University Press, 2008.
Juhasz, Suzanne. "Materiality and the Poet." In *The Emily Dickinson Handbook*. Ed. Gudrun Grabher, Roland Hagenbüchle, and Cristanne Miller. Intro. Richard Sewall. Amherst: University of Massachusetts Press, 1998.
Juhasz, Suzanne. *The Undiscovered Continent: Emily Dickinson and the Space of the Mind*. Bloomington: Indiana University Press, 1983.
Kant, Immanuel. *Critique of Judgment*. 1790. Transl. and intro. Werner S. Pluhar. Foreword by Mary J. Gregor. Indianapolis and Cambridge: Hackett, 1987.
Kateb, George. "Whitman and the Culture of Democracy." In *A Political Companion to Walt Whitman*. Ed. John E. Seery. Lexington: University Press of Kentucky, 2011.
Killingsworth, M. Jimmie. *Walt Whitman's Poetry of the Body*. Chapel Hill: University of North Carolina Press, 1989.
Knapp, Steven, and Walter Benn Michaels. "Against Theory." *Critical Inquiry* 8 (Summer 1982): 723–42.
Kojève, Alexandre. *Introduction to the Reading of Hegel: Lectures on the Phenomenology of Spirit*. Assembled by Raymond Queneau. Ed. Allan Bloom. Transl. James H. Nichols Jr. Ithaca, NY: Cornell University Press, 1969.
Kramnick, Jonathan. *Actions and Objects: From Hobbes to Richardson*. Stanford, CA: Stanford University Press, 2010.
Kurke, Leslie. *The Traffic in Praise: Pindar and the Poetics of Social Economy*. Ithaca, NY: Cornell University Press, 1991.

Larson, Kerry C. *Imagining Equality in Nineteenth-Century American Literature.* Cambridge: Cambridge University Press, 2008.

Larson, Kerry C. *Whitman's Drama of Consensus.* Chicago: University of Chicago Press, 1988.

Liddell, Henry George, and Robert Scott. *A Greek-English Lexicon.* Rev. and augmented by Sir Henry Stuart Jones, assisted by Roderick McKenzie. Oxford: The Clarendon Press, 1940. Online edition accessed via Perseus Digital Library at Tufts University. www.perseus.tufts.edu/hopper/.

Loesberg, Jonathan. *A Return to Aesthetics: Autonomy, Indifference, and Postmodernism.* Stanford, CA: Stanford University Press, 2005.

Lorenz, Chris. "If You're So Smart, Why Are You under Surveillance? Universities, Neoliberalism, and New Public Management." *Critical Inquiry* 38.3 (Spring 2012): 599–629.

Lukaçs, Georg. *History and Class Consciousness: Studies in Marxist Dialectics.* Transl. Rodney Livingstone. Cambridge, MA: MIT Press, 1971.

Margolin, Victor. "Design History and Design Studies." In *The Politics of the Artificial: Essays on Design and Design Studies.* Chicago: University of Chicago Press, 2002.

Marx, Karl. *Capital: A Critique of Political Economy.* Vol. 1. Intro. Ernest Mandel. Transl. Ben Fowkes. London: Penguin, in association with New Left Review, 1976, 1990.

Masteller, Richard N., and Jean Carwile Masteller. "Rural Architecture in Andrew Jackson Downing and Henry David Thoreau." *NEQ* 54.4 (December 1984): 483–510.

Matthiessen, F. O. *The American Renaissance: Art and Expression in the Age of Emerson and Whitman.* New York: Oxford University Press, 1941.

Matz, Robert. *Defending Literature in Early Modern England: Renaissance Literary Theory in Social Context.* Cambridge: Cambridge University Press, 2000.

McGann, Jerome. *Black Riders: The Visible Language of Modernism.* Princeton, NJ: Princeton University Press, 1993.

McGill, Meredith. "Common Places: Poetry, Illocality, and Temporal Dislocation in Thoreau's *A Week on the Concord and Merrimack Rivers.*" *American Literary History* 19.2 (Summer 2007): 357–74.

McIntosh, James. *Thoreau as Romantic Naturalist: His Shifting Stance toward Nature.* Ithaca, NY: Cornell University Press, 1974.

Merish, Lori. *Sentimental Materialism.* Durham, NC: Duke University Press, 2000.

Messmer, Marietta. *A Vice for Voices: Reading Emily Dickinson's Correspondence.* Amherst: University of Massachusetts Press, 2001.

Michaels, Walter Benn. *The Gold Standard and the Logic of Naturalism.* Berkeley: University of California, 1987.

Michaels, Walter Benn. *The Shape of the Signifier: 1967 to the End of History.* Princeton, NJ: Princeton University Press, 2004.

Miller, Cristanne. *Emily Dickinson: A Poet's Grammar.* Cambridge, MA: Harvard University Press, 1987.

Mitchell, Domhnall. *Measures of Possibility: Emily Dickinson's Manuscripts.* Amherst: University of Massachusetts Press, 2005.

Montrose, Louis. "Of Gentlemen and Shepherds: The Politics of Elizabethan Pastoral Form." *ELH* 50.3 (Autumn 1983): 415–59.

Moon, Michael. *Disseminating Whitman: Revision and Corporeality in Leaves of Grass.* Cambridge, MA: Harvard University Press, 1991.

Moon, Michael. "Solitary, Singularity, Seriality: Whitman vis-à-vis Fourier." *ELH* 73.2 (Summer 2006): 303–23.

Moretti, Franco. *Distant Reading.* London: Verso, 2013.

Neçipoglu, Gülru. *The Topkapi Scroll: Geometry and Ornament in Islamic Architecture*, Contrib. Mohammad al-Asad. Los Angeles: Getty, 1996.

New, Elisa. *The Line's Eye: Poetic Experience, American Sight.* Cambridge, MA: Harvard University Press, 1998.

New, Elisa. *The Regenerate Lyric: Theology and Innovation in American Poetry.* Cambridge: Cambridge University Press, 1993.

Noble, Mark. *American Poetic Materialism from Whitman to Stevens.* Cambridge: Cambridge University Press, 2015.

Otter, Samuel. *Philadelphia Stories: American Literature of Race and Freedom.* New York: Oxford University Press, 2010.

Ovid. *Metamorphoses.* Ed. David Raeburn. Intro. Denis Feener. New York: Penguin, 2004.

Oxford English Dictionary Online. Oxford: Oxford University Press, 2015. www.oed.com.

Paul, Sherman. *The Shores of America: Thoreau's Inward Exploration.* New York: Russell & Lowell, 1958.

Paulson, Ronald. "Introduction." William Hogarth. *The Analysis of Beauty.* Ed. Ronald Paulson. Paul Mellon Centre for British Art. New Haven, CT: Yale University Press, 1997.

Perry, Imani. *More Beautiful and More Terrible: The Embrace and Transcendence of Racial Inequality in the United States.* New York: New York University Press, 2011.

Petrino, Elizabeth A. *Emily Dickinson and Her Contemporaries: Women's Verse in America, 1820–1885.* Hanover, NH: University Press of New England, 1998.

Pindar. *Pindar's Victory Songs.* Transl. Frank J. Nisetich. Foreword by Hugh Lloyd-Jones. Baltimore, MD: The Johns Hopkins University Press, 1980.

Plato. *Phaedrus.* Transl. Robin Waterfield. Oxford: Oxford University Press, 2002.

Price, Kenneth. *Whitman and Tradition: The Poet in His Century.* New Haven, CT: Yale University Press, 1990.

Prown, Jules David. "Mind in Matter: An Introduction to Material Culture Theory and Method." *Winterthur Portfolio* 17.1 (Spring 1982): 1–19.

Puttenham, George. *The Art of English Poesy: A Critical Edition.* Ed. Frank Whigham and Wayne A. Rebhorn. Ithaca, NY: Cornell University Press, 2007.

Puttenham, George. *The Arte of English Poesie.* London: Harding and Wright, for R. Triphook, 1811.

Raffel, Burton, transl. *Poems and Prose from the Old English.* Ed. Alexandra H. Olsen and Burton Raffel. Intro. Alexandra H. Olsen. New Haven, CT: Yale University Press, 1998.

Rancière, Jacques. *Aisthesis: Scenes from the Aesthetic Regime of Art.* 2011. Transl. Zakir Paul. London and New York: Verso, 2013.

Rancière, Jacques. *Dis-agreement: Politics and Philosophy.* Transl. Julie Rose. Minneapolis: University of Minnesota Press, 1999.

Ray, Reginald A. *Touching Enlightenment: Finding Realization in the Body.* Boulder, CO: Sounds True, 2014.

Reynolds, David. *Walt Whitman's America: A Cultural Biography.* New York: Alfred A. Knopf, 1995.

Reynolds, Sir Joshua. *Discourses on Art.* Ed. Robert R. Wark. New Haven, CT, and London: Yale University Press, 1975.

Rilke, Rainer Maria. *The Letters of Rainer Maria Rilke, 1910-1926.* Transl. Jane Bannard Greene and M. D. Herter Norton. New York: Norton, 1969.

Romero, Lora. *Home Fronts: Domesticity and Its Critics in the Antebellum United States.* Durham, NC: Duke University Press, 1997.

Rossi, William. "Poetry and Progress: Thoreau, Lyell, and the Geological Principles of *A Week*." *American Literature* 66.2 (June 1994): 275–300.

Said, Edward W. *The World, the Text, and the Critic.* Cambridge, MA: Harvard University Press, 1983.

St. Armand, Barton Levi. *Emily Dickinson and Her Culture: The Soul's Society.* Cambridge: Cambridge University Press, 1984.

Saltz, Laura. "'Corn Grows in the Night': Thoreau, Actinism and the Natural Laws of Rhyme." In *Imponderables: Photography and the Science of Light in American Romantic Literature.* Unpub. MS.

Sattelmeyer, Robert. "Walden: Climbing the Canon." In *More Day to Dawn: Thoreau's Walden for the Twenty-first Century.* Ed. Sandra Harbert Petrulionis and Laura Dassow Walls. Amherst: University of Massachusetts Press, 2007. 11–27.

Schiller, Friedrich. *On the Aesthetic Education of Man; In a Series of Letters.* Transl. and ed. Elizabeth M. Wilkinson and L. A. Willoughby. Oxford: Clarendon Press, 1982.

Schneider, Richard J., ed. *Thoreau's Sense of Place: Essays in American Environmental Writing.* Foreword by Lawrence Buell. Iowa City: University of Iowa Press, 2000.

BIBLIOGRAPHY

Schor, Naomi. *Breaking the Chain: Women, Theory, and French Realist Fiction*. New York: Columbia University Press, 1985.
Schor, Naomi. *Reading in Detail: Aesthetics and the Feminine*. New York: Methuen, 1987.
Seaton, Beverly. *The Language of Flowers: A History*. Charlottesville: University Press of Virginia, 1995.
Segal, C. P. *Pindar's Mythmaking: The Fourth Pythian Ode*. Princeton, NJ: Princeton University Press, 1986.
Sewall, Richard. *The Life of Emily Dickinson*. New York: Farrar, Straus and Giroux, 1974.
Silverman, Kaja. *World Spectators*. Stanford, CA: Stanford University Press, 2000.
Smith, Martha Nell. *Rowing in Eden: Rereading Emily Dickinson*. Austin: University of Texas Press, 1992.
Sokolowski, Robert. *Introduction to Phenomenology*. Cambridge: Cambridge University Press, 2000.
Steiner, Deborah Tarn. "Pindar's 'Oggetti Parlanti.'" *Harvard Studies in Classical Philology* 95 (1993): 159–80.
Steiner, Deborah Tarn. *The Tyrant's Wit: Myths and Images of Writing in Ancient Greece*. Princeton, NJ: Princeton University Press, 1994.
Steiner, George. *Martin Heidegger*. Chicago: University of Chicago Press, 1978.
Stewart, Susan. *Poetry and the Fate of the Senses*. Chicago: University of Chicago Press, 2002.
[Stowe, Harriet Beecher.] Christopher Crowfield. *House and Home Papers*. Boston: Ticknor and Fields, 1865.
Sucitto, Ajahn. *Turning the Wheel of Truth: Commentary on the Buddha's First Teaching*. Boston: Shambhala, 2010.
Thanissaro Bhikku, transl. "Rohitassa Sutta: To Rohitassa." *Anguttara Nikaya* 4.45. http://www.accesstoinsight.org/tipitaka/an/an04/an04.045.than.html (accessed July 22, 2015).
Thoreau, Henry David. *Excursions*. Ed. Joseph J. Moldenhauer. Princeton, NJ: Princeton University Press, 2007.
Thoreau, Henry David. *Journal*. Gen. ed. Robert Sattelmeyer. Princeton: Princeton University Press, 1997.
Thoreau, Henry David. *The Journal of Henry David Thoreau*. Ed. Bradford Torrey and Francis H. Allen. Foreword by Walter Harding. Boston: Houghton Mifflin, 1906. Reprint, New York: Dover, 1962.
Thoreau, Henry David. "Pindar." *The Dial* 4 (January 1844): 379–90. In *Translations*. Ed. K. P. van Anglen. *The Writings of Henry D. Thoreau*. Princeton, NJ: Princeton University Press, 1986.
Thoreau, Henry David. *Walden*. Ed. J. Lyndon Shanley. *The Writings of Henry D. Thoreau*. Gen. ed. Robert Sattelmeyer. Princeton, NJ: Princeton University Press, 1971.

BIBLIOGRAPHY

Thoreau, Henry David. *A Week on the Concord and Merrimack Rivers*. 1849. Ed. Carl Hovde, William L. Howarth, Elizabeth Hall Witherell. Intro. John McPhee. Princeton, NJ: Princeton University Press, 1980.

Tiffany, Daniel. *Infidel Poetics: Riddles, Nightlife, Substance*. Chicago: University of Chicago Press, 2009.

Varela, Francisco J., Evan Thompson, and Eleanor Rosch. *The Embodied Mind: Cognitive Science and Human Experience*. Cambridge, MA: MIT Press, 1991.

Varela, Francisco J. *Ethical Know-How: Action, Wisdom, and Cognition*. Stanford, CA: Stanford University Press, 1992.

Vendler, Helen. *On Dickinson: Selected Poems and Commentaries*. Cambridge, MA: The Belknap Press of Harvard University Press, 2010.

Walls, Laura Dassow. *The Passage to Cosmos: Alexander von Humboldt and the Shaping of America*. Chicago: University of Chicago Press, 2009.

Walls, Laura Dassow. *Seeing New Worlds: Henry David Thoreau and Nineteenth-Century Science*. Ed. George Levine. Science and Literature. Madison: University of Wisconsin Press, 1995.

Wardrop, Daneen. *Emily Dickinson and the Labor of Clothing*. Durham, NH: University of New Hampshire Press, 2009.

Warner, Michael. "Whitman Drunk." In *Publics and Counterpublics*. New York: Zone Books, 2005. 65–124.

Weisbuch, Robert. *Emily Dickinson's Poetry*. Chicago: University of Chicago Press, 1975.

Whitman, Walt. *Leaves of Grass: Comprehensive Reader's Edition*. Ed. Harold W. Blodgett and Sculley Bradley. New York: New York University Press, 1965.

Whitman, Walt. *Leaves of Grass: A Textual Variorum of the Printed Poems*. 3 vols. Ed. Sculley Bradley, Harold W. Blodgett, Arthur Golden, and William White. New York: New York University Press, 1980.

Whitman, Walt. *Prose Works 1892*. Vol. II, *Collect and Other Prose*. Ed. Floyd Stovall. *The Collected Writings of Walt Whitman*. Gen. series eds. Gay Wilson Allen and Sculley Bradley. New York: New York University Press, 1964.

Widmer, Edward L. *Young America: The Flowering of Democracy in New York City*. New York: Oxford University Press, 1999.

Williams, Raymond. *Culture and Society: 1780–1950*. New York: Columbia University Press, 1958, 1983.

Wrathall, Mark. A. *Heidegger and Unconcealment: Truth, Language, and History*. Cambridge: Cambridge University Press, 2011.

INDEX

Ahmed, Sara, 198n23
Alcott, Louisa May, 47
aleatory materialism, 31, 82, 88, 89
aletheia (ἀλήθεια), 6–7, 24
Althusser, Louis, 81, 88, 89, 119
Anacreon, 41, 42, 43
Antigone, 171
Arendt, Hannah, 32, 103, 111, 207n49
Aristotle, 22, 197n13
Armstrong, Isobel, 199n44

Barthes, Roland, 18, 101, 102
Beam, Dorri, 200n57
Being, 3, 6–11, 35, 64–67, 111, 113, 121–127, 134–140, 181–182, 189–192
Bennett, Jane, 82–84, 109, 177
Bernstein, Susan, 16, 121, 125, 135, 138
Best, Stephen, 198n32
Bourriaud, Nicolas, 196n8
Brown, Bill, 109–112, 120, 211n100
Buddhism, 12, 34–35, 120, 216n65
Buell, Laurence, 40, 48, 74, 204n7, 211n105

"Cædmon's Hymn," 79, 134, 183, 209n84
Cameron, Sharon, 122–124, 131
  on Dickinson, 105–106, 123, 132, 214n29, 218n94
  on Thoreau, 38–39, 47–48, 53, 191, 208n49
capitalism, 20, 32, 98–102

Carson, Anne, 21–24, 106, 109, 156
Cavell, Stanley, 205n22
Celan, Paul, 185
Chaldean Oracles, 42–43
Cheng, Anne Anlin, 225n48
Cicero, 30, 114, 116, 150
Coomaraswamy, Ananda, 54–56, 129, 188, 202
cosmos, 3, 12, 23, 161–162, 164, 174, 181–182, 192

De Man, Paul, 15
deconstruction, 14–19
decorum, 23, 28, 149–150, 154, 166–168, 180
deixis, 79–80
democracy, 28, 30–32, 144, 155, 157–158, 164–173, 176–178, 180, 196n8, 223n27, 227
Derrida, Jacques, 14, 199n44, 221n7
Descartes, René, 8
Detienne, Marcel, 22–23, 116, 134
Dickinson, Emily, 1–3, 10–12, 22, 29–30, 90–139, 144, 164, 181, 183–188, 193
Dimock, Wai Chee, 165, 171, 225n57

eidos, 14, 132, 158, 162
Emerson, Ralph Waldo, 47, 61–62, 97, 209n76, 223n27
  "The Poet," 2, 42

INDEX

environmentalist criticism, 40–41, 88, 107
Epicurus, 81, 119
epinikion, 26
equality, 158, 167–179, 183, 227n71
Erkkila, Betsy, 98–99, 157
esteem, 163, 165–166, 170, 174, 176, 192

Ferguson, Frances, 71–72
Ford, Andrew, 21–28, 201n60, 203n92
formalism, 16, 22, 81, 98, 102, 180, 221n9, 230n119
François, Anne-Lise, 40
Fraser, Nancy, 165–166, 192
freedom, 13, 167, 182, 193, 220n4
Fusell, Edwin, 220n4
Fuss, Diana, 97, 213n6

Glassie, Henry, 17
Grabar, Oleg, 35, 153, 196n9, 201n71
Grier, Katherine C., 17, 85, 86
Grossman, Allen, 34, 122, 123, 132, 136, 137, 157–158, 162, 165, 171, 173, 185, 186, 218n89
Guillory, John, 226n70

Hegel, G. W. F., 11, 100, 182
Heidegger, Martin, 5–12, 28–30, 33, 35, 62–67, 81, 88, 97, 110, 121–126, 134–139, 180–181, 196n10
  Being and Time, 8, 9, 11, 64, 126, 135, 197n13, 198n31
  Dasein, 8–9, 11, 64, 66, 121, 126, 148, 181, 228n86
  the Open, 30, 122–127, 130, 131, 134, 136, 139, 140, 181, 190, 192–193, 218n94
  "The Origin of the Work of Art," 122, 124, 135, 138–139
  What Is Called Thinking?, 42, 62–63
Heise, Ursula, 88
historicism, 12, 19, 33, 97, 203n100
Honig, Bonnie, 171, 174
Howe, Susan, 1, 106, 125, 126

industrial design, 16, 20, 100, 207n46
intention, 4, 63–64, 66, 68–72, 75–76, 82–83, 107

interpretation, 9, 39, 59, 60, 199n32
Izenberg, Oren, 185–186, 192, 214n31

Jackson, Virginia, 107–110, 112, 215n40, 218n94
Jameson, Fredric, 33, 203n100
Johnson, Barbara, 184, 186, 224n44, 229n97
Juhasz, Suzanne, 96, 216n46

Kant, Immanuel, 14, 44, 68–69, 71–72, 88, 209n75
Kateb, George, 157, 176
kleos poetry, 21, 24–28, 163
Knapp, Steven, 15, 107
Kojéve, Alexandre, 100, 182
Kurke, Leslie, 26–27, 163–165

Larson, Kerry, 157, 180, 227n71
liberalism, 32, 144, 165, 172, 211n102
Loesberg, Jonathan, 69, 71, 209n75
Lukács, Georg, 100, 198n31

manners, 166–168, 179, 180, 223n27, 226n61
Marxism, 11–12, 19, 33, 99–102, 203
material culture, 1, 13, 15–19
materialism, 81, 89, 222n11
McGann, Jerome, 98–99, 102
metaphor, 103–104, 130, 220n4
Michaels, Walter Benn, 15, 106–108, 203n100
mimesis, 11, 13, 18, 95
Mitchell, W. J. T., 106, 109
Moon, Michael, 148, 221n9
Moretti, Franco, 230n119
Morris, William, 20, 98

Neçipoglu, Gülru, 16, 18
New, Elisa, 29, 50, 52, 67, 113, 139–140, 218n89

the Open. *See under* Heidegger, Martin
Otter, Samuel, 226n61

Parmenides, 6, 28, 64
performativity, 22–26, 153, 180–181

INDEX

phenomenology, 6–12, 33, 97, 124, 181, 199n32
Pindar, 26–28, 134, 163–165
Plato, 7, 21, 25, 196n9
poststructural theory, 13, 14, 15, 102
praise poetry, 80, 162–163
Prown, Jules David, 17
Puttenham, George, 30, 149–156, 179, 223n26

Quintilian, 217n77

Rancière, Jacques, 32, 171–174, 177, 196n8
Reynolds, Joshua, 13, 14
rhetoric, 80, 114–116, 150, 154, 221n8
Rousseau, Jean-Jacques, 15

Said, Edward, 182
Schiller, Friedrich, 13–14
Schor, Naomi, 14–15, 217n77
Silverman, Kaja, 7, 9, 111–112
Simonides, 21, 24–27, 106, 163, 202n84
St. Armand, Barton Levi, 98, 103
Steiner, Deborah, 26, 27,
Steiner, George, 8, 66, 181, 228n86
Stewart, Susan, 29, 79–80, 132, 134, 149, 185, 210n85

Stowe, Harriet Beecher, 85, 211n102
Sucitto, Ajahn, 216n65

Thoreau, Henry David, 1–3, 26, 29, 37–89, 164, 191–192
  Journal, 29, 37–40, 43–62, 67–81, 83–84, 86–87, 191, 208n49
  Walden, 1, 10, 29, 40, 45, 47–48, 50, 53–55, 85–86, 191
  A Week on the Concord and Merrimack Rivers, 41, 74
Tiffany, Daniel, 31, 201n65

Varela, Francisco J., 120
Vendler, Helen, 130

Walls, Laura Dassow, 47–49, 224n46
Warner, Michael, 157
Weisbuch, Robert, 95–96
Whitman, Walt, 1–3, 30–31, 141–193
  Democratic Vistas, 2, 166–167
  Leaves of Grass, 22, 141–143, 148, 173
  "Song of Myself," 144–146, 151–155, 160–161, 170, 174, 177–180, 225n57
Williams, Raymond, 19–20, 230n118
Winnicott, D. W., 186

www.ingramcontent.com/pod-product-compliance
Ingram Content Group UK Ltd.
Pitfield, Milton Keynes, MK11 3LW, UK
UKHW041302180426
11947UKWH00009B/625